Spiritual Motivation

Spiritual Motivation

New Thinking for Business and Management

Edited by

Jeremy Ramsden, Shuhei Aida and Andrew Kakabadse

First published 2007 by
PALGRAVE MACMILLAN
Houndmills, Basingstoke, Hampshire RG21 6XS and
175 Fifth Avenue, New York, N.Y. 10010
Companies and representatives throughout the world

PALGRAVE MACMILLAN is the global academic imprint of the Palgrave Macmillan division of St. Martin's Press, LLC and of Palgrave Macmillan Ltd. Macmillan® is a registered trademark in the United States, United Kingdom and other countries. Palgrave is a registered trademark in the European Union and other countries.

ISBN-13: 978-0-230-54291-4   hardback
ISBN-10: 0-230-54291-3   hardback

This book is printed on paper suitable for recycling and made from fully managed and sustained forest sources.

A catalogue record for this book is available from the British Library.

A catalogue record for this book is available from the Library of congress.

10 9 8 7 6 5 4 3 2 1
16 15 14 13 12 11 10 09 08 07

Printed and bound in Great Britain by
Antony Rowe Ltd, Chippenham and Eastbourne

Aufklärung ist der Ausgang der Menschen aus seiner selbstverschuldeten Unmündigkeit. Unmündigkeit ist das Unvermögen, sich seines Verstandes ohne Leitung anderer zu bedienen... Faulheit und Feigheit sind die Ursachen, warum ein so grosser Teil der Menschen... gerne zeitlebens unmündig bleiben und warum es anderen so leicht wird, sich zu deren Vormündern aufzuwerfen.

I. Kant

Contents

List of Figures and Tables

Figures

Tables

Notes on the Editors

Shuhei Aida is Professor Emeritus at the University of Electro-Communications in Tokyo. He has also been staff engineer at TDK Corporation, research scientist in the National Biomedical Research Foundation (Washington, DC) and a research fellow in the Institute of Industrial Science at the University of Tokyo. Graduating in industrial management at the University of Electro-Communications, and in electrical and electronics engineering at the University of California, Berkeley, he obtained his doctorate in applied physics from the University of Tokyo in 1968. He is or has been Visiting Professor at the Cybernetics Laboratory of the Italian CNR and at Cranfield University, UK. His research interests include eco-technology (founding the International Eco-technology Research Centre at Cranfield in 1986) and EcoDesign, which he first proposed in 1971. He has published about 150 papers and 30 books in the fields of systems engineering, information technology and global environmental issues. He is a member of a number of Japanese academic and governmental advisory committees. Currently he is Chairman and CEO of the Human Media Foundation, Japan, and Director-General of the Cranfield Japan Centre in Tokyo. He has received the Mainichi Cultural and Publishing Award and has been decorated 'Al Merito della Repubblica Italiana' by the President of the Republic of Italy.

Andrew Kakabadse is Professor of International Management Development at Cranfield School of Management. He has been Visiting Professor at a number of US, Australian and Chinese universities. His areas of research cover boards and top teams, the governance of enterprises and the governance of governments, international relations and conflict resolution. He has published 26 books, over 145 articles and 16 monographs. Andrew has consulted and lectured in the UK, Europe, the USA, SE Asia, China, Japan, Russia, Georgia, the Gulf States and Australia. He was also Vice Chancellor of the International Academy of Management and has been Chairman of the Division of Occupational Psychology, British Psychological Society, 2001. He holds positions on the boards of a number of companies. He is editor of the *Journal of Management Development* and sits on the editorial board of the *Journal of Managerial Psychology* and the *Leadership and Organisation Development Journal*. He has also been adviser to a Channel 4 business series.

Jeremy Ramsden is Professor of Nanotechnology at Cranfield University. Graduating in natural sciences from Cambridge University, and obtaining his doctorate from the Ecole polytechnique fédérale in Lausanne, he carried out postdoctoral studies at Princeton University and from 1988 to 2000 was based at the Biozentrum of Basel University. He is or has been Visiting Professor at universities in Argentina, France, Georgia and Japan, and is also Director of Research at Cranfield University at Kitakyushu. His research interests cover nanophotonics, biomacromolecular interactions, self-assembly and self-organization processes, computational evolution and information flows in living organisms and other complex systems. He has published about 150 papers in these areas, as well as several encyclopaedia articles and books, and has chaired several international conferences devoted to biomacromolecular interactions. He is currently Editor-in-Chief of the *Journal of Biological Physics and Chemistry*, and of *Nanotechnology Perceptions: a Review of Ultraprecision Engineering and Nanotechnology*. He is President of the Collegium Basilea (Institute of Advanced Study), and chairman of several international academic-industrial research-focused networks.

Notes on the Contributors

Peter Allen is Head of the Complex Systems Management Centre in the School of Management at Cranfield University. He is also an Invited Professor in the Economics Department of the University of Paris I. His research is directed towards the application of the new ideas concerning evolutionary complex systems to real world problems. He has a PhD in theoretical physics, was a Senior Research Fellow at the Université Libre de Bruxelles 1972–1987, where he worked on the theory of complex systems with Ilya Prigogine, and has worked for over two decades on the mathematical modelling of change and innovation in urban, social, economic, financial and ecological systems, and the development of integrated systems models. Professor Allen has written and edited several books and published well over 200 articles in a range of fields including ecology, social science, urban and regional science, economics, systems theory, and physics. He has been a consultant to the Canadian Fishing Industry, Elf Aquitaine, the United Nations University, the European Commission and the Asian Development Bank. He is an Editor-in-Chief of the journal *Emergence: Complexity and Organization.*

William Batty led the Built Environment Group at Cranfield University before taking up the challenge of working in Japan (at Cranfield University at Kitakyushu), since April 2001, to develop research partnerships with industry and academic research institutions. His experience in the UK included design consultancy for buildings and building environmental services systems, energy management, and research into the development of novel building environmental services systems. His current work in Japan is focused on energy management within the public sector, designing energy- and cost-efficient building services that provide comfortable indoor environments, the development of innovative energy-saving technologies, designing for environmentally conscious urban developments, and life cycle design. He is Visiting Professor at the Faculty of Environmental Engineering of the University of Kitakyushu.

Lorne Denny is the newly appointed Priest-in-Charge at Holy Trinity, Milton-next Sittingbourne, Kent. He was ordained in 2001 and served as non-stipendiary curate in the parishes of Jericho and then Cowley, in Oxford, where for 21 years he taught English and directed plays at Magdalen College School. He was educated at Pembroke College, Oxford, the Institute of Education, London and the St. Alban's and Oxford Ministry Course.

Kaneyuki Hamada graduated in Control Engineering from Kyushu Institute of Technology, and thereafter spent over 25 years with Yaskawa Electric

Corporation. In 1999 he became CTO, Yaskawa Siemens Automation & Drives Corporation, and in 2002 Director and CTO, Yaskawa Electric Corporation, taking on the responsibility for corporate planning in 2003. Since 2005 Mr Hamada has been President and CEO of Ye Data, Inc. He is also a sometime Fellow Researcher at Shanghai Jao Ton University.

Peter A. Hunter spent his early career as a Navigation Officer in the Merchant Navy, then as an Officer in the Royal Navy, including a stint at the Royal Naval Strategic Systems School. On leaving the Royal Navy he spent six months in Venezuela as a consultant for Corpoven, the National Oil Corporation of Venezuela. Since then he has worked in the North Sea drilling industry and in South America as a management consultant for Shell, BP, Deutag and KCA Drilling. During that time he developed the 'Breaking the Mould' philosophy and methodology, a distillate of his corporate experience, now also described in the eponymous ground-breaking book. Peter took his first degree at Sunderland, and has an MSc in Underwater Technology from Cranfield Institute of Technology. He is presently owner and Director of Hunter Business Consultancies Ltd.

Nada Korac Kakabadse is Professor in Management and Business Research at the University of Northampton, prior to which she was a Senior Research Fellow at the Cranfield School of Management. Before entering academia, Nada was a Senior Information Technology Officer with the Australian Public Services Department of Employment, Education and Training. She has worked for international organizations in Scandinavia, the Middle East and North Africa, as well as for the Canadian Federal Government. She has co-authored seven books, contributed almost 50 chapters to international volumes and published over 100 scholarly articles. Current areas of her research interest focus on governance, corporate social responsibility, leadership and boardroom effectiveness, leadership and governance of governments, the addictive effect of information and communications technology (ICT), and strategic sourcing.

Simon Knox is Professor of Brand Marketing at the Cranfield School of Management, and is a consultant to a number of multinational companies, including McDonald's, Levi Strauss, JohnsonDiversey, BT and Exel. Upon graduating, he followed a career in the marketing of international brands with Unilever plc in a number of senior marketing roles in both detergents and foods. Since joining Cranfield, Simon has published over 100 papers and books on strategic marketing and branding, and he is a regular speaker at international conferences. He is a Director of the Brand Management Development Centre at the School of Management and is currently leading a research team looking at the impact of corporate social responsibility on brand management.

Masayuki Koyanagi is currently President of HABA Laboratories, Inc., a company that he established in 1983. He started business with high-purity squalane-based cosmetics and nutritional supplements developed as the result of in-house research. The HABA group now has a Japan-wide network to manufacture and sell a wide range of safe cosmetics and nutritional supplements. Mr Koyanagi is a graduate of Keio University, where he majored in economics.

Toshiro Ono is Professor of Mechanical Engineering in the Department of Intelligent Mechanical Engineering at Okayama University of Science (OUS). After his graduation in mechanical engineering from Osaka Prefecture University in 1960, he obtained his doctorate in aeronautical engineering from Kyoto University, where he remained as Assistant Professor of Applied Mathematics and Physics. He became Associate Professor of Mechanical Engineering at Osaka Prefecture University in 1968, and Professor from 1983 to 2000. His major fields of interest are control theory, measurement science and robotics, and their applications to dynamic weighing problems, dynamic multiple measuring methods, robotic systems for rehabilitation, etc. He is a Member of the Japan Academy of Engineering, an SICE Fellow, a Permanent Member of the Japan Society of Mechanical Engineers (JSME), etc.

Masato Shinagawa is presently Professor at the Information Technology (IT) Centre, Hosei University. He has been a Visiting Professor at Osaka University. After graduation from the Faculty of Law at the University of Tokyo he joined the Ministry of Posts and Telecommunications, later managing sections of the Telecommunications Bureau. In 1991 he became Councillor to the Minister, in 1993 was appointed Head of the Tohoku Regional Bureau of the Postal Services Administration Office, and subsequently Head of the Postal Savings Bureau (1996) and Head of the Broadcasting Bureau (1997). In 1999 he became Deputy Minister of Posts and Telecommunications, and retired from office in 2000. Mr Shinagawa was President of the International Telecommunication Union Association of Japan, Inc. (ITU-AJ) from 2000 to 2002. From 2003 to 2005 he was Vice-President of the NTT Data Corporation. He has also been an adviser to Nikko Cordial Securities, is an external auditor of Biznet Corporation, and was a member of the management council of the Tsukuba University of Technology.

Homare Takenaka is Chairman and CEO of the LBS Co., Ltd, an affiliated company of IBM Japan established in 1993. After graduating in economics from Keio University he joined IBM Japan in 1960. After various positions in marketing and headquarters functions, he was promoted to branch manager for the distribution industry in Tokyo, appointed manager of personnel planning in 1974, and in 1976 was nominated as administrative assistant to the Vice-President of Personnel at the IBM Corporation headquarters in New

York. He was appointed regional manager of the SEIBU sales office in 1980, and nominated Director of Communications for IBM Japan in 1983, being elected to the board of directors two years later. He became Director of External Relations in 1987, and the following year was promoted to Managing Director, external relations, later becoming Senior Managing Director. He became an advisor to IBM Japan in 1995. He served as Chairman of the Keidanren's subcommittee for 'Improvement of the Business Environment for Foreign-Affiliated Companies in Japan' subcommittee in 1993 and 1994, and has been a member of several government councils and economic organizations from 1988 to 1995. In 1999 he published the book *IBM Japan: Wonderful Route from ICBM*.

Yutaka Ujiie leads the industrial cluster research project in the Research Institute of Economy, Trade and Industry (RIETI) since 2005. After graduating in economics at Tohoku University, he joined Nikko Securities Ltd in the business planning division of the Nikko Research Centre in the Corporate Business Division, and also worked on intellectual property matters and mergers & acquisitions. In 1999, SBF Inc. was established in Palo Alto, California, and Mr Ujiie became President & CEO. He has also been some-time IT industrial promotion adviser to the Governor of Osaka Prefecture, and docent at Tohoku University Graduate School of Engineering.

Foreword

Frank R. Hartley

For many years the name of Cranfield has been synonymous with excellence in both management and technology, and stands at the cutting edge of both the research to advance the underpinning science and the development of the technology itself. The latter comprises the entire production cycle, including manufacturing, logistics and the organization and governance of companies, aspects in which the Cranfield School of Management is esteemed for its excellence.

Cranfield was founded (as the College of Aeronautics) in 1946, and during these first few decades of its existence the progression – overall – in many or most of the domains of human activity with which it is concerned could be at least approximated reasonably well as linear. There are, however, enough examples, especially in the micro-nano and ultraprecision engineering fields, of which Moore's 'law' is perhaps the best known example, showing that in reality the progression is exponential, with the implication that sooner or later reality will irremeably diverge from the facile linear extrapolation.

This in itself strongly motivates the search for new approaches, which will undoubtedly have to encompass the entire span of production, as described above, from the underpinning science to questions of the organization of ensembles of production.

This may, however, be insufficient. Corporate and political misdemeanours, often perpetrated by individuals, have proliferated in recent years. At a national level, in the UK, this has been officially recognized, and the response was the establishment of the Nolan Committee in 1994.

This is the stage on which this book enters. It is an attempt to redress the imbalance created by past neglect of ethical questions and to imbue a new rectitude into corporate, political and public life. The especial novelty and uniqueness of this attempt is above all due to the assimilation of Japanese philosophical notions. For many years Cranfield has been privileged to have strong links with Japan, of which the Cranfield University Japan Centre in Tokyo and Cranfield University at Kitakyushu on the Kitakyushu Science and Research Park (KSRP) are living examples, and is fortunate to be able to draw upon a distinguished array of authors from industry and academia, who have contributed chapters to this book.

It is my earnest desire that this book will inject new impetus into the now global problem of motivation and ethics in a rapidly changing world. That about half of the book is devoted to very practical ways in which this can be achieved is in the best tradition of Cranfield being above all an institution interested in finding practical, workable solutions to real problems.

Preface

Jeremy Ramsden

Our world is currently challenged by three extraordinary phenomena which, as far as we know from all the annals of recorded human history, have never before been present simultaneously. These three are: ultrahigh technology, material abundance, and ethical chaos.

Extraordinary phenomena demand extraordinary responses, and that is the motivation for this book. But first let me elaborate on the three extraordinary phenomena or challenges.

As Raymond Kurzweil has shown admirably in his writings, technological progress is typically characterized by exponential increase. Over the last two decades it has been concretely and indisputably codified in the form of Moore's 'law', applicable to that most characteristic of contemporary technologies: the very large scale integrated (VLSI) electronic circuit. Electronic circuitry arguably influences our living environment more extensively and profoundly nowadays than architecture, which for millennia has played a dominant role. The seemingly unstoppable miniaturization and concomitant increases in sheer processing power have led to machines with intelligence already equal to the intelligence that previously human fulfillers of certain roles were allowed to exercise in those roles, and a further exponential increase in that processing power will, apparently inevitably, steadily erode our human advantage over machines and possibly give new meaning to the presently somewhat discredited term 'artificial intelligence'.

In parallel, and bearing some relation to that increase in machine intelligence, although the connexion cannot be very clearly defined, is the increasing complexification of our world. Electronic circuitry is an excellent example: the latest processors already surpass the ability of electronic engineers to consciously oversee the design of such immense collections of components and interconnexions. In the future, if the present rate of increase of component density on electronic chips is to continue to be matched by concomitant increases in the sophistication of the circuitry, some kind of automated, even self-evolving design process will be very necessary. The same holds for the programs written to render the chips functional. The seemingly endemic bugs in widely used commercial software are evidence enough of the inability of even the largest software companies to fully control and oversee the programs that they produce and sell. That it is possible to sell them at all, despite their all too evident deficiencies, presumably has something to do with the intrinsic allure of new, high technology, which is in some way connected to our theme, although we cannot really go into it here.

Whereas in their early days high-speed digital computers were well out of public view, used only in scientific research institutes, and then slowly entered the commercial and military spheres, nowadays they are a common household item. Likewise with the Internet, created initially for the convenient exchange of large electronic data files between researchers, and also used extensively by western scientists to communicate efficiently with their colleagues behind the Iron Curtain, in the days when telephone and post had to be used with circumspection, and were respectively very costly and very slow. Nowadays, along with playing games, connecting to the internet is probably the most common use made of the ubiquitous home computer, which in terms of processing power greatly surpasses that of the very large machines used for data analysis in radio astronomy and other fields in universities in the 1970s.

The Internet, more than anything else, more than the web of more traditional means of communication and even more traditional means of transport that have linked the world quite effectively for centuries, signifies global interconnexion. The implications of that interconnexion are vast and still evolving. An amazing fusion of cultures is underway, implicating everything from the design of cities and skyscrapers through the language and style of novels, popular music and other cultural 'memes' such as food and drink. To be sure, organized religion has for millennia had a global outlook. Missionary activity has been an integral part of the work of the Christian church since the death of Christ. Schisms and abutting against the spheres of influence of other religions have ensured that, while Christianity may be represented in all corners of the globe, it is by no means dominant. Nevertheless, there have been remarkably few attempts to attempt a global synthesis of all that might be considered most admirable and worthy of retention from each of the world's major religions in order to create a new global religion on a par with the new global language (English) and the global style of current popular music. We shall return to this point under the discussion of the third extraordinary phenomenon or challenge, ethical chaos.

Mechanization, of which increasingly intelligent automation is but a manifestation, has been greatly responsible for the incredible material abundance now enjoyed by the western world. The enormous advantage created by having been the first to develop large-scale industrial production of artefacts has turned out to be unbeatable. Even the time when certain key raw materials considered indispensable by the West, such as coffee, cocoa etc., were becoming increasingly expensive and there were serious attempts to develop artificial, though doubtless less palatable, substitutes, belongs to the past. As is now all too frequently lamented by the poor producers, prices of these commodities are now very low. Equally low are the prices of sophisticated manufactured goods. Considering the amazingly sophisticated technology behind the laptop computer, commercial prices – which continue to fall year by year – are incredibly low. The myriad of manufactured conveniences large and small necessary for us to enjoy a comfortable lifestyle are produced at relatively less and less cost (and increasingly in places such as the People's Republic of China).[1]

In short, we are living in a kind of El Dorado that in the past was only dreamed of.[2] And according to the protagonists of full-blown nanotechnology, the Drexlerian vision of molecular manufacturing carried out by personal nanofactories requiring only electricity and piped acetylene, or some similar hydrocarbon feedstock, will usher in an age of even greater material abundance,[3] in which the main social problem might be finding useful employment. That could indeed lead to the kind of society envisaged by E. M. Forster in his short story 'The Machine Stops', in which the population lives in underground cubicles equipped with only the minimum of material necessities, and spends the time communicating with small groups of friends – much as we already do, to an increasing extent, with the Internet.[4] Such considerations are beyond the scope of this book, however. What is of concern is that the present organization of manufacturing, which has led to this state of great material abundance, has also led to the emergence of vast corporations, far more powerful, in terms of the resources that they can mobilize, than all but the governments of the largest countries. Whereas in the past, governments, whether ruled by a benign autocrat or democratically, provided the ethically-based legal framework fully accepted by the population, the relative size and influence of the increasingly numerous vast global corporations effectively mean that the ethical imperative to provide a framework of conduct has passed to a large extent to these corporations, placing them in a role for which they appear to be still largely unprepared.

Although the contrast between the values embodied in a government and their absence in a corporation is greatest when the government is overtly linked to historical values, typically religious, at least formerly and at least

---

[1] There are, of course, large swathes of the world to which this does not apply, and in which the vast majority of the population lives in poverty, and makes little use of convenient manufactured artefacts. It is well beyond the scope of this book to address that matter.

[2] In the short term, there is still some chance that there will be shortages of essential commodities and hence battles for resources. Much depends on the rate of technical progress, whether such a phase will be interposed before universal plenty sets in, and, one might add, on those battles not being carried out with such ferocity that humanity is destroyed (as is still technically possible with present nuclear stockpiles, even in this post-Cold War era).

[3] See S. Burgess, 'The (Needed) New Economics of Abundance', *Nanotechnology Perceptions* vol. 2 (2006) pp. 107–109; and R.A. Freitas Jr, 'Economic impact of the Personal Nanofactory', *Nanotechnology Perceptions*, vol. 2 (2006) pp. 111–26.

[4] Forster's underground denizens spent much of their time delivering lectures to small circles of listeners; the modern equivalent would be writing weblogs or blogs.

externally shared by the vast bulk of the population,[5] it is inevitably present even in the modern secular state – one has only to consider at the example of Turkey. The re-emergence of a kind of religious fervour in many countries, even if unconstitutional, might be a growing trend in the future, albeit unwelcome, and it is therefore not inconceivable that it is the great multinational corporation that will in future become the standard-bearer of a right and rational set of values that both affirm our essential humanity and ensure that human activities do not destroy the very environment in which we live.

Here, it is already generally recognized that Japanese corporations, both great and small, are in the van of a trend that elsewhere in the world is only just beginning to become apparent. Apart from the constant striving to improve, the people employed by corporations in Japan are considered not so much as employees but rather as partners or associates; they are valued very highly and reciprocally give a high level of commitment to the corporation. That would appear to be an excellent starting point for this book, and makes the inclusion of a large number of Japanese contributors entirely appropriate. It might be remarked that the existence of these corporate values in Japan is a reflexion of the typical Japanese worldliness, in the sense of a commitment to daily realities (which gives a sense of immediacy) and an absence of transcendental values. This worldliness appears to have been a characteristic of Japanese society as far back as literary and pre-literary records allow us to infer.

Elsewhere, it may be that such a reversal of the relative importance of governments and private commercial corporations has at least in part been responsible for the ethical chaos that we see around us. Whereas in the past it was governments who granted the charter, i.e. the legal right to exist, to the corporation; now, corporations have the power to destabilize governments, or to render their power ineffective. Beyond a few corporate guidelines, however, it is unlikely that the employees of these corporations will receive any particular ethical instructions. The loyalty of the employee is expected to be directed towards that of the employing corporation regardless of any ethical considerations (and without the sense of partnership so characteristic of Japanese corporations), and even well-meaning attempts to alert the public at large about corporate misdemeanours typically fizzle out, and almost invariably result in severe problems for the individual instigating the attempt.[6] Beyond loyalty to the corporation lies the ethics of the boardroom, directed towards maximizing 'shareholder value', which is in many cases

---

[5] An example is the 'Fid. Def.' (fidei defensor) still embossed on British coins as an inalienable duty of the Head of State.

[6] The same is unfortunately true of some public bodies, most notoriously the Commission of European Communities, in whose corridors, alas, duty and principle appear to have become subordinate to self-interest and expediency.

unsustainable and anti-human. It is perhaps at that level that the necessity for change is the most urgent.

At the same time, many of the attempts made by groups (non-governmental organizations, NGOs) such as ETC Group (Action Group on Erosion, Technology and Concentration) constituting themselves independently from any commercial corporation, although doubtless well-meaning, are all too frequently based on dubious or even false premisses.[7] The image of unscrupulous corporations being held in uneasy check by largely ignorant pressure groups hardly encourages confidence in the possibility of a future world dominated by inspiring and liberal values.

The most obvious signs of ethical chaos might be quite minor things such as dropping litter in the street, youths not giving up seats in suburban trains and trams to the elderly, conducting loud conversations (possibly using a mobile telephone) in crowded trains or on aircraft, and so on. The slogan recently seen on a police car in a major UK city, 'tackling crime, disorder and fear', is typical, and surveys have established that the police, rather than medical doctors or priests for example, are held in the greatest esteem by the population of Germany. One does not know where all this will lead. Nevertheless, the existence of the first two extraordinary phenomena or challenges (ultrahigh technology and material abundance) alone ensures that we are facing an unprecedented situation in human history, hence comparison of any seeming decline with that apparently experienced by Rome before its downfall, etc., may not be relevant. The quantitative differences between our present civilizations and those of Rome etc. are so great as to have become qualitative. At the same time, although it is periodically fashionable to invoke doomsday scenarios of a collapsing civilization, in the spirit of Oswald Spengler, there is actually little hard evidence in favour of such a view, only uncertainty about how the future will develop.

It is on such a stage that this book enters. The contributing authors are all from the UK or Japan. Why? This is not by chance, but is a perfectly rational consequence of history. The UK invented, or initiated if you prefer, the Industrial Revolution, and the information revolution and the nanotechnology revolution are not essentially different, and may be considered to be manifestations of the same phenomenon. Therefore the UK certainly has a claim to play a part in constructing a new future that is already and will be even more heavily moulded by these industrial phenomena. Japan was almost at the opposite end of the spectrum of development – still in the feudal age when the Industrial Revolution in Europe was its height. The remarkable achievement of Japan in so wholly modernizing its economy in such a relatively short space of time, such that it is now the leader in several of the most

---

[7] A very small, but well-documented, example can be found in D.M. Berube, 'The Magic of Nano', *Nanotechnology Perceptions*, vol. 2 (2006) pp. 249–56.

important and sophisticated areas of global industrial technology, gives it an indisputable claim to contribute to this book. Beyond that, however, Japan has always shown, from the earliest times when it was subject to influences from China and Korea, down through the tentative contacts made by Europeans at the end of the Middle Ages (who for example introduced firearms, which, it may be noted, rapidly spread throughout the islands), to the great swathes of foreign cultures assimilated in the twentieth century, a remarkable and effective ability to discriminatingly adopt foreign ways that were felt to be superior to the existing ways. This utterly objective and heuristic approach, alongside which the essential spirit of the nation still remains untouched and untouchable, has nowhere else been carried out to such tremendous effect, and is an example to the whole world.

At the same time, Japanese worldliness, already alluded to a few paragraphs earlier, giving a very strong sense of immediacy, has led to the development of abilities to react swiftly to unforeseeable changes. This mentality seems to be thoroughly embedded within Japanese thought at all levels, and contrasts to the same ideas being enunciated by only a very few of some of the more remarkable European thinkers such as Clausewitz (of whose ideas very effective practical use was made for many decades by Napoleon Bonaparte), and not being shared at all by the vast majority of the population. Undoubtedly, this gift has also been very important in the historical development of the Japanese nation.

It is not the intention here to develop the theme of why certain nations have played and play the roles they do; we might just remark that island nations – with the inevitably strong maritime traditions that follow from their geographical location (it will not escape the notice of the reader that the ability to swiftly react to unforeseeable changes is precisely what is required of the Master of a ship, especially a sailing vessel) – on the margins of their continents appear to have the ability to play leading roles at critical junctures. The roots of these abilities might be quite prosaic and not even particularly complimentary: the proverbial English laziness may have engendered the equally proverbial English love of machinery, whose purpose is after all first and foremost to save effort. The Japanese seem to have an equal love of and admiration for machinery. Another feature uniting the two nations is their mutual love of practical action, which is definitely placed above thought and reflexion. That is certainly one of the factors responsible for the still noticeable mutual incomprehension reigning between the English and their continental cousins (here it might be added that some of the earliest works written in English, such as Langland's 'Piers Plowman', already hinted at an awareness of the economic aspect of life – and that was still well in the Middle Ages).

It is well known that the Japanese samurai is above all a man of action, who values science (knowledge) only if it is of practical use, and does not strive for objective truth. Actions are governed by the tripod of wisdom (*chi*), benevolence (*jin*) and courage (*yu*). This is the soil from which the remarkably humane structures of Japanese corporations sprang.[8]

Although rooted in particular cultures, those of Japan and Britain, this book makes a strong claim for universality of appeal. It therefore unashamedly sits in the van of cultural globalization: our aim is indeed to find a set of principles that can be adopted throughout the world: anything less will inevitably be felt to be inadequate; and just as no one quality was the exclusive patrimony of bushido, the ethical code of the samurai, but it was the aggregate that was unique, so we also anticipate that it is the aggregate of the content of this book that will offer a unique and new way of thinking for the leadership of corporations. Hence the reader must work too in order to make his or her synthesis from the different contributions presented here. We also know that the omnipresent Internet has essentially swept parochialism away; this places a huge implicit imperative on us to blend, distil and select, and in the fire of the still to allow old associations to break and new ones to form.

There are, of course, numerous books about corporate life and organization. The modern genre was really invented by the late C. Northcote Parkinson. Although much of his writing was anecdotal, the anecdotes were constructed with such wit and erudition – and a few mathematical equations – that they made an excellent read. His work was also admirably concise. Later imitations have been very definitely epigones. They combine turgidity of prose with devastating triviality of content. The anecdotes are neither witty nor erudite but, in compensation, purport to describe incidents that really happened – the reader has of course little chance of verifying that. However, the physical volume of the books is partly due to the fashion of printing them in a large font, possibly so that they can be read on aircraft passing through zones of turbulence. At any rate airport bookstalls seem to be their favourite repositories – and even though the publishers claim that millions of copies are sold, to the extent of actually printing that claim on the covers, I have personally never actually seen someone buying one.[9]

The samurai's ethics were above all directed towards fulfilment of military duties, and we are well aware that in the supposedly pacifist latter half of the twentieth century, military values have been increasingly downgraded, although a few management gurus nevertheless retained an affection for certain

---

[8] To give a counter example, it is barely conceivable that the kind of horrible fates – slow death by asbestosis – to which employees of the Australian building materials enterprise James Hardie have been left would have been encountered in Japan. That is admittedly perhaps an extreme case; the cold cynicism of the Hardie management vis-à-vis its employees aroused negative comment even from the most dispassionate business and economy commentators.

[9] According to L.S. Hyman (*Financial Times*, 25 November 2005) there are over 200,000 business books of that type (in his amusing words 'low content self-help books for attention deficit disorder afflicted executives') currently available.

classics such as Sun Tzu's *The Art of War*. As a result, bushido, the ethical code of the samurai, would not appear *a priori* the first place to look for input to a new universal set of ethical values for the corporations of the twenty-first century. Nevertheless, the wars in the Middle East, and above all the US-led invasion of Iraq in 2003, happening long after this book was first conceived, have thrust militarism back onto centre stage, and the all too well documented atrocities of a peculiarly gruesome and inhuman nature perpetuated on the inmates of prisons like the notorious Abu Ghraib by US troops,[10] and the vast scale of civilian casualties,[11] proportionately far exceeding those of even the First World War, have thrust ethics and militarism firmly into the centre of general attention, and further confirmed today's ethical chaos. The perhaps naïvely plaintive question voiced by millions upon millions is 'why has it been necessary to abandon all semblance of humanity in order to purportedly save it?' Perhaps ethical chaos is too mild a term – the world has tied itself in an ethical knot worse than that faced by Gordian, and it is clear that any book attempting to create a new ethical framework for corporations must also encompass the conduct of a war such as that one. Besides, the complicity in fighting such a war of numerous large and influential corporations, whose aims are so inextricably intertwined with the aims and goals of the military forces, starting from the supply of ordnance and provision of transport and going through to the 'reconstruction' so laughably – and profitably (to the corporations) – being attempted in Iraq,[12] that in essence they are the same, indistinguishable from one another, makes ethics for one applicable to the other.

The current 'morality' of many corporations today – and largely endorsed by commentators – tend to gravitate down to the simple statement that it is wrong to discriminate between groups of customers (i.e. one group of customers has no right to tell a supplier to cut off business with another). Hence it is not immoral to sell a gun to a criminal, or a bomb to a terrorist, and as is well-known and documented almost daily, this is exactly what is happening around the world. The US response to the alarming rise of shooting incidents in schools, in which teachers are attacked by pupils, has been calls to provide the teachers with guns (*sic*). Clearly this 'morality' is inadequate, and is only mentioned here to show that the need for a new direction is so overwhelming that sometimes it is hard to recognize the presence of the need, because it is so all-pervasive.

---

[10] S.H. Miles, 'Abu Ghraib: Its Legacy for Military Medicine', *The Lancet*, vol. 364 (2004) pp. 725–9.

[11] L. Roberts *et al.*, 'Mortality Before and After the 2003 invasion of Iraq: Cluster Sample Survey', *The Lancet*, vol. 364 (2004) pp. 1857–64; G. Burnham *et al.*, 'Mortality after the 2003 Invasion of Iraq: a Cross-Sectional Cluster Sample Survey', *The Lancet*, vol. 368 (2006) pp. 1421–8.

[12] See e.g. U. Tilgner, 'Babylon der Rambos', *Schweiz global*, issue 4 (2005) pp. 5–8.

From the beginning of this Preface, it will have been apparent that the three extraordinary phenomena or challenges set down there are very strongly interrelated with one another. Thus, for example, there is a strong current of opinion asserting that technology itself leads to immorality. I shall myself return to this theme in Chapter 7, but already here it must be stated that the seemingly inexorable development of technology itself poses some undeniable problems. Although technology already realized or on the threshold of realization is often presented as the solution to pressing problems (e.g. the genetically modified organism (GMO) lobby presents this particular technological solution as the way to overcome food shortages in many parts of the world – admittedly that particular problem is not especially an ethical one), in nearly every case the technology that already exists, and that in some cases has existed for decades, is adequate to solve the problem under consideration. This applies in particular to many of the issues associated with energy and raw material sustainability. The problem is rather that we simply do not know how best to make use of the technology at our fingertips – and that is what we call the ethical problem associated with technology.

This issue is particularly apparent in the context of the current debates about nanotechnology. Alongside the material superabundance that it promises are the largely unknown risks associated with the presence of nanoparticles in the environment, and (somewhat farther in the future) with the possible uncontrolled replication of nanoscale assemblers (known as the 'grey goo' scenario). Actually, the level of ethical debate currently associated with envisaged applications of nanotechnology is probably at a higher level than in any of the previous technological revolutions that have taken place, which is certainly a welcome trend. And in that vein, discussion of 'accountability', or better 'responsibility', is becoming more are more firmly embedded in corporate culture, although as the still ongoing James Hardie affair demonstrates,[13] movement towards more responsible conduct is taking place at very different rates around the world.

The response of some to the generally accepted deficiencies in the behaviour of certain corporations has been to call for more regulation (as shown, for example, by the activities of the Better Regulation Task Force, BRTF). But do we really believe that that will provide an answer? Strictly speaking, as yet we cannot give a final, definitive answer to that question. More research, along the lines of historical surveys of past attempts, and complex systems modelling of the type described in Chapter 6, is clearly needed to discover the nature of the influence of regulation on the evolution of society and corporations. The fundamental contribution of this book is not towards laying down a possible regulatory framework, however: its fundamental message is that improvement can only come through knowledge combined with personal inner reform.

---

[13] See footnote 8.

Acknowledgements

The idea to publish this book originally started from the 'Spiritual Motivation Forum' organized by Cranfield University Japan Centre, and eventually became a joint project between the Human Media Foundation and the Cranfield School of Management. The editors thank each of the authors who contributed to this book, people from the industries that supported us, Kieko Mombayashi for assistance with the translations of those essays that were originally written in Japanese, and Alex Kessler for her indefatigable assistance in preparing the English typescripts.

Prologue

Lee Teng-hui

I was a student of Taipei High School in the old education system when I encountered the book called *Bushido* for the first time. It hit me like a thunderbolt, combining as it does a certain way of living with the personality of Nitobe Inazo, a person whom I respect greatly.

Many people tend to think of bushido as a ghost of the feudal age. However, once you read the book written by Nitobe Inazo with a lot of soul carefully and earnestly, you will soon find that this is a very shallow and superficial reaction. I have found myself repeatedly asking 'why bushido now?', not only Japan and the Japanese but also myself, because I firmly believe that each member of society needs to rediscover and take another look at 'pointers to the way of life' at this critical epoch. I feel strongly that we cannot see the future of a nation and its people without asking this big question.

I cannot help feeling that the young people who will be in charge of the future of Japan tend to lose sight of guidelines for the future. Adults who have not shown firm attitudes and beliefs should be held liable for most of this, because children grow up regarding their parents as a role model. In the confusion of their society after the war, Japanese adults have sought the values of materialism and mammon under the slogan of 'high growth', ignoring excellent spiritual values previously developed worldwide. Nobody can blame a young generation that has seen the lifestyles of their parents headed in the materialistic direction. This trend may not be completely unrelated to the materialism of Marxism that spread so widely after the Second World War.

Where has the resolute lifestyle gone, as symbolized by the expression 'A samurai, even when starving, acts as if his stomach is full'? The young generation is supposed to take charge of the future based on a grand plan for a hundred years, and being contented with honesty and poverty. Therefore, it is not difficult to imagine the big shock that young people received when they realized that elite bureaucrats, politicians and top leaders such as corporate managers who should have shown good examples of philosophy and ideas about how to live by providing leadership to that generation are actually making frantic efforts to feather their own nests without thinking of the future of public matters such as the nation and its people. Moreover, nobody would voluntarily, without hesitation take responsibility for a big failure of their company or the nation caused by their own lack of leadership. They just think they can solve the problem only using 'public money', which is a punitive tax collected from the citizens. Is this attitude what 'serving the public' means in current society?

The reason why I am emphatically recommending a re-evaluation of 'bushido' is that I would like Japan and the Japanese to recall their original spiritual values clearly and eagerly. I would like them to rethink seriously what their unique 'history' is and what their unique 'tradition' is.

In short, it attributes the issue of how to sublate or *aufheben* the two seemingly antithetical concepts of tradition and progress. However, such a lifestyle in which we choose one of the two is the height of absurdity: making light of 'tradition' because of making too much 'progress'. It is said that recently young people tend to lean too much towards the materialistic aspect, and as a result they are focusing on superficial 'progresses', not noticing the importance of spiritual 'tradition' and 'culture' that should form the basic premiss. It is because of firm tradition as the base that we can build up wonderful progress. Without tradition there cannot be progress in any real sense. On the other hand, progress should not be treated lightly just because tradition is important. The simple pursuit of progress without thinking about what tradition is and what progress is will make the future of the nation and its citizens gloomy.

I know very well that various systems and directions of New Japan have changed significantly since I left Japan to be reborn as a Taiwanese. Moreover, it is also an undeniable fact that the change that had been brought about by the big 'progress' became one of the driving forces to build one of the world's great economic powers. However, if Japan abandons the most important tradition for both the nation and its people in order to obtain progress, I wonder whether it can be truly be labelled 'progress'.

After all, irreplaceable traditions, including good customs, manners and a unique culture that originated from the country, having taken root and after having been nurtured, cannot vanish away easily – even if Japan, its system and other things may change.

There were similar discussions in the air when Dr Nitobe Inazo was alive, and he expressed his concerns about it in his book *Bushido*. He was particularly concerned about the possibility that drastic 'progresses' might drive out traditional values.

However, I do not simply worry about the situation. Fortunately I was educated and spent my impressionable youth in the wonderful tradition that the great seniors in the Meiji era like Nitobe Inazo, Uchimura Kanzo, Nishida Kitaro and Suzuki Daisetsu left us. Since the dawn of history, Japan has made remarkable advances and splendidly established a unique tradition of its own without being swallowed by the omnipresent rushing torrent of changes. This is the reason why I am not worried about it so much.

For example, Chinese characters, kanji, were once introduced from China to Japan. Did it drive the Japanese language away? Precious ancient Japanese cultural heritage did not vanish because of that; rather, the tradition was strengthened after the stimulation from new 'progresses'. In fact, Japanese people utilized the newly introduced Chinese characters to create a new Japanese culture with a mixture of Chinese characters and Japanese phonetic characters in order to address their own needs. I think this way of the Japanese to create new things is very valuable.

The Japanese have been blessed with such rare ability and spirit since ancient times. After introducing foreign culture with dexterity, they will remake it into forms more convenient and more suitable for themselves. This way of creating 'new culture' is quite important for the growth and development of a country for the future. Endowed with such natural ability, the Japanese cannot discard their precious heritage and traditions such as Bushido and Japanese spirit so easily. Their mental attitude as Japanese must return the Japanese people to that way ultimately.

Why do we need to esteem such traditional values so highly? Let me explain the reason using a Judaeo-Christian story that boils down to the matter of 'justice'. I feel that many contemporary Japanese have lost the proper sense of justice. Consider this episode in the Old Testament. A prophet in Moresheth called Micah used to be a farmer. In Jewish society in those days, about 2,700 years ago, the exploiting class severely oppressed the agrarian class, and there was no social justice. Therefore Micah became a prophet and began preaching social righteousness, justice. This is the universal truth he wrote, applicable to the modern world:

'Woe to them that devise iniquity, and work evil upon their beds! When the morning is light, they practise it, because it is in the power of their hand. And they covet fields, and take them by violence; and houses, and take them away: so they oppress a man and his house, even a man and his heritage. Therefore thus saith the Lord; Behold, against this family do I devise an evil, from which ye shall not remove your necks; neither shall ye go haughtily: for this time is evil.'[1]

In essence, Micah already preached the fundamental proposition 'How should a human live?' 2,700 years ago. Leading others means working hard night and day for justice, and it is only when a person has the mental attitude or mettle to give their blood for justice that they can manifest real leadership.

Translated by
Kieko Mombayashi

---

[1] Micah, chapter 2, verse 1 to chapter 2, verse 3.

Part I
Core Elements

1
Contemporary Challenges to Sustainable Industrial Civilization

Homare Takenaka

1.1 Postwar footsteps of Japanese society

An amazing fact still fresh in our minds is that Japan, which suffered from devastating damage in the Second World War, had almost miraculously recovered only a few short decades later. It is undeniable that Japan had good luck in terms of the postwar economic and security environment it encountered. However, I think the most important factors that enabled this recovery to happen were the good qualities of the Japanese people, such as diligence, honesty and high standards of education, as well as a well-established mutual trust among people in society.

To start with, the Japanese people should recognize and be proud of their outstanding achievements; through their own efforts the Japanese people have realized some of the most fundamental wishes of human beings, such as economic affluence, high educational standards, low crime rates, longevity, and so on. These are among the goals that people on earth have been pursuing since the dawn of history.

Nevertheless, despite these excellent achievements, the Japanese people now seem to be gripped by vague discontent, uncertainty and frustration about both the current situation and what will happen in the future. What has caused the confusion and chaos witnessed in various areas of current Japanese society, such as politics, economics, education and society? What have the Japanese people gained and lost during this period, when they made the best possible efforts to realize economic prosperity, and actually achieved it?

In order to build a bright future for Japanese society, it is important to examine these issues again and to think about appropriate measures that may have to be taken for the future. I hope that these reflexions are also of value to other countries in the world experiencing a similar malaise.

1.2 Changes in the environment that surrounds Japan

The incidents encountered in daily life and reinforced through reports in the mass media have made one feel increasingly uneasy about the current and future Japan. One notices young girls making themselves up on trains, youngsters who do not give their seats up to the elderly or handicapped, or violent attacks committed by children, various scandals perpetrated by social leaders, a flourishing subculture of fraudulent activities, and suicide victims amounting to some 30,000 people per annum, as examples. Incidents like these that have not even been imagined in the past have become occurrences that are not unusual these days, amplifying our uneasiness.

Concerning possible fundamental factors that have triggered this state of alarm, I would like to draw attention to the following three items:

1.2.1   An affluent society achieved during a short period of time

The economic prosperity realized during a relatively short interval is a critical factor. As a result of the Japanese people's strenuous efforts to pursue an economically affluent society, Japan has achieved its now almost legendary 'miraculous' economic success in the world. However, this success was realized too quickly and resulted in the creation of an imbalance between material affluence on the one hand and mental immaturity on the other in Japanese society taken as a whole. In other words, although we have succeeded in achieving our primary goal of economic prosperity, we have not yet found those new principles and rules that would be required to maintain a certain social order under the new environment in which we find ourselves.

A basic core philosophy, which played a decisive role for the Japanese people after the war, has been the national slogan, 'Catch up with Western countries'. The highest priority was placed on social and economic affluence and on higher productivity achieved through teamwork. Everybody was expected to behave as a good member of the total team, and considerations of the total team and loyalty to the group have been regarded as virtues. Yet when economic success became a reality and had reached a level equal to that observed in western countries, the Japanese people no longer had examples to follow and started to feel at a loss, which is where they stand at present.

We have been required to face a new situation, which has led us to question our own identities, and to enquire about a new possible goal at which to aim.

Under the national policy of increasing wealth and military power in the Meiji era, and with the slogan 'Catch up with the West and overtake it', we always had competitors that were running ahead of us, and therefore the objectives were clear. The spiritual core that had led Japanese people in such a social environment was, 'Compare ourselves with others and decide what we should do', which has become the deeply-rooted traditional base for our thoughts and activities. Expressions like 'shame-sensitive society', 'flexible thinking and actions according to circumstances', 'not afraid of being poor but afraid of not being equal' are some examples to represent these characteristics.

Once the Japanese had achieved the desired objectives and began enjoying material affluence without spiritual maturity, they became conceited with the illusion, 'There is nothing to learn from Western countries' and their traditional spiritual core lost its power to discipline themselves by learning from others.

Although we Japanese succeeded in realizing a materially rich society, we have not yet established a new spiritual base that should be the key for making our future brighter. Japanese society desperately needs leaders to guide it with a vision for the future, and with a corresponding philosophy and principles that should constitute a new social basis.

1.2.2 Advent of the information society and its social impact

In addition to the material richness, another factor that has influenced the traditional spiritual base of Japan must be information technology (IT) innovations, that incidentally exemplify almost perfect globalization.

The advances in information technology, such as the rapid development and spread of television, innovative ways of data processing and communication brought about by a combination of computers and telecommunications, and the emergence of the Internet, have together engendered a revolutionary influence on every sector and area of our society. The amazing progress that has taken place in information technology now enables us to send the same information to all people at the same time, completely beyond conventional barriers such as distance, time, age and others. This enablement has brought about fundamental changes in the traditional values and ways of doing things in our society. Especially, the influence on children and juveniles is immeasurable. After all, the source of intellectual growth of a human being is basically 'information', and it should preferably be provided according to the stage of growth of the individual and his or her ability to digest it in order to transform the information into useful nutrients for sound individual growth.

In the pre-information society, the first information providers to children were their parents, grandparents, elder brothers and sisters, and senior people from the neighbourhood. This role was eventually partially taken over by schoolteachers, but nevertheless the information was conditioned and provided using traditional information channels and matched to the growth level of the children.

The advent of the information society has completely changed the conventional form of information transmission. Two things will happen to a child who is since birth exposed to the flood of information now provided by the various media. First, the number of separate channels that supply information as a source of intellectual development has increased dramatically, and the information the child typically receives exceeds its own capability to digest it, and also surpasses the capability of the child's parents or teachers as educators to manage and supervise it. Furthermore, parents and teachers themselves cannot digest the relevant information appropriately, being themselves inundated with various kinds of information from all over the world.

Children will tend to obtain more information and knowledge on particular subjects than their parents, grandparents or teachers. This is already happening! Consequently, their authority and esteem as educators or leaders will be diminished.

Secondly, children buried in a flood of information that exceeds their ability to digest it will have to accept it as it is, creating their own world without the proper guidance of their seniors about ways of interpreting the information. Hence the children find themselves in circumstances in which they have neither leaders nor educators who can help them perceive the nature of society and point out good examples. Consequently, the development of educators for this new era must be one of the most pressing needs in our society.

1.2.3   The progress of globalization

Epoch-making progress in transportation technology and information technologies has made the world rapidly smaller. Information from all over the world can now be shared instantly, and the interdependence of countries has become much closer than ever before. On the one hand, such an environment, where many kinds of resources like people, goods, funds, information and know-how travel the globe freely, is quite wonderful and could serve to produce new values created through using the wisdom of as many people as are concerned in the world.

On the other hand, rapid globalization is also one of the factors causing confusion in the formerly rather clearly apprehended spiritual aspect of Japanese society. As I mentioned earlier, the traditional base of Japanese spiritual guidelines has been judgement by circumstances and position relative to others. No other clear independent principles for people to think and judge their own thoughts and behaviours have existed. At least, to judge our own selves by comparison with others has been the main pole for most Japanese.

According to the famous book *The Study of Atmosphere* written by Yamamoto Shichihei,[1] the final responsibility of important decision-making rests with the atmosphere in Japanese society. In a society in which a rather homogeneous membership has been predominant for a long period of time, tacit understanding has played a very critical role and may be said to have built such a society in which important matters are indeed decided by the atmosphere.

The 'society of the Japanese, by the Japanese, for the Japanese', built on the historical and geographical conditions that were unique to Japan and which had hitherto functioned quite well is now faltering as a result of the onslaught of expanding globalization. Under circumstances leading inexorably to increasing international interdependence, a minimum requirement for the Japanese people would be to be able to explain their own way

---

[1] Yamamoto Shichihei, *Kuuki no Kenkyuu* (*The Study of 'Atmosphere'*). Tokyo: Bungeishunju, 1997.

of thinking and doing to people of other countries and to people with different cultures.

In order to establish real collaborative relations with other countries in the world that have different histories, cultures, values, ways of thinking and customs, it is indispensable that the Japanese should have a clear idea of their vision, and the capabilities for communicating well beyond the Japanese themselves. We have to concede reluctantly that under the new global circumstances, it is impossible to make the idea that 'The atmosphere should be a decision-maker' work in the world. Essentially a new type of Japanese person equipped with a philosophy and principles that can be applied to the world is now sought for in order to allow Japan to survive and prosper in the contemporary world situation apparently heading for complete globalization.

1.3 The search for new leaders

Here we discuss how to find Japanese leaders for establishing a bright future of Japan; in order that Japan will develop its potential as a country able to play a key role in the globalizing world, the most important thing should be to develop individuals with a universal mindset and mode of thinking that are internationally robust. Furthermore, it is extremely important to regain diligence, honesty, fairness and faith in Japanese beauty, which has lost its traditional critical weight in the minds of the Japanese people distracted by the pursuit and attainment of economic affluence. We have to steep ourselves anew in the refreshing aether of Japanese spiritual beauty, which has been cherished for so long in our national history. I firmly believe that creating a new value in cooperating with people in other countries to build a better world would be the way to secure continual existence and development of not only Japan but also those other countries in the twenty-first-century world.

Many of the traditional values and thoughts developed in Japanese society as part of the code to discipline human conduct – what we can call ethics – could be universally accepted in their essence. To study and expand understanding of this essence, that became formalized in Japan as bushido, and relate it to common features found in English chivalry for example, is a wonderful project. The goal of such a project must be to achieve a real fusion between east and west, applicable to the new global business society, and be positively perceived and universally accepted. It will significantly contribute to developing future leaders with a firm identity and philosophy, the essential nature of which has never before been so keenly felt.

Translated by
Kieko Mombayashi

2
The Book of Five Concepts for Management: Based on Miyamoto Musashi's *The Book of Five Rings* – The Spirit of Being Well-skilled in Wielding Both the Sword and the Pen

Shuhei Aida

Miyamoto Musashi's *The Book of Five Rings*, which is considered to contain the basic principles of bushido, describes martial art in five ways: the principles are compared to 'earth, water, fire, wind and emptiness' in Buddhism and expounded in five corresponding chapters. It is very interesting to apply the meaning of these principles to management thinking today. It can be said that the apprehension of the market economy, corporate management and dynamism in our twenty-first-century global society, based on personality, experience and knowledge, shares something in common with the perspective of the martial artist.

In his '*Book of Five Rings*' Musashi states that the strategics expounded in his book can be applied not only to man-to-man combat but also to group-to-group fights, and, furthermore, to social life in general. His ideas are convincing because they stem from his own experiences of fierce fighting. Let us read it and figure out what the five chapters of *The Book of Five Rings* mean in an interpretation drawing on modern systems science.

Considering that Miyamoto Musashi's knowledge as a martial artist is the basic platform for a leader, it can be recognized that the concept of 'person, goods and money' in corporate management has been changing drastically in recent years. In modern society, the quality and abilities of the workforce should be noted. In terms of goods, a series of processes, from material procurement and a production site to distribution and consumption by society, should be accorded notice. Moreover, they are required to maintain harmony with the planetary ecological system at all levels. The creation of an eco-design industry should be taken into consideration from this viewpoint.

Alongside changes in the market economy, the allocation of investment or money to make profit has also been changed. It is necessary not only to promote the efficiency and streamlining of the production site, but also strategies

Table 2.1 Correlation between Musashi's *Book of Five Rings* and contemporary management systems

Chapter name	Chapter theme	Interpretation in modern systems thinking
The Earth Chapter	Frame of mind in swordsmanship	Cultivation of holistic approach/Real image of the system can be identified by synthesis.
The Water Chapter	Swordsmanship in strategics	Analytical techniques and conceptual power/Real image of the system can be identified by analysis.
The Fire Chapter	Technique in battle with an opponent	Practice of management techniques/Real image of the system can be identified by practice.
The Wind Chapter	Comparison of your style with other styles	Synthesis through criticisms of management/Real image of the system can be identified by considering conflicting ideas. Dialectic development.
The Emptiness Chapter	Stance/No stance	Management philosophy/Real image of the system can be identified by experience.

to change the site in deficit into one that lays 'golden eggs' should always be implemented with the perspective of investment and participation in the future of the business. It is important to steer each business appropriately into the right power balance in the market economy and to assess the direction and anticipated conclusion, as well as the time expected to get there. Furthermore, having the motivation to provide something that truly contributes to people in the world with one's own business is important. Based on the modern systems methodology, the following five chapters can be compared (see Table 2.1).

The Earth Chapter: the general statement of Musashi's strategics – cultivation of a holistic approach

In this part of the book Musashi gives a general statement of his basic concept of strategics. He points out the importance of employing every reasonable means for the desired purpose, based on the holistic principle. In modern terms, this is essentially the system architecture of human activity. He wrote that he had named the first chapter the Earth Chapter, in order to pave the way for what followed. *Hyoho*, or strategics, is the code for warriors to follow as well as the art of winning. In order to take hold of true strategics, both small things and big things need to be understood, and one should seek profoundly. This is the Way and paving the way for the True Way at the same time.

In terms of systems methodology, this chapter explains the approach of holism aiming at 'Truth is in Synthesis'. Synthesizing means becoming like water in nature, as is written later in the 'Water Chapter'. Water is not solidified and can change its shape according to the container, even into a square or round shape. It can be a drop of water, or assemble to form an ocean. This allegory insists on the utilization of experience and wisdom in a positive way that the individual has cultivated, with a pure mind like clear blue water putting all other distracting thoughts away.

In other words, it is important to think of business management in a holistic manner. If one can master the principle of swordsmanship in order to defeat one's enemy at will, it follows that in principle one can defeat or win over all the people in the world. Winning over one person or winning over 1,000 people begin with the same principle. A leader should judge the big picture by paying attention to small matters. This is like building a great statue of Buddha based on a miniature model.

This Synthesis chapter can also be identified with Kantian exploration or holism as it takes an overall examination, and in a sense denies atomism. It claims that building systems and constructing functions resides neither in inorganic theory (the accumulation of data) nor in the importance of human experience, but in both of them. Specifically, it means neither collected data nor theory has truth on its own.

Many theories are constructed based on collected data, and the data are collected based on the existing theories. In this sense, data and theory are inseparable and tautology is an ever-present danger. The point is that when considering any problems or issues, two or more alternative ideas or models need to be built, in order to make the whole picture of the system to be examined more clearly apparent.

In today's world, being full of changes, data as such do not hold as much significance as formerly. The collected data may have transient utility based on forecasting, but when the matrix in which the data are embedded, or the standard of the measurement, is changed from that prevailing originally, the data will lose their significance. For example, the data of a big bank that went bankrupt and was closed down might be useful as academic material, but not for a comprehensive economic forecast.

Human vitality should be exerted in an integrated manner utilizing six potential powers: physical strength, courage, energy, judgement, power for decisive implementation and ability. This is what was advocated as systems science then. One word should be enough for a wise man to know ten, and Miyamaoto Musashi wrote that 'With the one, know the ten thousand – this is the principle of the martial arts' in his *Book of Five Rings*. Here is the essential challenge for synthesis. Aiming at the exertion of one's ability in order to cope with various changes at all levels will become important challenges also in business management.

The Water Chapter: swordsmanship in Musashi's strategics – the improvement of analytical techniques and conceptual power

A leader should pattern himself after water as the foundation and let his or her frame of mind be like water, considering the water state as the ideal and aspiring to that state of mind.

Water changes its shape according to the container, even into a round or square shape, and one drop of water can form a stream by gathering together with others, eventually becoming a big river that runs slowly and magnificently to the ocean. In the master's strategics, it is important to take an overall view from the smallest part. The clear blue colour of water, its unfettered and flexible form and its purity can be considered as the symbol of the idea that 'Nature consists of itself'.

The Japanese language makes no clear distinction between singular and plural forms. Samurai is samurai; no matter how many samurai we mean we do not say samurais in the plural form. In Musashi's strategics, the opponent was always one, no matter how many enemies there were. This is the basis of the natural philosophy, 'Stance/No stance', in Musashi's swordsmanship.

The basics of management thinking is to analyse the targeted phenomenon and thing and to comprehend the constituent elements in order to obtain a comprehensive image of dynamism. Analytical techniques and conceptual power exist together here, mutually exclusive and complementary to each other at the same time. Physical and chemical analysis methods can be used as a concrete approach. Methods and choices challenge the manager's conceptual power to understand a business system comprehensively.

In an ecosystem, the process by which a living organism digests what it eats and stores it in its body as nutrition embodies a savage system of 'analysis and synthesis' of nature that thoroughly excludes others. In business management, it is necessary to take the system of 'analysis and synthesis' as a similar reference example. Therefore, the application of the concept of 'analysis' to business management is indispensable, as well as taking the concept of 'synthesis' into consideration: the two have a complementary existence.

In modern systems thinking, this is called 'synthesis by analysis' and is a basis of that thinking. It is a basic process observed in many areas.

In the philosophy of science it is said that truth lies in analysis and it starts from analysing the targeted system down to the minimum unit that can be observed comprehensively. Based on this principle, various methods (of analysis) should be utilized for the purpose of analysis. Ultimately it should enable the results of the analysis to be accumulated; that is, to grasp the total image of business management.

This idea is called Leibniz exploration, after the philosopher who first advocated it. The philosophy of analysis is a basic concept of modern science and was also called 'atomism', because at that time an atom was considered to be the smallest indivisible unit of substance. The notion of atomism established the foundation of scientific analysis. However, it is very important for a business manager to accept the fact that conflicting and exclusive notions like atomism and holism can always exist at the same time in the various systems targeted.

Atomism and holism encompass physical and chemical analyses as artificial methods and decomposition processes of a self-organizing character that take place in nature, like the digestion process within a living body. Furthermore, it is also an important exercise to always question oneself what conceptual power apart from self-interest and selfishness exists as challenges in one's mind.

The 'element-reduction method', which has often been used conventionally, is one of the ways of thinking along the lines of reductionism, and it regards the whole as nothing but the sum of its sub-elements. The reduction method evaluates the characteristic traits of each element in the system with a single norm, and comprehends the properties and attributes of the whole organization simply by collecting them. However, in order to comprehend complex systems such as the natural environment or a business, each element should be observed and assessed at different levels, and if the results from the assessment are simply added up and the power to synthesize them is absent, it is obviously pointless.

It is a real nonsense to judge international issues from the standpoints of different cultures or different ways of personality assessment. The human value of a complex system lies in the fact that each of the constituent elements has individual conceptual power. Here is the reason why system thinking counts. It advocates 'analysis and synthesis' as exclusive with respect to each other, but simultaneously having a complementary existence.

The Fire Chapter: techniques in battle with an opponent one knows – management as practical philosophy

As fire changes quickly by growing big or becoming small, it is described as the symbol of battle. We feel that it is easy to see what is large, and difficult to see what is small. Moreover careful observation shows that it is difficult for a large group of people to change direction quickly, so it is not hard for us to foresee their next move. The movement of a small group of people is less easy to see in that sense. On the other hand, as an individual person can change things upon a sudden idea, it is hard to foresee the next step of another individual. The Fire Chapter expounds the daily training to acquire the ability to cope with changes in an emergency and prescribes in detail precautions regarding how to fight.

This chapter can be compared with the dictum 'Truth is in practice', the logic of Singer, a pragmatic philosopher working in America in the early twentieth century, who aimed to establish a multiplicative model. The importance of pragmatic experience is often emphasized. For instance, giving an engineering student an assignment to repeatedly conduct an experiment in physics will bring about the desired results naturally: the purpose of the experiment is to enhance learning effects by taking control over all the events, large or small, that the student may encounter in the process, who learns 'the experience of successes'. In practice, experience of successes will bring about the next success. You may have failure sometimes but even so, you will get something out of it and learn an idea that could lead you to success.[1] As an example of the value of experience, consider that the experience acquired in the Gulf War increased the hit probability of missiles remarkably in the Iraq War, namely from 30 to 80 per cent, disregarding advances in missile technology *per se*.

Learning individual matters and synthesizing them will create appropriate ideas to deal with complex issues such as global environmental ones. The scenario of a virtual world based on them will enable a future society to be developed by activating the potentiality of the real world.

The Wind Chapter: understanding the way of other styles and comparing them with one's own – the process of synthesis with criticism[2]

The Wind chapter explains the importance of knowing other styles of martial art as well as your own style, and comparing them with your style. You cannot know yourself without knowing others. Unless you believe in the Way earnestly and master the True Way, a little distortion of mind could lead you far from the True Way and you will find yourself in the wrong way. Musashi's 'strategics' place priority on becoming well aware of this principle. One should recognize the importance of accumulating techniques of reasonable swordsmanship without being deceived by which style your opponent will take or by what is behind his behaviour. This is the basis of Musashi's 'natural philosophy': 'Wind blows freely and, the wind, as well as water, is source of Japanese aesthetic feelings.'

---

[1] Recent computer simulations that can be played like games incorporate unexpected events too. However, they are likely to be quite different from the experience of using real machines or tools. Above all, huge differences could exist between a real battlefield and a simulation in the laboratory.

[2] 'If you do not know others, it is difficult to understand yourself. There are always heretical understandings, no matter in what Way or affair you conduct yourself. If you put your energy into such an understanding day by day and your mind is wide of the mark, though you think, "This is a good Way", you will not be on the time path when seen from the correct position. If you do not attain the True Way, a small warp of the mind will later become a large one' (extract from *The Book of Five Rings*, translated by William Scott Wilson).

It is the very exploration of Hegelian dialectic. The study of complex systems has something in common with the journey in pursuit of virtual and real worlds by considering their dual nature. All the data are generally a bunch of figures and the figures themselves are meaningless. The conception is that when one idea is combined with a contrasting idea, the data become meaningful information for the first time. This is also a significant concept for business management.

For example, through the process of integrating conflicting management policies, the ideal aspect of business management will be understood. This is the logic that dictates that any issues need to have at least two completely conflicting expressions. In order to resolve a conflict, other thinkings or ideas should be understood thoroughly, and in that spirit, various kinds of system thinking should be examined fully. Moreover, the ability to provide guidance towards a new solution with discussions not denying criticism but including it is an essential attribute of the excellent leader.

The process suggested in the extract from the chapter quoted at the beginning of this section (footnote 2) has something in common with coexistence phenomena in ecosystems. It resembles the phenomenon that multiple animals repeat intense competitions and collaborations to coexist and compartmentalize. As an example of 'mutualism', in which creatures share benefits, when you put multiple bacteria in a beaker, they battle with each other at first but eventually they will create a new mode of coexistence in order to establish a stable society after finding their complementation *modus vivendi*.

Here one may mention that while a commensal organism takes benefits one-sidedly and attacks another until it dies, a mimicking organism changes itself as if it tried to gain other organisms' favour to protect itself and prosper. It is interesting to note that similar phenomena can be observed in human society. In addition, in most of the cases, synthesized stability in a global way can be introduced into the natural world system when these three phenomena – mutualism, commensalism and mimicry – are inherent there.

Natural wisdom is inherent in the natural ecosystem. In modern civilization, the 'fallacy of composition' may arise because no natural wisdom that we should take as a great example is lurking there. Flashpoints could become larger or smaller, and have a distinctive power that may be allegorized as being like smoke. Locating the whereabouts of the smoke is also a challenge for 'synthesis with criticism' in order to create a new management philosophy by using objections and criticism in a useful way.

Conflicts or contentions between individuals in business management assume similar characteristics when they arise between groups. The point is to grasp the big picture and to study what the other side does carefully. The big points are easy to see but the small points are hard to see, because things done by a big number of people cannot be changed rapidly, so they are easy to capture; on the other hand, as an individual person can change things according to his own idea, it is hard to foresee the next step.

Observation is always important to cope with every situation. When one encounters criticism and objection, one should take time until one can consider it with one's senses, rather than hasten to solve it instantly or emotionally. This is a key point of *The Book of Five Rings*, which can be applied effectively in many aspects of life as well. In brief what is described in the Wind Chapter means dialectic development in philosophical terms.

The Emptiness chapter: conclusions – experience creates management philosophy

Emptiness means something with no shapes, which cannot be recognized, and with no beginning or ending. Achieving the secret is to be released from the secret: attaining the state of perfect freedom in the Way of martial arts. There are no esoteric techniques or secrets in Musashi's 'strategics', it is simply necessary to control the scene, using the sword naturally and fighting against the opponent in the course of nature. This is what he means by the Way of Emptiness. One can fully display the greatest power by following the operation of nature at will: responding to the time and place, realizing the appropriate rhythm spontaneously and defeating one's opponent; one can fight against one's opponent by following the natural rhythm. This is the Way of Emptiness, which is the 'True Way' according to Musashi's natural philosophy. This chapter explains how to proceed to the Way of Truth naturally.

In terms of systems theory, this chapter can be compared with Locke's philosophical expression 'Truth is in experience', which forms the basis of his empirical philosophy, which is the philosophy underlying many empirical philosophies. Generally, modelling business management means making a model based on empirical rules. For example, one has the idea that the complicated phenomena that a manager encounters every day can be reduced to a simple empirical observation and its validity should be assured by consent at the directors' board meeting. In addition, philosophical empiricism emphasizes the difference between *Taiken* and *Keiken*. (Both Japanese words are translated as 'experience' in English.) It maintains that *Taiken* ends with physiological stimulations only, but *Keiken* forms a philosophy. This means that a standard of value related to information interpretation changes empirically in the information society, and this is an important issue for business management in particular, although to expand this point more here would be beyond the scope of this chapter.

A particular point to notice here is denial of the information interpreted by authority as well as making use of intuition coming from the manager's experiences: as is so often the case, most of the information disseminated by the mass media or trade papers tends to be a one-sided interpretation by those in power or by knowledgeable people. One requires insight to be in a position to counter it.

On the whole, the correctness of business management can always be justified by direct results – with no logical verification required. Working based on experience starts from experiential criteria for the judgement of individuals, such as raw data on site, observation and other sensory inputs that comprise a model based on expanded general facts. A model of economic prospects is an example. It is often affected by the personal experiences of experts, and therefore the presence of experts among managers is highly valued. The importance of gaining experience can be found here.

Nevertheless, the 'direct results' justifying a particular management policy are themselves judged by varying criteria, as is so prominently apparent from even a simple perusal of the financial columns of daily newspapers. The achievement of quarterly, annual or quinquennial profits requires very different decisions in most cases, and other issues, such as maintaining social harmony among employees, or preserving the surrounding environment in a pristine state, bring their own management exigencies. In the information society, the experience of television companies generally shows that profits are inversely related to intellectual content and aesthetic appeal, and this trend is similarly apparent elsewhere, as in the motion-picture industry based in Hollywood.

The Emptiness Chapter focuses on the importance of training oneself and gaining experience both mentally and physically. As a master of martial art, one can learn the art totally – from 'frame of mind or way of thinking', posture, the way of using the eyes, to the way of holding the sword, how to assume a posture of defence, how to strike with one's sword and the way of carriage of the feet. The same goes with managers. Their experience should be full of what they have undergone in life, embodying their force and significance as professionals. In a sense, in what has neither beginning or end, neither the entrance nor secrets might be counted as experience, *Taiken*. Experience or *Keiken* forms philosophy, as is said in empiricism.

Translated by
Kieko Mombayashi

Appendix: The life of Miyamoto Musashi

The famed swordsman Miyamoto Musashi was born Shinmen Takezo in Harima Province and may have fought at Sekigahara under the Ukita as a common soldier. Perhaps unsurprisingly, he makes no mention of this in the brief autobiography in his book, rather confining himself to his achievements in single combat. He claimed to have defeated his first opponent (a certain Arima Kihei) at the age of 13, following this up with a victory over 'a powerful martial artist called Akiyama of Tajima province'. After 1600 Musashi drifted to Kyoto and became involved in a well-known battle with members of the Yoshioka School of swordsmanship, emerging victorious. He wrote that he engaged in sixty duels without suffering defeat once, and was noted for his skill at handling two swords at once. He was also remembered for employing a simple bamboo sword, which he used to deadly effect.[3]

Much of Musashi's life between 1600 and 1640 is the stuff of legend; some have postulated that he served at Osaka Castle from 1614 to 1615 on the defending side, taking quite a few heads in the process. In a similar vein, he is sometimes said to have helped quell the Shimabara Rebellion of 1638 – a theory which, like his glories at Osaka, is impossible to verify. On the other hand, many of the important events described in Yoshikawa Eiji's famous novel *Musashi*[4] have a basis in reality, including his battle with the Yoshioka School, his defeat of the noted spearman Inei (chief priest of the Hôzô-in), and his duel in 1612 with Sasaki Kojiro, another famed swordsman.[5] Less well known is his skill as a painter, his works including a number of self-portraits and naturescapes.

Musashi the man must have been a forbidding figure: he was said to have rarely bathed or changed his clothes and suffered from a somewhat disfiguring skin condition. Following his duel with Sasaki, he seems to have focused his energies on perfecting his style of swordsmanship, spending much time in travel and reflexion – thus epitomizing the image of the brooding wanderer-samurai.

In 1640 Musashi accepted service with the Hosokawa clan, and three years later, in Higo Province, began work on his great book, *Gorin no shô* (*The Book of Five Rings*).[6] He finished this influential work on swordsmanship in May 1645, the year of his death.[7]

---

[3] http://www.samurai-archives.com/musashi.html
[4] Yoshikawa Eiji, *Musashi*. Tokyo: Kodansha, 1981. Originally published in serialized form in the *Asahi Shimbun*.
[5] The newspaper *Asahi Shimbun* noted in 1988 that at least one Edo Period source questioned Musashi's duel with Sasaki, stating that Musashi was not alone at the fight, and that his followers killed Ganryu after he had been knocked down to the ground.
[6] Miyamoto Musashi, *The Book of Five Rings* (trans. Thomas Cleary). Boston, MA: Shambhala, 1993.
[7] See also Thomas Cleary, *The Japanese Art of War*. Boston, MA: Shambhala, 1991 and Stephen Turnbull, *The Lone Samurai and the Martial Arts*. Hampstead: Arms and Armour Press, 1990.

3
A View of Bushido

Masato Shinagawa

'Bushido', or the code for the Japanese warrior, has two very contrasting associations, *'Bushi* warriors regarded as model citizens for commoners' (Ihara Saikaku, novelist, 1642–1693), and 'Samurai, high class idlers' (Miura Hiroyuki, historian, 1871–1931). The differences in the two associations are largely attributable to the conflicting meanings in the kanji (Chinese) characters of 'bushido'; in Japanese *bu* means martial power, *shi* means a person having an acknowledged position, and *do* means way or code. *Bu* changed the nature of its meaning as samurai swords and lethal weapons became symbols of status and objects of art for their aesthetic quality. *Shi*, who were originally armed warriors-in-waiting as guards of the court, became officials (civilians) engaged in the management of feudal estates. *Do* was also transformed from the 'code' for *bu* into various professions, with the tendency of 'code' as the meaning of *shi* growing stronger. *Shido*, or the 'code' for *shi* in its broader sense, which includes feudal lords, became associated with superordinate concepts such as the 'code for government' and the 'way of heaven'. Another aspect to be considered is the conflict between 'royalty' and 'loyalty,' which can be differentiated into 'intra-castle bushido' and 'extra-castle bushido'. This will be elaborated on below.

Intra-castle bushido

In intra-castle bushido, the stability of the 'castle' – defined as the place, typically an enclosed fortification, serving as the home for its inmates – itself becomes an important goal. Each day the warriors were constantly close to death. There was no way of knowing when one might be confronted with death, or placed in a position where avenging was expected. The interest of the *bushi* was solely centred around their relation with the feudal lord; the rule was that *Shi* render service for the one who knows him'. This rule, actually imposed by the *shi* themselves, shows that the balance of 'to know' (equivalent to the distribution of rewards) and 'the services rendered' has always been a point of great interest. At the same time, Buddhism also provided a framework for the thoughts and feelings of the warriors in preparation for death, which could indeed occur at any time. *Iki*, or chic elegance, was highly valued among the commoners, who expressed it in the form of *ikuji*, or state of having strength in bushido (Kuki Shuzo, philosopher, 1888–1941) and supported *bushi* in their existentialist being. One other factor that should be mentioned is that in the dense human relations of the intra-castle environment, *shudo*, or homosexuality sometimes became a mode of life.

Extra-castle bushido

The range of regions defined as extra-castle consists of the areas within the feudal domain, within the nation and the world. With regard to whom 'services should be rendered' being the target of loyalty, the *bushi* is confronted by the choices that they have to make, whether it should be for the 'lord himself', the 'feudal clan', the Tokugawa Shogunate government that lasted for several centuries, Japan or the Emperor.

The military code[1]

The canon of swordsmanship, which was passed down through the Yagyu family, making generations of Yagyus feudal lords and shogun teachers of the period, had to overcome the contradiction concerning loyalty by returning from the state interpreted as 'the sword that makes men live' developed for the 'peaceful period' back to 'the sword that kills' developed for the 'turbulent period'.

Tami, or common people for whom the *bushi* in the intra-castle bushido had little regard, now became subjects of interest. The *bushi* were requested to become 'role models' for the people by 'enlightening' them on *shiki* or Morale under the direction of their own fellow *bushi* class member (Hashimoto Sanai, 1834–1859, surgeon and statesman belonging to the Fukui clan; regarded as dangerous for his liberal ideas, at 25 he was executed by the Tokugawa government). In addition to those models that were not 'models who only write and preach' (Yagyu Munenori), there were also 'those of great uses on great occasions' (ibid.) meaning 'models' who demonstrated or led by their own actions.

'Bushido' in two forms

So far, I have extracted how *bushi* and *bushido* were perceived, and how they functioned, from mainly classical writings of the Edo period or before.

---

[1] After Yagyu Munenori, a feudal lord and teacher of shoguns in swordsmanship, 1571–1646.

In Japan, there are many works written on 'bushido' interpreted as 'subjects or retainers', but very few works on 'bushido' interpreted as 'lord or master'. The *'Constitution of Seventeen Articles'* by Prince Shotoku (574–622), and the much later *'Omeikan Isho'* by Hosoi Heishu (scholar, 1728–1801) may perhaps be counted as the only examples.

I do not know of any book discussing 'shogun', the highest-ranking *bushi*, or for that matter, 'lords'. Many tales or anecdotes on superior feudal rulers have been compiled in books, but I know of no writing that systematically discusses monarchs. All the writings on bushido discuss only retainers' bushido. A point of interest is the influence, or lack of it, from the ethical codes, or religions. Confucianism and Buddhism were introduced at about the same time into Japan. Of these two teachings, Buddhism, having affinity as *butsudo*, or 'Buddha's *do*', seems to have harmonized closely with bushido. I have noticed that three writers on bushido, Yagyu Munenori, Ihara Saikaku and Kenko the Priest (1283–1350), form a little group quite distinct from the other writers. Bushi *do* as seen by them has very little influence from Confucianism, while the influences of Buddha's way, and furthermore *shudo*, homosexuality, among *bushi* of the same clan, are strong. This prevents them from seeing out of the castle, especially *joka* or the lord's domain around the castle.

The famous *'Hagakure'*, the book of teachings for *bushi* of the Nabeshima Clan, may be summarized as a kind of 'office politics' for the intra-castle zone. The *'Family Traditional Book on the Military Code'* (Yagyu Munenori) may also be classified as an intra-castle crisis management text, in spite of its discussion on 'heaven's rule'.

'Ryushi Shinron' (Yamagata Daini, scholar, 1725–1767) was the first book on bushido in the context of *jogai*, or extra-castle, and *joka*, the lord's domain around the castle areas. In this work, discussions on the justifiable causes, the transformation of *bu*, martial power, contradictions arising from same persons serving as warriors and civilian officers, in other words, discussions on 'bushido' as 'government' where mutual conflicts occur between *bu* and *shi*, and bushido centred around the extra-castle area were provided. In order to encapsulate all these ideas, I offer a representation of the structure of bushido in the form of a topological diagram, (Figure 3.1) based on an idea I got from the *'Structure of Iki'* (Kuki Shuzo).

Terms given at each of the apices of the diagram have been taken from *'Budo Denraiki'* (Ihara Saikaku), *'Heiho Kaden-no-sho'* (Yagyu Munenori), *'Ryushi Shinron'* (Yamagata Daini), and *'Iki no kozo'* (Kuki Shuzo). If the currently popular rule of the five 'W's (when, where, what, who and why) and one 'H' (how) is applied to the writings of bushido, HOW was very much discussed, but WHAT was not. HOW, equivalent to *do*, transforms into self-purpose, hence the momentum towards a discussion of the five 'W's is effete. The custom of the wearing of swords by the *bushi* had as its goal the provision of an insignia of social rank, which is not seen in any other culture, and is one

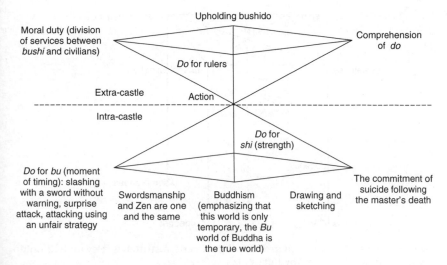

Figure 3.1   The topology of bushido

illustration of HOW becoming a self-purpose. It was on the eve of the Meiji imperial restoration that the *bushi* were pressed for discussions on the five 'W's of bushido and how to put the results into action. The intra-castle bushido holds HOW as its self-purpose was not able to give a solution or demonstrate standards of action. Intra-castle bushido actually brought about the fall of the Tokugawa Shogunate according to Fukuchi Ochi (journalist, 1841–1906), and extra-castle bushido, which was able to demonstrate the five 'W's and the practice of conjoining them with one 'H', gave birth to the Meiji restoration. The extra-castle bushido saw its consummation in a coincidental writing of Alfred P. Sloan, which in effect asserts that 'the organization follows the strategy'. This is equivalent to the demonstration and practice of the five 'W's and one 'H'.

The next figure (Figure 3.2) illustrates some of the aesthetic aspects of bushido. The apices connected by the edges of the parallelepiped, such as spirit and austere elegance, always indicate some degree of opposition. The same applies to apices that would have to be connected by a diagonal line, such as spirit and indecency. All such apices are associated with adversarial relationships. The rectangles crossing vertically along the P,O axis, and which are generated by cutting the parallelepiped according to the two sets of diagonals of the top and bottom squares, show value confrontation in the *für sich* framework and non-value confrontation in the *être pour autrui* framework.

The point of intersection of the two diagonals of the bottom square is labelled O, and the point of intersection of the two diagonals of the top square is labelled P. OP is a straight line along which the rectangles representing *für sich* and *être pour autrui* cross each other. This line signifies concrete universals within the system of elegance.

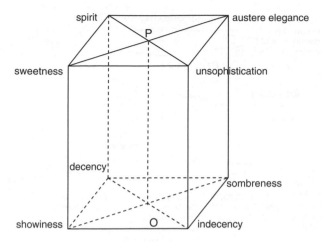

Figure 3.2   A sketch of the interrelationship of certain attributes relevant to bushido (extracted from *'Iki no kozo'* by Kuki shuzo)

The normal axis OP vertically bisects the rectangles representing *für sich* and *être pour autrui*. In consequence, we can deduce that the rectangle constructed from O, P, spirit and decency has value and the one constructed from O, P, unsophistication and indecency has anti-value (i.e. the antithesis of value). The one made of O, P, sweetness and showiness represents positivity and the one made of O, P, austere elegance and sombreness represents negativity.

Table 3.1 summarizes the essential elements of bushido in the form of proverbs.

In Japan, the Chinese character *shi* is very popular, and is used in words that denote professions or titles for example, *gakushi* (graduates of universities, bachelor of arts or bachelor of science), *bengoshi* (lawyer), *kenchikushi* (architect), *koninkaikeishi* (certified public accountant – CPA), *daigishi* (congressman), *bunshi* (writer), etc.

Etymologically, shi is one who saburau, or keeps waiting on the alert, so 'shi' is also a servant. Shi serves whatever the preceding character(s) represent. The way for the one who serves the people of the nation (city, town or village) is extra-castle bushido – that is, the way of a public servant. At present, we are confronted with the crisis of not only the public servants in the narrow sense of the word but of *shi*. I sincerely hope that a lively discussion on *shi* in the twenty-first century will arise.

The famous sentence, 'A woman is not born a woman, she becomes a woman' can also be applied to *bushi*: 'A *bushi* is not born a *bushi*, he becomes a *bushi*'. I would also like to note, that in conclusion of our study on the writings of 'bushido' that 'one is not born . . . *shi*, he becomes a . . . *shi*, even in the era of Heisei.[2]

---

[2] The name of the current era in Japan.

Table 3.1   Three proverbs summarizing samurai life

Proverb	Action in life
A samurai acts as if his stomach is full even when he is starving.	Live a simple and humble lifestyle.
A samurai keeps his word once he has said it.	Deeds must correspond to his words.
Since all samurai exist in the same circumstances, they must sympathize mutually and help each other.	They must act with integrity and with thoughtful attention.

Biographical notes

Writing a chapter on history is in effect a deliberate sampling of the entire record. The range of samples used in this chapter is as follows: 'Constitution of Seventeen Articles' by Prince Shotoku (574–622), 'Tsurezuregusa', an essay by Priest Kenko (1283–1350), 'Hojo-ki', an essay by Kamo-no-Chomei (1155–1216), 'Heihou Kaden-no-Sho' (Canon of Swordsmanship) by Yagyu Munenori (1571–1646), 'Tosenpuron' by Hoashi Banri (1778–1852), a high-ranking bushi of the Hiji Clan and a scholar in natural philosophy, 'Ryushishinron' by Yamagata Daini (1725–1767), a royalist scholar who was regarded as dangerous and executed, 'Seidan' by Ogyu Sorai (1666–1728), a scholar highly respected by the Shogunate government, 'Keihatsuroku' by Hashimoto Sanai (1834–1859), 'Ninjo Bushido' and 'Shosetsu Nippon Fudoki' by Yamamoto Shugoro (1903–1967), a novelist, 'Nippon Seishin, Relance da alma japoneza' by Wenceslau de Moraes (1854–1929), the Portuguese Consul-General in Kobe, who, after his wife's death, moved to her home town of Tokushima and spent the rest of his life there, 'Kokushijo-no-shakaimondai', or 'Social Problems in Japanese History' and 'Rekishi-to-jinbutsu,' or 'History and People' by Miura Hiroyuki, a historian (1871–1931), 'Kinsei Kijinden,' or 'Eccentric People in Modern History,' by Ban Kokei (1733–1806), 'Gakumon-no-susume' by Fukuzawa Yukichi (1835–1901), an enlightenment thinker, 'Maruyama Masao Kogiroku, or Lectures by Maruyama Masao, Vol. 6' by Maruyama Masao, a political philosopher (1914–1996), 'Iki-no-kozo' by Kuki Shuzo (1888–1941), 'Iriki Bunsho' by Asakawa Kanichi (1873–1948), a historian, 'Bushido' by Yamaoka Tesshu (1836–1888), a statesman, 'Oboegaki Bakumatsu no Mitohan,' or 'Notes on Mito Clan at the end of the Edo period,' and 'Buke-no-josei,' or 'Women in Bushi family', by Yamakawa Kikue (1890–1980), a feminist writer, 'Chushingura, or Vendetta by the loyal ronin of Ako in 1702, vol. 1, and vol. 3,' compiled by the City of Ako, 'Hotokuki', or the 'Record of Ninomiya Sontoku, farmer, economist and leader' (1787–1865), by Takada Takayoshi (1814–1890).

4

Chivalry: From the Knights of the Round Table to the Nolan Committee

Jeremy Ramsden

The purpose of this chapter is to trace the development of the ideal of the English gentleman, starting from the medieval knight, and ending in ethics by committee. Brief references to contemporaneous developments in Japan will be made, but the reader is asked to refer to Chapter 2 for a fuller account of bushido. The connexion between right behaviour and knowledge will be made, and the status of the scholar in the Middle Ages will be discussed, and how that evolved into the professional scientist of today.

At the time when bushido was emerging as a way of life in Japan, Europe was still immersed in the Middle Ages, whose dominant poles of the mind were, as Huizinga has remarked,[1] chivalry and social hierarchy. The whole medieval system of ideas actually put chivalry in a dominant position. The latter is perhaps not so very different from the structure of Japanese society, and hierarchy is moreover readily perceived to be a ubiquitous form in nature, and hence does not seem particularly unnatural. It must therefore have been a considerable advance to state, as did the Gregory the Great, 'omnes namque homines natura aequales sumus', taking up an idea put forward earlier by Seneca. This concept of the equality of all men was an essential part of chivalry, along with the idea that true ability is based on virtue.

The central figure of chivalry is the heroic knight, the European equivalent of the samurai. The knight errant was typically poor, and often had no social obligations. There was a fantastic and useless side to his nature, which is very well typified by the story of the quest of the Holy Graal, part of the adventures of King Arthur's Knights. The Holy Graal is sometimes associated with the Last Supper, sometimes with a mysterious and magical vessel, and many knights died in the vain quest for it, the Round Table was scattered, and Arthur's kingdom was weakened by the neglect of ordinary duties.[2]

---

[1] J. Huizinga, *The Waning of the Middle Ages*. London: Arnold, 1924.
[2] See for example A. Lang (ed.), *The Book of Romance*. London: Longmans, Green & Co., 1902.

Despite the uselessness and tragedy associated with that quest, the ideal of chivalry had a great hold on the mediaeval mind. It was constantly celebrated by writers, and served as a model to all men as a sublime form of secular life, paralleling, and in some ways rivalling, the life of faith, as practised by monks. Although then, as now, the majority of the inhabitants of the nations that called themselves Christian (and even some popes, notably Boniface VIII) were actually pagans, in the sense of paganism being 'a state of acquiescence, or merely professional activity, unaccompanied by sustained religious experience and inward discipline',[3] nevertheless medieval thought was saturated with Christian concepts, and medieval theology sprang from intense feeling. The contrast between acquiescence and intensity is one of many possible examples of those violent juxtapositions that are so characteristic of the Middle Ages. The church coloured the whole life of most individuals, not only through its omnipresent ceremonies marked by vivid colour and movement, but also in the way that it was somehow able to satisfy the often vague human longings felt by most of us: in short, the church interpreted life and gave meaning to it. Yet at the same time it was all part of a sort of game, and when those intense feelings led those dubbed heretics astray, the root of antipathy towards them was simply that they did not play the game.

One pillar of virtue was the idea of courtly love. Here we see traits of compassion, sacrifice and fidelity contrasting with those of the fierce and violent warrior. Courtly love as a notion embraced all ideas appertaining to a noble life. The deliverance of the virgin, as a literary motif, long predated the Middle Ages, but it was no less intense for that. Love is the source of a constant renewal of energy and enthusiasm for life; of course, the erotic element is frequently present. In the concept of chivalry, the romantic worship of a woman was as necessary a quality of the perfect knight as was the worship of God. The latter, however, was by no means the exclusive province of the knight, given that at that time all of Europe was essentially Christian, and even though, as pointed out above, the vast majority of people in reality lived as pagans rather than by faith, nevertheless they were constantly surrounded by the church, whose presence was an integral part of their lives.

The church takes some credit for having preserved the notion of learning in the monasteries during the Dark Ages (*ca* 400–600 CE), albeit that the learning mostly comprised the regurgitation of erroneous Greek ideas and tended towards the stultification of thinking. As the Middle Ages got under way, certain elements do not appear particularly encouraging for the development of a vigorous life devoted to the pursuit of pure, disinterested and effective knowledge. Jean Gerson, sometime Chancellor of the University of Paris, notoriously inveighed 'contra vanam curiositatem' in a treatise, with 'vanam'

---

[3] F.M. Powicke, 'The Christian Life', in C.G. Crump and E.F. Jacob (eds), *The Legacy of the Middle Ages*. Oxford: Clarendon Press, 1926.

doubtless defined conservatively. Yet knowledge was nevertheless steadily but surely growing. Among the most outstanding medieval figures are Fibonacci, Roger Bacon (Oxford and Paris), Jean Buridan (Paris) and Nicholas da Cusa (Basel). This period witnessed the triumphal birth of modern science, the epoch – long predating the Renaissance, it should be noted – in which the oldest European universities in the modern sense were founded, such as those of Bologna, Paris and Cambridge.[4] In that epoch efforts were made to unite all philosophy in a single centre.[5]

Scholarship was ranked together with knighthood, and vestiges of this equality can still be seen today in the robes and ceremonies held in universities on the days for awarding degrees, which not uncoincidentally resemble those of the ceremonies used to confer knighthood on a person. In essence, knighthood and the doctorate of science were sacred forms of the two superior functions of courage and knowledge, both expressed by a ceremonial consecration. Chivalry also coloured thought and the development of knowledge, perhaps most significantly by ensuring that the notion of thought transcending the limits of the feasible, so important for innovation and discovery, was firmly embedded in the mind of the scholar.

At the same time, ethics as represented by church doctrine remained essentially fixed and unchanging. The general teaching of the dominant Roman Catholic Church even today is still based on the writings of St Thomas Aquinas (1226–1274), and the authority of the much earlier St Augustine (353–430) was appealed to by Protestants and Catholics alike even after the Reformation.[6] Based on such incontrovertible historical evidence, Buckle has argued powerfully that all improvements in our standards of behaviour, in other words our ethics, are derived from advances in knowledge,[7] for while behaviour has undoubtedly improved, only knowledge has advanced, while the theory of ethics has essentially remained static. Important ethical thinkers associated with the Renaissance, such as Erasmus, were not particularly associated with the church; more significant were the various communities of thinkers who happened to be living in the same place at the same time – a good example is Basel in the early sixteenth century, where Erasmus (ethics), Paracelsus (medicine), Amerbach (law) and others were all living and working at the time,

---

[4] See S.L. Jaki, *The Road of Science and the Ways to God*. Edinburgh: Scottish Academic Press, 1978; and P. Duhem's monumental *Le Système du Monde*. Paris: Hermann, 1913–79.

[5] This movement, which began with the Irishman John Scotus Erigena in the ninth century, is known as scholasticism.

[6] Furthermore, the Roman Catholic Church at least remains on the whole hostile to science, the latest evidence for which can be found in the sermon preached by Pope Benedict XVI in Ratisbon on 12 September 2006.

[7] H.T. Buckle, *History of Civilization in England*. London: Longmans, Green and Co., 1869, vol. 1.

and where the University had been but recently established, and whose students were still enthusiastic about the thrill of new knowledge.

Post-Reformation, a real flowering of knowledge took place in the Elizabethan era, marked by such luminaries as Francis Bacon, Galileo, Kepler and Descartes, and also remarkably vigorously creative literary figures such as Marlowe and Shakespeare. Yet still more was to come: the century that followed saw Pascal, Boyle, Newton and Wren,[8] and what are perhaps the two most remarkable intellectual dynasties of all time in the western world, the family of Johann Sebastian Bach and their descendants, and the Bernoulli brothers and their descendants.

One of the prices to be paid for this vigorous development was the splitting of knowledge into rival faculties. As has been said, the Renaissance 'departmentalized our major interests', and this departmentalization has remained with us ever since, with the notable exception of the attempt to fuse art, sport and industry together in the early years of the USSR. Only now is there a growing and seemingly successful movement among scientists to break down the by now extremely firmly embedded inter-faculty boundaries.

With the arrival of the so-called Enlightenment, the accelerating rush of the preceding few centuries slowed down and became somewhat diverted. Voltaire is usually considered as the embodiment of the Enlightenment, and although he was indeed a prolific writer, his actual contributions to knowledge cannot be put in the same league as those named in the preceding paragraph. The ideas of another Enlightenment luminary, Adam Smith of Scotland, are still being vigorously debated to this day, with no real end in sight, in contrast to the glacial immutability of Newton's laws from the preceding century. The contributions of Kant will be more fully discussed in Chapter 7; the exuberant vitality of Beethoven remains a monument to this day, of course, and the same can be said of Goethe, even though his scientific endeavours were not all marked by the peerless excellence of his poetic work. The giant Euler was a sometime member of that group, which included Voltaire, who brought modern Western European civilization to Germany and Russia. Within the context of this chapter, Henry Cavendish is the most relevant representative of the epoch, and he will be discussed more fully below. The point we want to make here is that in some ways the Enlightenment was retrograde, for example with its emphasis on the unthinking application of physics to all human activity, in other words it promoted an overly mechanical and reductionist viewpoint of the universe, along with an undercurrent of the picturesque but effete idea that nature is self-revealing.[9]

---

[8] For an authoritative and comprehensive account of the developments sketched with extreme brevity here and in the following paragraphs, with the omission of many important names, see H.T. Pledge, *Science since 1500*. London: His Majesty's Stationery Office, 1939.

[9] On this point see J.J. Ramsden, 'Paracelsus: the Measurable and the Unmeasurable' *Psyche: Problems, Perspectives*, vol. 4 (2004) pp. 52–88.

Finally, we come to the golden age of science and engineering, ushered in by Berzelius, Davy, Thomas Young and others,[10] which began in roughly 1850 and lasted for about 100 years,[11] when the really seminal ideas that have shaped modern physics were formulated by Boltzmann, Einstein, Helmholtz, Maxwell, Planck and others. No less remarkable were the great engineers of that period, figures such as I.K. Brunel and the Stephenson brothers, and in other fields the contributions of Darwin and Faraday must also be mentioned. What motivated them? Apparently an unswerving devotion to making man's estate on Earth a more pleasant, dignified or uplifting one.

What had happened to the knight errant meanwhile? Essentially, he fades away in the Renaissance. It is as if the entire energies of European humanity were so completely taken up by the tremendous intellectual developments taking place at that time as to be unable to pursue the old ideas of equality and courtly love. And not only were tremendous developments taking place in the realms of the mind alone – that epoch was marked by highly significant technological developments, in a very large part triggered by the enormous influx of concepts and technologies from China that ensued upon the return of the Polos, especially Marco (1254–1324). Examples are the efficient equine harness; the technology of iron and steel, gunpowder and paper; the mechanical clock; and basic engineering devices such as the driving belt, the chain drive and the standard method of converting rotary to rectilinear motion, to name but a few.[12] Arriving at a time of anyway actively developing ideas in Western Europe, these ideas took root in very fertile soil, as is clear from the results. Rapid technological developments were able to take place and be fully implemented. Printing, another Chinese invention, but whose realization in Europe incorporated the innovation of movable type, was established by Johannes Gutenberg soon after 1450 in Mainz. The importance of this development for the dissemination of knowledge can scarcely be underestimated. Cities such as Basel that rapidly built up printing industries became magnets for scholars, seeing the possibilities offered by the facilitation of getting their work disseminated.

Comparable developments in technology took place in Japan following the arrival of the Portuguese, the first Europeans to land, in 1543 (see the comparative chronological Table 4.1 on the next page).[13] Firearms were introduced

---

[10] See Pledge, *Science since 1500*, [8]for a much more comprehensive account.

[11] When, incidentally, the word 'scientist' was first coined.

[12] See J. Needham, 'Science and China's Influence on the World', in *The Legacy of China* (ed. R. Dawson). Oxford: Clarendon Press, 1964.

[13] As might be expected from the geographical proximity of the two countries, people from Korea and China introduced technologies such as weaving, metal-casting, brewing, writing etc. at a much earlier epoch, around 500–700 CE, immediately preceding the establishment of the capital at Nara. Later relations with China were marked by hostility (as exemplified by the two expeditionary forces sent to attack Japan in the 13th century, both defeated by the Japanese).

Table 4.1 A brief chronology of Europe and Japan

Britain & Europe	Japan	
1100–1450 *Middle Ages* Fibonacci, Roger Bacon, Jean Buridan, Nicolas da Cusa, Universities of Bologna, Cambridge, Paris	794	*Heian Period (until 1185)*
	850–950	*Age of Enlightenment*
1450–1550 *Renaissance* Erasmus, Macchiavelli, Copernicus, Paracelsus	1185	*Kamakura (military) government*
1550–1650 *Elizabethan age* Francis Bacon, Galileo, Shakespeare, Kepler, Descartes		
1650–1750 Pascal, Boyle, Wren, Newton, Bach, Bernoulli	1392–1573	*Muromachi Period* Luxury architecture, art and drama. First Portuguese landed (1543). Firearms, sugar etc. introduced.
1750–1850 *Enlightenment* Voltaire, Euler, Adam Smith, Kant, Klopstock, Cavendish, Goethe	1603–1868	*Edo Period (Tokugawa government)* First Englishman (William Adams). Knowledge of astronomy, medicine etc. Book of 5 Rings (1643). First book on Bushido (~1760). Treaties of commerce with USA, Britain, Netherlands, France, Russia (1858).
1850–1950 *Golden age of science & engineering*	1868–present	*Meiji restoration* Capital moved to Tokyo. Abolition of feudalism.

shortly thereafter and this technology rapidly spread throughout the whole country. The first Englishman to set foot on Japanese soil, William Adams, landed in 1600, and treaties were concluded with the Dutch Republic and England a few years later, and led to many further technical innovations being introduced into Japan.

In this epoch the social structure of Japan comprised the powerful Shogun (the 'Lord of Lords') at the core, who dominated the daimyo (feudal lords), among whom the country was divided up into fiefs (but they were required to spend a portion of the year at the capital, then Kyoto, in the proximity of the Shogun). One notices the similarity to the social structure in England at the time, with the king at the centre attempting to keep the barons controlling the rest of the country under his control. Samurai served the daimyo, much in the way that knights served the barons in England, and the European knight errant found his counterpart in the masterless samurai (ronin) who wandered around the country. Rather separate from this militaristic structure was the Emperor and the court nobles (kuge), with very little power, and the towns-folk (chonin) who busied themselves with trade and industry. This structure was to remain essentially in place until the Meiji restoration in 1868.

In Europe, the burgeoning intellectual and technological developments enormously increased civic power, simply as a consequence of the wealth accruing from the implementation of new technologies.[14] One of the consequences of this wealth was that a far greater number of people were able to devote at least some of their time to the observation of nature,[15] an activity so characteristic of the English gentleman.[16] The Royal Society of London was founded in 1660,[17] and the Society started the world's first scientific journal in the modern sense, its *Philosophical Transactions*, in 1665. The early volumes display a catholic curiosity about everything (the titles of some articles chosen randomly are: *On some other not-common springs at Basel and in Alsatia* (vol. 1); *Inquiries for Hungary and Transylvania, Inquiries for Egypt, Inquiries for Guinea* (vol. 2); *Some observations concerning Japan* (vol. 4)).

Henry Cavendish (1731–1810) was a prominent figure in the second century of the Royal Society. Having had a large fortune bequeathed to him by an

---

[14] See for example M.M. Postan and E. Miller (eds), *The Cambridge Economic History of Europe*, especially vol. 2, *Trade and Industry in the Middle Ages*. Cambridge: University Press, 1987, 2nd edn.

[15] J.J. Ramsden, *The New World Order*. Moscow: Progress Publishers, 1991.

[16] He seems to have emerged as a concept around that time, as witnessed for example by the appearance of H. Peacham's book *The Compleat Gentleman*. London: Francis Constable, 1622.

[17] This was a Europe-wide trend. The Accademia dei Lincei had already been founded in 1603, and the Académie des Sciences (Paris) was founded in 1666. Russia was about a century behind in this development, the St Petersburg Academy being founded in 1725.

uncle, he devoted the whole of his life – apart from three years at Cambridge University (which he left without a degree) – to scientific investigations. One of his most famous experiments, whose success was dependent on the elimination of even the most minute disturbing forces, was the determination of the constant *G* giving the magnitude of the gravitational force between two masses. He also gave the first full description of hydrogen, and established that water resulted from the union of hydrogen with oxygen.

Cavendish epitomized the post-medieval gentleman as the imago of the union of the medieval knight and the medieval scholar, working with unimpeachable personal ethics as a dispassionate observer of nature. The two, ethics in personal life and the professional nature-observing work of the scientist, are inseparably interrelated. The painstaking extraction of 'truth' (in the sense of conditional information or knowledge that is usually called 'theory') from the unconditional information or facts revealed by experiment and observation, through highly creative leaps of the imagination, requires the utmost honesty both in the contemplation of those facts and in the formulation of the theory. The scientist views with peculiar horror the misdeeds of those who depart from that norm,[18] blatantly contravening the unwritten laws of scholarship.

It should therefore come as no surprise that one of the most eloquent descriptions of a 'gentleman' was that formulated by Cardinal Newman in a work dedicated to conceptualizing knowledge and universities:

> ... one who never inflicts pain ... and is mainly occupied in removing the obstacles that hinder the free and unembarrassed action of those about him ... he is tender toward the bashful, gentle toward the distant, and merciful towards the absurd[19] ... he guards against unseasonable allusions, or topics that may irritate ... he makes light of favours when he does them, and seems to be receiving when he is conferring ... he never speaks of himself except when compelled ... has no ears for slander or gossip. .. is scrupulous in imputing motives to those who interfere with him ... and interprets everything for the best[20] ... he is never mean or little in his disputes, never takes unfair advantage, never mistakes personalities or sharp sayings for arguments, or insinuates evil which he dare not say out aloud. ... he observes the maxim of the ancient sage, that 'we should conduct ourselves towards our enemy as if he were one day to be our friend' ... he has too much sense to be affronted by insults, is too well employed to remember

---

[18] One of the most prominent and well-documented examples in recent times was the fraudulent reporting of invented data by J.H. Schön, B. Battlogg and others at Bell Laboratories.

[19] This is of course the Pauline sentiment of being 'all things to all men' (1 Corinthians 9, 22).

[20] A sentiment lampooned, perhaps a trifle unfairly, by Voltaire in *Candide*.

injuries or to bear malice . . . he is patient, forbearing and resigned . . . he submits to pain because it is inevitable, to bereavement because it is irreparable, and to death because it is his destiny . . . if he engages in controversy of any kind, his disciplined intellect preserves him from the blundering discourtesy of better, perhaps, but less educated minds, who, like blunt weapons, tear and hack instead of cutting clean, who mistake the point in argument, waste their strength on trifles, misconceive their adversary, and leave the question more involved than as they find it. He may be right or wrong in his opinion, but he is too clear-headed to be unjust; he is as simple as he is forcible, and as brief as he is decisive. Nowhere shall we find greater candour, consideration, indulgence: he throws himself into the minds of his opponents, he accounts for their mistakes; he knows the weakness of human reason as well as its strength . . .[21]

The idea of a gentleman has since become inseparably linked with Englishness. Even if this would never normally be asserted by any Englishman, it suffices to look at numerous continental European (and, one may add, Japanese), commentators. Karel Čapek, in his witty *Letters from England*,[22] writes of the (English) gentleman as 'one you can trust without reducing the distance between you', and of (after a visit to a London club) 'the silence of a gentleman among gentleman'. It includes not only ideas of coolness under fire and the 'stiff upper lip' (that exactly parallel those attributes of bushido described in Chapter 2), but also the idea of the sportsman with a keen conception of fair play and fairness. It is actually highly significant that there is not even a word for 'fairness' in other European languages. The closest the French can get to it is probably 'juste', but that is not really equivalent (or, at best, comprises only a small part of it), and the Germans have meanwhile borrowed the English words 'fair' and 'unfair' as they are. Perhaps the last word on this point should be said by Sir Hans Krebs, that very distinguished scientist who arrived as a refugee and made England his home and place of work:

> British society . . . where people of many different dispositions, races, convictions and abilities live together harmoniously, and yet vigorously. We [refugees] saw them argue without quarrelling, quarrel without suspecting, suspect without abusing, criticize without vilifying or ridiculing, praise without flattering, being vehement without being brutal. We saw what Robert Browning said of his dog, 'strength without violence, courage without ferocity'. These are some of the characteristics of the soul of this country . . . if proof were needed that these attitudes are prevalent traits of

---

[21] J.H. Newman, 'Knowledge and Religious Duty', in *The Idea of a University*, based on lectures given in 1852 by Dublin, and published in 1859.

[22] (Translated by P. Selver). London: Geoffrey Bles (1925).

the British way of life, I would say: which other language uses in its everyday life phrases equivalent to 'fair play', 'gentleman's agreement', 'benefit of the doubt', 'give him a chance', 'understatement', phrases indicative of a sense of justice, of a sense of perspective, of tolerance, of humility, and, above all, respect for humanity? Quite a few languages have to use the English words when wishing to express the sentiments lying behind these phrases and I am sure that this is not an accident.[23]

Moving the clock not so very many years forward brings us to the 1980s and the era of Thatcherism, of the competitive, thrusting dealmaker, of business exemplifying the very apotheosis of the sentiment described by Weir: 'beneficial undertakings had been proved profitable; [later] it was assumed that a business, as long as it is profitable, does not require to be proved beneficial'.[24] This is the ethos of the modern business school, the anvil on which the lean and the mean are forged. The sentiments described with almost panegyrical eloquence by Newman, Čapek and Krebs appear alien to this era, which moreover seems to have continued up to the present. Gentlemanliness is a neglected concept. And paralleling this decline in business ethics is a similar decline in the way of doing science. It must, however, be said that this decline is not driven by the individual scientist, who would much prefer to continue to work in the fashion of Henry Cavendish, but by governments, to whom most scientists are nowadays beholden for all but the most abstract, theoretical work requiring no more than a pencil and a piece of paper for its execution. The main current way of financing, and hence inevitably of choosing and directing, topics for investigation is through the competitive grant award. Massively criticized by scientists such as the late Sir Peter Medawar when it was first introduced into the UK in the 1960s, it nevertheless continued to penetrate the scientific world, until today it overwhelmingly constitutes the principal mode whereby science is carried out. Administered by the hugely unpopular research councils, the grant award system is now dysfunctional to the extent that even the most cursory examination of the state of affairs must conclude that the research councils actually hinder research in the United Kingdom, rather than facilitate it. The system works by inviting proposals for research to be carried out to be submitted by a scientist to one of the research councils. These proposals constitute a description of the planned research in half a dozen pages or so, to be written in a rather closely prescribed bureaucratic format, together with a budget and some further text under such rubrics as 'relevance to beneficiaries', the content of which almost inevitably comes close to what Thouless has dubbed 'non-communicating discourse' (NCD). These proposals

---

[23] From an address delivered on 8 November 1969 in the Livery Hall of the Sadler's Company in London.

[24] A. Weir, *The Historical Basis of Modern Europe*. London: Swan, Sonnenschein, Lowrey, 1886.

are then evaluated by other scientists who write brief reports on them (the peer review process). A survey of the content of these reports reveals that in almost every regard the precepts of gentlemanliness enunciated by, for example, Newman are blatantly disregarded. How often have scientists despaired of the waste of time spent in writing these proposals (typically a quarter of the working time of a scientist is now spent in writing them), when they are rejected by their peers who 'tear and hack instead of cutting clean, who mistake the point in argument, and waste their strength on trifles'?

In short, the whole system is built on the ethos of the time server, for whom duty and principle are subordinate to self-interest and expediency. It is therefore unsurprising that the quality of scientific research in Britain has been in decline for some time. The Save British Science Society was founded in 1986, and only weariness at having so often repeated the same message, the need for which continues to be so glaringly obvious, to continuingly obstinately deaf ears, has diminished the impact of the message. Even the layman can concur with one of the main evidential arguments promulgated by the movement spearheaded by Sir Peter Medawar and others, that the grant award system has not been and would have been incapable of being responsible for any of the main innovations in the twentieth century, such as the transistor and penicillin, multiplication of examples of which would be perfectly superfluous here, and whose benefits to humanity are universally admitted. A particularly contentious point is the enormous level of detail required in the budgets and research plans, to the extent that since so much advance knowledge of the work that should be done is required to be already available in the proposal, one may doubt whether fresh research is needed at all. It is unfortunate that even Russia, which enjoyed a more enlightened system based on the earlier European model right up to the end of the Soviet Union, has now adopted the grant award system with all the rude energy of the imitator.[25]

It seems that the basis of the work of the research councils has never been subject to fundamental scrutiny, by which I mean asking why they are there. Three possible answers come to mind: to allow an optimal distribution of limited funds; to prevent inappropriate work from being carried out; and to prevent heresy. The first reason probably provided the justification for setting up the system in the first place. Given that funds are limited, what could be better than subjecting the scientists to a Darwinian-like selection procedure from which the best projects would emerge?

---

[25] The trend is also mirrored in other countries. For example, Switzerland's Secretary of State for Science, Charles Kleiber, has avowed the intention of financing research in Switzerland exclusively via competitively-funded projects. The only barrier towards the implementation of this policy is the opposition of the universities, which fall under the jurisdiction of the cantons, which in Switzerland's confederation are independent enough from the central government to be able to maintain, to some extent, the old-fashioned gentlemanly way of doing science.

Unfortunately this procedure has become dysfunctional because the ratio of proposals to funded projects is now unreasonably low, such that only a minor fraction of even those proposals awarded the highest possible marks can be funded, and hence the selection is essentially random. Taking into account the cost of maintaining the whole research council infrastructure, plus the cost of writing the proposals and of the peer review, from this point of view it is clear that the system now delivers very poor value for money, and it would be better to simply disperse the available funds according to some minimally bureaucratic system, such as in order of receipt of proposals. For it must be remembered that the criteria of eligibility to submit a proposal are very stringent: only fully accredited academic staff may apply, who have already gone through a Darwinian-like selection procedure to obtain their posts. It may therefore be reasonably supposed that they are fully capable of proposing sensible research. As for the second possible reason for the existence of the research councils, clearly this carries with it the great danger of falling into the same trap into which the Soviet Union fell regarding biological research under Lysenko. What is, or is not, appropriate? Anything other than strict scientific criteria of excellence have no place in the selection of research projects. Furthermore, no scientist worth his or her salt is willingly going to spend time on a problem that is not important. The final reason can be dismissed by virtue of the fact that ultimately the output of any project is going to be written up and submitted for publication in a peer-reviewed journal. Bad science is simply not going to see the light of day. And although the system has been somewhat undermined of late by the emergence of the so-called 'online journals', with a lighter or even absent peer review process (publication is essentially paid for by the authors, i.e. on the same basis that commercial advertisements are accepted), it is probably robust enough to weather such perturbations. Good evidence for that is, for example, provided by the fact that the misdemeanours of Schön, Battlogg *et al.* (see footnote 18) alluded to earlier did not take very long to be exposed and corrected once they had been published and circulated worldwide.

It is part of the current policy of the research councils of the United Kingdom that the research work that they pay for has industrial relevance, and indeed concrete support of a project by an industrial concern is practically a prerequisite for obtaining a research grant. This policy, so obviously conceived to obtain a favourable opinion of the Treasury with regard to diverting government revenues into scientific research, mirrors a trend in science that was in the past closely associated with the development of militarism and state-sponsored belligerence, notably in Germany. Commenting on the situation in that country around the beginning of the First World War, Frederick Scott Oliver perceptively wrote,

the close alliance between learning and the bureaucracy does not seem to be altogether satisfactory. For thought loses its fine edge when it is set to cut millstones of state. It loses its fine temper in the red heat of political controversy. By turning utilitarian it ceases to be universal; and what is perhaps even worse, it ceases to be free. It tends more and more to become the mere inventor of things which will sell at a profit; less and less the discoverer of high principles which the gods have hidden out of sight.[26]

This policy was doubtless to a great extent responsible for the early military successes of Germany in both the First and Second World Wars, although ultimately events turned out not to be to Germany's advantage. As far as the present situation is Britain is concerned, a properly quantitative and independent survey of the actual return on the research council's investment in terms of benefits to the economy of the country never seems to have been carried out.

Paralleling these rather depressing developments in the institutional organization of science, which correlate with the alarming decline in the number of undergraduates in subjects such as physics, chemistry and engineering, are trends in fields far more visible to the public at large, notably in business and politics. In politics, the decline in standards of conduct had become so bad that in 1994 the then Prime Minister, John Major, announced the setting up of a Committee on Standards in Public Life, whose terms of reference were

> to examine current concerns about standards of conduct of all holders of public office, including arrangements relating to financial and commercial activities, and make recommendations as to any changes in present arrangements which might be required to ensure the highest standards of propriety in public life. For these purposes, public office should include: ministers, civil servants and advisers; members of parliament and UK members of the European parliament; members and senior bodies of all non-departmental public bodies and of national health service bodies; non-ministerial office holders; members and other senior officers of other bodies discharging publicly-funded functions; and elected members and senior officers of local authorities.[27]

The first chairman of the Committee was Lord Nolan, hence it has come to be known as the Nolan Committee. It has set out 'Seven Principles of Public Life', which it believes should apply to all in the public service. These are:

> **Selflessness:** holders of public office should act solely in terms of the public interest. They should not do so in order to gain financial or other benefits for themselves, their family or their friends.

---

[26] F.S. Oliver, *Ordeal by Battle*, 2nd edn. London: Macmillan, 1915.
[27] Hansard (HC), 25 October 1994, col. 758.

Integrity: holders of public office should not place themselves under any financial or other obligation to outside individuals or organizations that might seek to influence them in the performance of their official duties.

Objectivity: in carrying out public business, including making public appointments, awarding contracts, or recommending individuals for rewards and benefits, holders of public office should make choices on merit.

Accountability: holders of public office are accountable for their decisions and actions to the public and must submit themselves to whatever scrutiny is appropriate to their office.

Openness: holders of public office should be as open as possible about all the decisions and actions that they take. They should give reasons for their decisions and restrict information only when the wider public interest clearly demands it.

Honesty: holders of public office have a duty to declare any private interests relating to their public duties and to take steps to resolve any conflicts arising in a way that protects the public interest.

Leadership: holders of public office should promote and support these principles by leadership and example.

The Committee has been very active (nine reports published up to 2003). Prior to the ninth report, 308 recommendations had been made, about 250 of which had been accepted and implemented by the British government. These recommendations included many things that one was surprised to learn had not been implemented by mutual consent since time immemorial, such as 'making the agendas and minutes of meetings of the governing bodies of public sector organizations publicly available', and 'publishing audit reports of public sector bodies'.[28] Some of the recommendations have been very detailed, such as 'to require parliamentary agreement for the two special adviser posts in the Prime Minister's office with executive powers, and limit those powers to work carried out in the Prime Minister's office', or, from the first report,

> Each executive NDPB [Non-Departmental Public Body] and NHS body that has not already done so should nominate an official or Board Member entrusted with the duty of investigating staff concerns about propriety raised confidentially. Staff should be able to make complaints without going through the normal management structure, and should be guaranteed anonymity. If they remain unsatisfied, staff should also have a clear route for raising concerns about issues of propriety with the sponsor department.

---

[28] These reports are all freely available, hence will not be summarized in any detail here.

Recent events in other countries of the European Union, such as in Hungary in the autumn of 2006, have shown how very far standards have fallen in political life generally, and the work of the Nolan Committee could doubtless be applied beneficially to most other European nations.

The work of the Nolan Committee continues, with each new public misdemeanour by a politician engendering a new report and new recommendations. It is difficult to establish whether these recommendations have any real effect, not least because they are not implemented pre-emptively. The scandals that sustain the popular press appear to be as frequent as ever, and no consequential audit of the degree to which current standards conform to the implemented recommendations of the Committee appears to have been carried out. The cumulative collection of implemented recommendations is now already so large that those to whom they apply have to allocate significant effort in order to acquaint themselves with it. This situation mirrors that prevailing in general regarding the laws of the country. The idea of the English gentleman being a walking constitution, acting according to rules largely unwritten, with all the benefits that the concomitant flexibility implies for the conduct of human business, has been simply lost in the morass. The style of modern legislation is very much that of George Orwell's newspeak. An example, taken at random from the current Finance (No 2) Act 2005, Part 5, Schedule 4, Road Vehicle (Registration and Licensing) Regulations 2002, paragraph 1.-(1):

> the 'required declaration' means the declaration made to the Secretary of State by persons surrendering a vehicle licence or the keeper of the relevant vehicle to the effect that (except for use under a trade licence) he does not for the time being intend to use or keep the vehicle on a public road and will not use or keep the vehicle on a public road without first taking out a vehicle licence (or if appropriate a nil licence) for the vehicle.

The point here is that with this amazing proliferation of detail in legislation, the whole system becomes extremely rigid and inflexible, and every undesirable consequence can only be countered by the introduction of yet another Act and yet more explicit detail. Indeed, a direct consequence of this mass of detail is that if something advantageous to the perpetrator is not explicitly forbidden, it very likely will be done, regardless of any higher ethical consideration. Doubtless there is some mathematical proof of the futility of this 'dog chasing its tail' mode of regulating behaviour.

In the commercial sphere of industry and finance, present standards appear to be similarly low. The difference between the private sector and the public one is that whereas the existence and continuing work of the Committee on Standards in Public Life is possible and may even have some beneficial effect, in the private sector, with its huge inherent diversity and now globalization meaning that the lines of ownership are very likely to lead abroad, any kind of ethics regulated by committee is much harder to achieve. Of course, in theory the government could withdraw the charter of a company not acting in accordance with some Committee on Standards in Commercial Life, but by now it seems much too late to even contemplate the feasibility of such a move. Ethics by committee is akin to caulking a boat: it may work for a time, but is inherently unstable and can do nothing if the timbers themselves are rotten. The message of this whole book is that new thinking is the only solution to the impasse in which the civilized world now finds itself regarding the organization of its institutions.

5
Christianity

Lorne Denny

'God so loved the world that he gave his only Son Jesus Christ to save us from our sins, to be our advocate in heaven and to bring us to eternal life.'[1] These words, based on verses from the third chapter of St John's Gospel, are proclaimed at the beginning of innumerable services of Christian worship across the world. They mark the good news itself, the call to acknowledge our own need of that good news and the call to declare our belief in the saving power of Jesus Christ. They indicate that the Christian life begins in grateful and adoring recognition of what God has done for us and leads to hope in the promise of transformation into the sort of people God would have us be. As the central act of Christian worship continues, the Eucharist, Mass or Holy Communion, we hear the Scriptures and the Gospel presented and expounded afresh; we celebrate the Spirit-filled peace of the fellowship into which we are called; we re-present at the altar the signs of the loving sacrifice of his own life that Jesus Christ made for us all on the Cross; we receive the bread and wine, the spiritual body and blood, as food for our own new lives made possible by his dying and rising again; and we pledge ourselves to loving service of the world around us. All this we have been doing since the earliest days of the Church.

Accepting the standing, open invitation of any church to come and witness or share in such a service provides the easiest way of appreciating what we say we mean in the Christian faith. It certainly has the advantage over a chapter in a book, however much food for thought reading can offer. A service should, of course, itself offer food for thought but in the service the message and invitation are likely to be expressed not only in words but also in dramatic action, in music, in holy pictures and things, perhaps in beautiful smells, and, for those who have made their choice, the taste of the consecrated bread and wine themselves. All these are indications of how Christianity worships God who made and who loves this world in which we live and who calls us to enjoy the full potential of that world.

---

[1] Biblical quotations are from the Revised Standard Version.

But above all it is through coming to a real service, whether as bystander or participant, that we can begin to glimpse in the presence and the fellowship of other real people the greatest fact of all about Christianity: that its faith is incarnate, lived in ordinary flesh-and-blood and loving ordinary people, just as God has shown in suffering and dying among us in the person of Jesus Christ. So while coming together in prayer and worship is the special public expression, essential glue, duty and joy of our faith, it is by the response we make to Christ in our daily lives and interaction with others that we are both judged and known. We are reminded in the second letter of James that 'as the body apart from the spirit is dead, so faith apart from works is dead'. Being Christian may not turn us into good people in this life, but if our faith is real it should be making us into better people than we would have been otherwise!

We have begun by looking at what Christians most obviously do, going to Church, because ours is a living, present and visible faith, both timeless and of the here and now, a faith anyone can drop into or indeed out of, without man-made cost or penalty. When Christ at the Last Supper with his disciples before his death on the Cross broke bread and said, 'Take, eat; this is my body which is given for you; do this in remembrance of me', he both interpreted for us that death and also gave us the vital sign by which the Church is to gather together and be known; he gave us the focal point of our prayer and the enduring invitation to come to God through Him who knows us in all our frailty and mixed motives.

Let us now give some consideration to what had led up to the Christian call. For thousands of years before the birth of Christ, or before the common era (BCE) now used universally in dating, the ancient Hebrew people of the eastern Mediterranean world had been keeping oral and written records of history, ethical practice, prophecy and myth. The earliest extant manuscripts date from the third century BCE (neither the means nor any particular desire to preserve texts just because they were old having been a feature of the ancient world!) and before the beginning of the first century BCE these texts collated in Hebrew over many centuries had been translated into Greek as the Septuagint (after the 72 scholars thought originally to have been commissioned); it is this version of the Hebrew Bible that was in wide circulation at the time of the beginning of the Christian Church and which has become known to us as the Old Testament.

Jesus Christ was born in Judaea, part of the obscure Roman province of Palestine, about four years BCE, shortly before the death of Herod the Great. He was executed in or around 30 CE (Anno Domini traditionally) after condemnation by the Roman governor Pontius Pilate. The basic facts of his ministry and devoted following and of his death are recorded by the early Roman historian Tacitus (Annals of Imperial Rome, 115 CE) and the Jewish historian Josephus (The Antiquities of the Jews, ca 80 CE), for example, and not doubted by other ancient non-Christian sources, nor by most modern historians. That amounts to a good deal of disinterested authority for the historical life and death of a figure in the ancient world who wielded no political power and left no writings himself. What it does not give us, however, is any account of what it was that Jesus taught, what sort of person he was or the significance that he himself placed on his ministry and death. These things, our detailed knowledge of Christ, come from the four Gospels (Matthew, Mark, Luke and John) written in the middle to late first century BCE, with a gap of only thirty to sixty years after the events, remarkably close in time for ancient historical texts. By the middle of the second century, the four Gospels, together with important letters written by early Christian leaders, principally Paul, had been brought together to form what would eventually be called the New Testament. The two Testaments of the Holy Bible form the principal authority and yardstick of the Christian faith as embodied and witnessed by the Church.

Jesus Christ himself was born a Jew and Christians take their lead from him in reading the Old Testament as an account of God's dealings with a particular people highly conscious of their relationship with God and accountability to God, which prepares that people and ourselves for the coming of Christ into the world. The name 'Jesus' means originally 'God saves' and the name 'Christ', far from being some sort of surname, comes from the Greek 'Christos' for the Hebrew 'Messiah', anointed one. The Jews had long looked for a specially anointed saviour, someone they envisaged as a new king for the special triumph and deliverance of their race. It was the startling universality of the message of love brought by Jesus and his refusal to be bound by the tribal-priestly conventions of his time that provoked so much hostility in the Jewish authorities, leading to the calls for his death. In particular, they were infuriated by Jesus' identification of himself with God: the political anxieties of the leaders of an occupied people at an itinerant preacher being hailed as the new king were compounded by the offence taken at this apparent blasphemy. At the same time there were others, such as Judas Iscariot, the disciple who betrayed Jesus, who positively wanted him to assume an activist political role against the Romans and were disappointed when he did not. The coalescence of such misunderstanding, outrage and fear with the acquiescence of the Roman government led to the crucifixion of the man who had preached reconciliation and love between God and man and between all people, and who had breathed new, empowering life into all who believed in the divine goodness he embodied.

When Jesus identified himself with God he was making neither idle boasts nor woolly remarks of little significance. Rather, he was pointing to the essence of the meaning of his life as proclaimed in the Gospels, to the heart of the Christian faith. In this lies the chief stumbling block to the unbeliever, now as then, and the most compelling wonder to those who accept his claim. Almighty God is not a distant legislator whom we can only find or even think about by following the right rules of race or religion, nor is he merely a benevolent principle of life animating nature. Rather, he is the constantly creating and re-creating Lord and Father of all mankind who enters into and suffers the human condition through the person of Christ so that all of us may be raised up to share in his divine life insofar as we come to recognize his presence among us, the promise and call and the loving potential of Christ in the face of everyone we meet. The figure of the 'suffering servant' predicted by the Old Testament prophet Isaiah is Jesus of Nazareth, the healer and teacher of the Gospels who forgave even those who put him to death 'for they know not what they do' and who rose again from the dead on the first Easter Sunday, was seen by many and left his Spirit with the disciples to empower the Church and to vindicate once and for all the power of Love over death.

The suffering servant Jesus Christ is the one described in the Prologue to John's Gospel:

> In the beginning was the Word, and the Word was with God, and the Word was God. He was in the beginning with God; all things were made through him, and without him was not anything made that was made. In him was life, and the life was the light of men. The light shines in the darkness, and the darkness has not overcome it.

The first thing God is recorded as doing, in the first book of the Old Testament, Genesis, is speaking. In this ancient myth about creation and origins, it is the *Word* of God which expresses and enacts his love in bringing life, order and purpose to mankind.

Human beings, however, have needed more than the abstract assurance of that creative Word, that timeless expression of the will of God operating in the world. They have needed the physical, flesh-and-blood assurance of the Word, the walking embodiment of God's love, the intimate and immediate knowledge that God really cares and understands. They, we, have needed also the pressing call from one like us, though sent directly by God, to acknowledge our own failures and insignificance and accept the free and loving forgiveness that enables us to return to God the Father through the Son, his Word, the gate or connecting-door to eternal life. So, to return to the Prologue to John, Jesus Christ of the new creation was and is 'the true light that enlightens every man' and 'to all who received him, who believed in his name, he gave power to become children of God . . . And the Word became flesh and dwelt among us, full of grace and truth; we have beheld his glory, glory as of the only Son from the Father'.

Later in his Gospel, in the ninth chapter, John recounts how Jesus healed a man who had been blind from birth, anointing his eyes with mud or clay so that when he washed them his eyes were opened. Because this healing was carried out on the Sabbath, the Jewish day of rest, the Pharisees said that Jesus was a sinner, rather than a man of God and denied the reality of the healing, rejecting the once-blind man and afterwards going to stone Jesus. The ancient Jewish text, the Talmud, speaks scornfully of Jesus as a performer of sorcery; there can have been little doubt that during his three years of active ministry Jesus displayed extraordinary insight to physical suffering and caused wonderful healing. We hear stories today of remarkable recoveries and revivals sometimes inspired by religious faith, sometimes it would seem by inner strength that astonishes medical doctors; these events too remind us that there is no need to believe in magic in order to accept the essential truth of the accounts of Jesus' healing.

However, while Jesus clearly had great compassion for physical suffering, there is a wider significance to the account of the healing of the blind man, which lends it another sort of meaning for our understanding of Jesus himself, and of Christian faith, as indeed there is to other miraculous healings in the Gospels.

Just as Jesus himself is not doing wrong when he performs an active work of mercy in breach of the Sabbath rules, so the blind man cannot be seen as a sinner because he has been so afflicted and neither can his parents, despite the assumption at the time that such physical weakness must have been caused by moral turpitude. For Jesus, condemnation of individuals seems in any case to have been repugnant. He condemned sinfulness, to which we are all prone, but always loved the sinner, urging a new generosity of life rather than holding the past against someone; and his strongest rebukes were reserved for the hypocritical and the self-righteous. This teaches us to be wary, incidentally, of some sorts of apparently fervent Christians who link being born again in the Spirit with physical well-being or material prosperity. Just as the absence of these blessings cannot be attributed to wrongdoing, so having faith, or the sense of faith, cannot be assumed to lead to obvious signs of worldly happiness. The great Christian virtues of faith, hope and love are ends in themselves and although the Christian life is likely to entail a depth of inner peace, the feeling of being, or becoming, as one is meant to be, it is also a life in which we are called to share in the Way of the Cross, to be prepared lovingly to suffer for others as Our Lord suffered.

Sometimes Jesus' healing is an outward sign of the forgiveness of sins but as he says of the blind man, it is not to be assumed that physical suffering is anyone's fault: it is a part of the condition of the world, created, not itself divine, to be necessarily imperfect. Suffering can, however, generate and inspire goodness in others, or even in the sufferers themselves. After dismissing the idea that his blindness resulted from wrongdoing, Jesus says rather that it was 'that the works of God might be made manifest in him'. The most important thing in the face of suffering is not the apportioning of blame but our response to it. Inasmuch as we seek to follow Jesus' example, bringing comfort and hope, we become participants in God's work of creation and recreation. Insofar as, like the blind man, we recognize such goodness when we see it as 'the light of the world', we grow in faith. When Jesus heals the blind man with spittle and clay, he reminds us of the Genesis story of the original creation of man 'of dust from the ground'. So Jesus Christ shares in the constant work of God in creating and renewing the world. So it is that in the words which immediately prompt his opponents to begin stoning him, Jesus can say, 'I and the Father are one'. And so it is also that through lives oriented towards Christ we can ourselves be caught up in the loving purposes and activity of God, for Jesus the Son is in the Father and the Father in the Son.

We are initiated into the Christian life through the rite of Baptism 'in the name of the Father and of the Son and of the Holy Spirit', according to Jesus' instruction (Matthew's Gospel, 28, 19). After the example in the Bible of whole households being baptized into the early Church, this commonly takes place when we are infants and spoken for by parents and godparents. Of course, people are also baptized as adults, when the rite has not already been performed (or in some Christian circles when they do not accept the validity of infant baptism); and in any case all who have been baptized should afterwards be confirmed, when they can speak on their own behalf to pledge their commitment. In Baptism, the sign of the Cross is made on the person's head to mark the renouncing of the natural disposition towards sin, or self-centredness, and the person's acceptance of the claim of Christ. Water is then poured over them (or there may be immersion) to mark the washing away of the debilitating effects of that tendency to sinfulness and the person's rebirth in all the promise of newness of life. The enabling and transforming gifts of the Holy Spirit are prayed for, which may be marked with anointing. It is this rite of Baptism, normally performed by a priest in church but validly performed in an emergency by any other baptized Christian, which is the universal mark of membership of the Christian church, of whatever denomination. It is known as a sacrament, like the Eucharist or Mass, an outward and visible sign of an inward and spiritual meaning, in this case in essence the person's becoming a member of the body of Christ, the fellowship of all believers, departed, living and to come, under the headship of Jesus Christ.

We have so far considered at some length the meaning for us of God the Father and God the Son. But for Christians God is spoken of and fully invoked as 'Father, Son and Holy Spirit', as we saw in the description of the rite of Baptism: we believe in God as the 'Holy Trinity' and the third person of that Trinity is the Holy Spirit. The Holy Spirit is also understood to have been and to be present in God from the beginning and eternally. In those first verses in the Book of Genesis, when God brings order to the world through His Word, which may be understood as the Son, the Spirit of God is moving over the face of the waters. Like Christ the Son, the Spirit may be seen implicitly in the pages of the ancient Hebrew understanding of the world that form the Christian Old Testament. Then in John's Gospel (Chapter 14) in the New Testament, the coming of the Holy Spirit is made explicit. Knowing he is shortly to die, Jesus reassures his disciples of the life-giving strength with which the Holy Spirit will always fill the Church: 'But the Counsellor, the Holy Spirit, whom the Father will send in my name, he will teach you all things, and bring to your remembrance all that I have said to you'. This is 'the Spirit of truth, whom the world cannot receive, because it neither sees him nor knows him; you know him, for he dwells with you, and will be in you'. The moment when the 12 apostles (the inner core of disciples, now including Matthias after the death of the betrayer Judas Iscariot) become dramatically and intensely aware of the arrival of the Holy Spirit in the place of the earthly presence of Jesus is recounted in the second book of the Acts of The Apostles. As they are filled with the Holy Spirit, the apostles find the confidence and energy to speak in other languages and the mission of the Church to take the Gospel of Christ to all corners of the earth is begun. Vitally for our times as for theirs, a diversity of languages and races is no longer seen as frightening or an impediment to the worship of God, Father, Son and Holy Spirit. Christianity spread rapidly across the Mediterranean world, thanks largely to the arduous missionary work of Saint Paul, under the presidency of Saint Peter, and its progress towards becoming the most widely spread faith on the planet gained dramatic new momentum when Constantine made it the official religion of the Roman Empire early in the fourth century, and the long history of western Christendom began.

Undoubtedly the Christian banner has been stained and disgraced on countless occasions in the seventeen centuries since it was first associated with imperial power. There were follies and cruelties, especially during the Crusades of the Middle Ages against insurgent Islam, during the Spanish conquests in the Americas, during the internal wars of the Church at the time of the Reformation and during the colonizing of the British Empire. The twentieth century saw an advanced, nominally Christian European country attempt the extermination of the Jewish race, the very race which produced Jesus of Nazareth. People often behave appallingly and the tendency to bigotry, greed and barbarism latent in all of us is magnified exponentially within the collective mentality of the state and with the self-righteous zeal that the banner of faith can so paradoxically encourage.

Nevertheless, the Holy Spirit of God has indeed been active in the life of the Church and of individual Christians, as Jesus Christ said he would be. From those early days it has been the Sprit who has comforted the fainthearted and united believers in prayer. It is the Holy Sprit who kept together the pioneers of the early Church at Jerusalem, for all their divisions and it is the Holy Sprit who binds Christians in fellowship today, both in individual congregations, where at times the presence of the Sprit is so warm and enlivening as to be almost tangible, and across the continents. It is the Holy Sprit whose comfort strengthens us in hope when the world seems to be in a desperate state and when there are serious quarrels and fractures within the Christian community itself. The Holy Spirit enables us individually to be drawn closer to a real sense of the power and the love of God; through the Holy Spirit is generated intimacy with the one God who is greater than the skies and seas and yet stoops to serve and share with you and me.

For all the failures and divisions of Christians individually and institutionally in the Church, Christianity has been inspired and empowered by the Holy Spirit to influence the world for great good – often in ways that we now take for granted but without which our lives would be immeasurably poorer. In the West, the monastic communities of what we call the Dark Ages kept learning and scholarship alive through the long centuries before the Renaissance of wider classical culture and education. Many of our great universities and schools owe their existence to the Christian imperative both to train priests and to explore the wonder of creation through philosophy and through the empirical sciences. While faith has always been conscious – sometimes too conscious – of the limitations of rational enquiry and experiment as means to the kinds of wisdom and insight to which humans aspire, many scientists will testify that it is their faithful concern to appreciate and understand the gift of creation and human potential that has inspired research and discovery. It seems often to be the sense of God's loving purpose as an absolute truth that leads to the conviction that the pursuit of knowledge itself is both possible and desirable. Where that sense is lacking it is easy for the energy of curiosity to be dissipated in the production only of expedient techniques and the expression only of pragmatic opinions. Our great hospitals also have their origins in the expression of Christian compassion as hospitality and the relief of suffering. The attempt to engage with God – sometimes in awe, sometimes in argument – lies behind the beauties of our painting, our music, our literature, not to mention the often literally soaring achievements of the architecture of our cathedrals and churches. It is surely impossible to imagine the same power of endeavour without the motivation of celebrating the divine and of wrestling with the questions God poses for the conduct of our lives.

If much artistic activity has been in essence the varied attempts to explore and proclaim the Gospel of Christ, accompanying this has been the expression of Christian love for the Word of God Incarnate, Christ as reflected in the ordinary human beings with whom He connected himself. In the first half of the nineteenth century it was William Wilberforce and other evangelical Christians who achieved the abolition of slavery throughout the British Empire and caused the practice to be viewed with repugnance throughout the world. A similar passion to share Christ's love with equal respect for all lay behind the astonishing sacrificial life of Mother Theresa among the despised and rejected of Calcutta in the second half of the twentieth century. There are many more examples of the heroism of saints who have made profound and memorable impacts on the human condition, and whom Christians admire as exemplary for the way in which they have translated Christ's command to love one another directly into action. However, just as an obscure parish church or a temporary chapel off an anonymous corridor in a busy hospital can be as holy and refreshing a sanctuary as a wonderful gothic cathedral, so the presence of the Holy Spirit can be just as discernible in the God-centred lives of countless unfamed men, women and children for whom their faith is real and lived out in consideration for others. The Christian way of life to which most of us can aspire is aptly indicated in the poet William Wordsworth's homage to 'that best portion of a good man's life,/His little, nameless, unremembered, acts of kindness and of love'.

There are, of course, many good and thoughtful people who profess to have no faith. Indeed Christ himself suggests as much when he refers to 'other sheep, that are not of this fold' whom he must also bring (John's Gospel, ch. 10); and in his first letter, John writes 'if we love one another, God abides in us and his love is perfected in us' (ch. 4). But a world in which God was ignored, in which Christian faith was not widely taught and broadly practised would really be a dark age; and probably all the more so for being superficially illuminated with glittering distractions from facing up to our emptiness without God while there is still time to let Him into our lives. Perhaps there is something of that in large parts of the advanced world at the moment. We expect the undoubted benefits of material wealth and expanding choices to make us happy. We seek comfort and convenience; individual, often uncommitted lifestyles; the thrill of entertainment and instant information without the trouble of personal practice or acquired understanding. It seems as if life is to be consumed rather than enjoyed; we are always 'on the move' without being confident of our origin or our destination, a predicament the Californian poet Thom Gunn spotted back in the 1960s. We have made for ourselves so many enticing things and possibilities that we often lose our hold on who we really are and what is likely to bring us deep and lasting happiness. For all our excitement with the offerings of the 'leisure industry', the insecurity that often makes us work too hard and fill every spare minute with activity seems to prevent us from quietly enjoying time with ourselves, with others, with God. We have made a world where it is alarmingly easy to live indulgently and self-centredly; where there is always the appearance of something more exciting or more urgent than nurturing a committed relationship with God and our neighbour. However, the other side of all this is that we have the practical means to alleviate poverty and spread knowledge globally more than ever before. We must be capable of achieving these aims without ignoring the needs and claims of those untelevised lives and communities immediately around us, and without furthering spiritual impoverishment while improving physical conditions. We are indeed capable of this; but it will require a little discipline, or Christian discipleship.

A disposition towards God realized in loving recognition of the claims on us of our fellow creatures can be costly. There is in the parish church of Rye in south-east England a striking, contemporary life-sized crucifix. The figure of Christ is crowned with thorns and composed entirely of driftwood. So we are startled into awareness of the mockery to which the historical Jesus and the self-denying life today have been subject. So also through the driftwood we are called to acknowledge both the brokenness to which perfect love surrendered itself and at the same time the way the disparate, apparently insignificant and always flawed lives of each and every one of us have their vital parts to play in the saving, loving work that is His body in our world. And while the arms of the figure, as of the Cross, are extended in compassion, the head of the figure and the vertical beam of the Cross direct us upward in prayerful anticipation of the resolution and fulfilment of our transitory lives in the joyful spiritual reconciliation with Our Father in Heaven.

6
Complexity and Identity: The Evolution of Collective Self

Peter M. Allen

6.1   Introduction

Traditional science was based on the idea that there was an objective reality outside, and that we could study it and do experiments on it that allowed us to build, cumulatively, an increasingly accurate picture of that reality. Whilst for simple physical problems and for planetary motion this was a reasonable working hypothesis, for biological and social systems it has always been a problem. Experiments are not repeatable or transferable, and situations are historically evolved involving local, co-evolving contexts, and therefore can potentially all be unique and lacking in any generic behaviours or laws. Complexity science brings us face to face with this elusive reality. It tells us that we must accept uncertainty and admit that our cognition, our descriptions and our models are necessarily incomplete and temporary props to our current functioning. They help us make some sense of the past and the present, and are all we have to help us in taking steps into the future.

In reality, complex systems thinking offers us a new, integrative paradigm, in which we retain the fact of multiple subjectivities, and of differing perceptions and views, and indeed see this as part of the complexity, and a source of creative interaction and of innovation and change. The underlying paradox is that knowledge of any particular discipline will necessarily imply 'a lack of knowledge' of other aspects. But all the different disciplines and domains of 'knowledge' will interact through reality – and so actions based on any particular domain of knowledge, although seemingly rational and consistent, will necessarily be inadequate.

Wisdom requires an integrated view. These new ideas encompass evolutionary processes in general, and apply to the social, cultural, economic, technological, psychological and philosophical aspects of our realities. Often, we restrict our studies to only the 'economic' aspects of a situation, with accompanying numbers, but we should not forget that we may be looking at very 'lagged' indicators of other phenomena involving people, emotions, relationships, and intuitions – to mention but a few. We may need to be careful in thinking that our views will be useful if they are based on observations and theories that refer only to a small sub-space of reality – for example economics.

The underlying causes and explanations will involve other factors entirely and their effects will drive reality in ways that people will judge according to the concepts and constructs with which they articulate their values. What matters over time is the expansion of any system into new dimensions and conceptual spaces, as a result of successive instabilities involving dimensions additional to those the current 'system' appears to occupy.

This idea of evolution as a question of 'invadability', with respect to what was not yet in the system, was the subject of a very early paper by the present author.[1] Essentially then, systems are seen as temporary, emergent structures that result from the self-reinforcing non-linear interactions that themselves result from successive 'invasions'. History is written not only by some process of 'rational improvement' in its internal structure but more fundamentally by its dialogue with elements that are *not yet* in the system – successive experimental linkages that either are rejected by the system, or which 'take off' and modify the system irreversibly.

Rational improvement of internal structure, the traditional domain of 'systems' thinking', supposes that the system has a purpose, and known measures of 'performance', which can indicate the direction of improvements. But this more fundamental structural evolution of complex systems that results from successive invasions of the system by new elements and entities is characterized by emergent properties and effects that lead to new attributes, purposes and performance measures. In the next sections therefore, we attempt to show that this structural evolution is not in fact 'random' in its outcome, as successful invasions of a system are always characterized by the revelation of positive feedback and synergy, creating particular new, internally coherent structures from a growing, explosively rich set of diverse possibilities.

6.2 Dissipative structures – models of complexity

As is well known today, in systems with some degree of strong coupling between their elements, when a critical level of thermodynamic disequilibrium is reached then many amazing and surprising things can happen. One of the earliest and most studied cases was the 'Brusselator',[2] because of the intensive study it has received by the group at Brussels. It consists of a simple, fixed, non-linear reaction mechanism (6.1),

---

[1] P.M. Allen (1976) 'Evolution, Population Dynamics and Stability', *Proc Natl Acad Sci, USA*, vol. 73, pp. 665–8.
[2] G. Nicolis and I. Prigogine (1977) *Self-Organization in Non-Equilibrium Systems*. New York: Wiley Interscience.

$$A \longrightarrow X$$
$$B + X \longrightarrow Y + D$$
$$2X + Y \longrightarrow 3X$$
$$X \longrightarrow E \qquad \text{(6.1)}$$

where A and B feed the reaction, D and E are produced by it, and X and Y are intermediates. Let us suppose further that X is red in colour, and Y is blue. The kinetic equations are shown in equation (6.2), with the symbols in italics representing concentrations of the corresponding species,

$$\frac{dx}{dt} = A - BX + X^2Y - X$$
$$\frac{dy}{dt} = BX - X^2Y \qquad \text{(6.2)}$$

As is well documented, under conditions of chemical disequilibrium all sorts of moving or stationary patterns can emerge. For example, if we stir the reaction vessel, then at a certain critical reaction rate, instead of the system being uniform (a homogeneous mixture of red and blue, of X and Y) it suddenly begins to oscillate steadily from all red to all blue and back, in a perfectly rhythmic manner. Even if perturbed momentarily, it will return to this particular, stable beat. The random, incoherent movements and reactions of the molecules are abruptly transformed into disciplined, coherent, coordinated behaviour worthy of a good choir! If the reaction is driven harder then this regular behaviour changes frequency and can become chaotic. In a system that is not stirred all sorts of spatial and spatio-temporal structures can appear spontaneously: from simple left/right inhomogeneities, to expanding spiral waves of various well defined dimensions, to moving or stationary bands of red and blue – a whole bundle of different possibilities.

This process of self-organization is a remarkable phenomenon that strikes at the heart of some of our deepest preconceptions concerning physical systems. For example, if we take a particular spatial structure, then at the interface of 'red' and 'blue' there will clearly be fluxes of diffusing X and Y caused by the concentration gradients. Our normal reaction would be to say that they are 'explained' by the 'forces' that must exist between the zones. But in fact these forces themselves are generated by the spatial structure of which the interface is a part, and which in turn reflects the fluxes that are occurring in the system. If, for example, the coefficient of diffusion were modified, or the temperature, then the spatial structure itself would change or perhaps even disappear. In this sense, the 'cause' of this particular structure is the precise values of the fluxes, which in their turn, according to our simple preconceptions, result from this structure. Clearly, the circularity of the apparent 'causation' is showing up some weakness in our way of thinking about things.

Figure 6.1 Coloured patterns develop as the Belousov–Zhabotinski reaction is run in a Petri dish (shown here in greyscale)

We come upon the dilemma that faces anyone trying to understand a biological or social system. We can 'track' the energy flow in the Brusselator, or make balance equations (accountancy) for particular materials (carbon, nitrogen etc.); but these always *only indicate or reflect* the structure that had appeared in the system, and do not explain it, nor predict when some new structure may emerge. The 'explanation' behind a particular 'structure/flow' pattern lies in the history of instabilities it has traversed, and especially in the stability or instability of the structure at the moment we are observing it. What is new, and important, is that different solution branches can emerge which are qualitatively different from each other. We have, therefore, a *non-conservation* of symmetry, and hence of the number and nature of the 'qualities' which characterize the system. In one stride we have moved from the relative banality of simple arithmetic to the quantitative modelling of morphogenetic processes whereby structure and function emerge, where the qualitative differences of the living world appear, and in which we find creation instead of conservation.

Evolution represents a dialogue between the real, rich micro-detail of the system, and the simpler deterministic average behaviour that we have considered to be adequate to represent it. However, molecules do not really have aims and goals, and probably not interpretive frameworks and these are undoubtedly phenomena that arises as a result of evolution.

6.3   Our understanding of ecology

We may like to think that it is essentially human to consider that values are of vital importance for understanding the behaviour of the organism, but in fact this is important even for the evolution of simple organisms. For example, if values are what makes an individual decide to do one thing rather than another then organisms do it too. Even ants decide to go for the more concentrated sugar source, and any species (if it is persistent) must actually like what it hunts and eats, and must also live in terrain where its prey occurs. Similarly, prey species must know that they should avoid things that resemble their predators, hence they must also have values that drive their behaviour. Furthermore, these values must be capable of changing if the critical features of their prey or predators change, and each population will actually have variance around some average set of values, which will constantly be tested whether there is advantage in having a slightly different version. A fox may have a 'model' of rabbits, and will know places where and times when they tend to be found, and most certainly can recognize them, even on a dark night, and with scent, sight and sound. However, this is not enough to make a fox a fox. What is required is that it also *wants* to chase a 'probable' rabbit! So again, axiology, epistemology and ontology co-evolve. We can develop a mathematical model of the co-evolution of populations, and show how they must evolve over time, as internal diversities lead to mutually adaptive aims, goals and knowledge.

Can we extend the ideas and modelling methods from chemical kinetics – the population dynamics of reacting molecules – to ecosystems? What differences would exist between chemical kinetics and population dynamics of real populations? If so, can the lessons of self-organization then be transferred to ecosystems, and from there to social systems? Let us consider this by taking the following example. Consider an ecosystem, and let us attempt to model it using population dynamics. We can establish the different species that exist there, and then find out how many of each population there are. We can also, by sampling, find out which population eats which other population and calibrate the multiple plant/herbivore and predator/prey interactions. Once this is established, we can put the whole system of equations on a computer, and run it forward. What happens is shown in Figure 6.2.

This collapse of the (model) ecosystem is an astonishing result. It means that although the model was calibrated on what was happening at time $t = 0$ it diverged from reality as time moved forward. The real ecosystem stayed complex, and indeed continued to adapt and change with its real environment. But the model result shows us that the mechanical representation of reality differs critically from that reality. Our 'mechanistic epistemology' fails to represent reality!

What is missing? This can be discovered if we examine carefully the assumptions that we made in formulating our population dynamics. What happened is that the interactions of the real ecosystem form parallel food chains, with cross connexions and complications of course, but essentially with each level feeding on the lower one, some of these dying and others being eaten by the level above. The whole system of food chains loops back through death and micro-organisms that recycle all the carbon and minerals. When we run the population dynamics with the fixed, calibrated birth, death, capture and escape rates that we have found on average in the real system (in analogy with

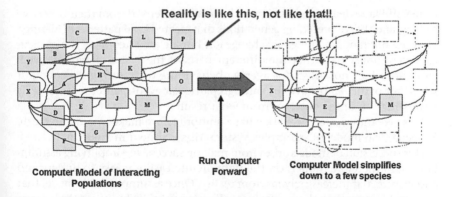

Figure 6.2 A calibrated ecosystem represented by the population dynamics of its constituent species collapses when run forward in time

chemical reaction rates), the food chain with the highest performance simply eliminates all the others. In other words, in the model, selection between metabolic chains operates and this selects for the highest performing chain. However, reality does not. The next step is to understand the discrepancy between the dynamic model and the original real system. *What is missing is the internal diversity of the populations – their individuality that comes from their genes and their particular history.* In chemistry, one molecule is identical to another, and the only difference is their spatial location. Dissipative structures can create spatio-temporal patterns because of this. But populations of organisms differ in many more ways – for example, in age, size, strength, speed, colour as well as location etc. – and so this means that whenever a population X is being decreased by the action of some particular predator or environmental change, then the most vulnerable individuals will be the ones that go first. Because of this the parameter representing the average death rate will actually decrease, as the distribution within the population X increases the average 'resistance'. In other words an ecosystem possesses, through the individuality of its populations, a multiple set of self-regulatory processes that will automatically strengthen the weak, and weaken the strong. In the same way that reaction diffusion systems in chemistry can create patterns in space and time, so in this more complex system the dynamics will create patterns in the different dimensions of diversity that the individuals inhabit. But neither we nor the individuals concerned need to know what these dimensions are. The process just happens as a result of evolutionary dynamics. In this way a model constructed using average population types interacting through average processes is not stable and will exhibit mutual adaptive adjustments all the time, rather then simply performing mechanistically.

So the internal diversity of individuals is actually a necessary, evolved part of a collective system. The diverse behaviours and decisions and apparent values and knowledge possessed by individuals are derived from their collective history, and that of preceding generations that created local patterns of identity. They are not random, nor easily changeable but are an outcome of the particular evolutionary path that the different parts of the system have followed. Evolution does not select for average behaviours with average events, but selects for particular behaviours through particular events, and the 'average' is a construction of the observer from what results.

This becomes clearer if we ask what assumptions we make in order to create a mechanical model of a complex system, this is shown in Figure 6.3.

This succession of models arises from making successive, simplifying assumptions, and therefore models on the right are increasingly easy to understand and picture, but increasingly far from reality. Once assumption 3 is made, that of average types, then the model loses all capacity to evolve, since these types are then fixed and only their relative numbers can change. No new types can appear. The operation of a mechanical system may be easy to understand but that simplicity has assumed away the more complex sources of its ability to adapt and change. They become more like 'snapshot descriptions' of the system at a particular moment, but do not contain the magic ingredient of micro-diversity that will really allow the system to undergo structural change and create a new, qualitatively different system, with some new variables and some emergent performance. The ability to adapt and change is still present in the 'evolutionary' model that only makes assumptions 1 and 2, but not those of average type and average behaviours.

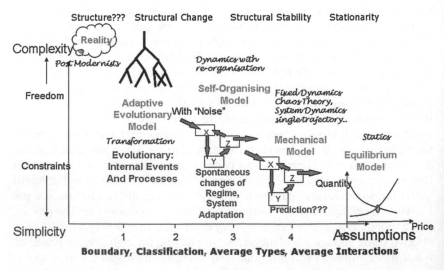

Figure 6.3   The results of successive simplifying assumptions that take us from a complex evolving system (upper left) to its mechanical representation (lower right). See also Table 6.1

The key assumption that we made that reduced the strategic view, including structural change, to the operational view where structural change is excluded[3,4,5,6,7,8] was an assumption that we could ignore the *internal diversity of the populations*. We see a pattern at the heart of complex systems thinking. The framework sorts or groups the factors into three categories, which are based on and build on the three sets of system factors. In specifying a more general model, three 'fundamentally different factors leading to the values of parameters in the working of the system' are identified:[9]

- The values of *external* factors, which are not modelled as variables in the system. These reflect the environment of the system, and of course may be dependent on spatial conditions. Temperature, climate, soils, world prices and interest rates are possible examples of such factors. (In the outside world, it could be that the system is seen as playing a 'role' in the outer world, and therefore fitting in to some outer purpose and axiology.)
- The effects of spatial arrangement, of juxtaposition and configuration of the entities underlying the system, affecting self-organizing and autocatalytic effects. Clearly in ecology the connexions reflect predator, prey, parasitic and cooperative roles, and therefore the structure of the system partly results from the aims and goals of the individuals (the ontology of the interacting agents). This must be true also in human systems.
- The values corresponding to the 'performance' of the underlying entities, due to their *internal* characteristics like technology, level of knowledge or strategies, but also the evolving values, aims and goals (axiology) and epistemology (beliefs, knowledge, skills) of the agents.

These three factors are all coupled by interaction, and so changes that occur in any one will affect the other two. This in turn will affect the environment

[3] P.M. Allen (1993) 'Evolution: Persistant Ignorance from Continual Learning', in *Nonlinear Dynamics and Evolutionary Economics*, eds E. Day and P. Chen. Oxford University Press, Chapter III, pp. 101–12.

[4] P.M. Allen (1994a) 'Evolutionary Complex Systems: Models of Technology Change', In *Chaos and Economic Theory*, eds L. Leydesdorff and P. van den Besselaar. London: Pinter.

[5] P.M. Allen (1994b) 'Coherence, Chaos and Evolution in the Social Context', *Futures*, vol. 26, pp. 583–97.

[6] P.M. Allen (2000) 'Knowledge, Ignorance and Learning', *Emergence*, vol. 2, pp. 78–103.

[7] P.M. Allen (2001a) 'Knowledge, Ignorance and the Evolution of Complex Systems', in *Frontiers of Evolutionary Economics: Competition, Self-Organisation and Innovation Policy*, eds J. Foster and S. Metcalfe. Cheltenham Edward Elgar.

[8] P.M. Allen (2001b) 'A Complex Systems Approach to Learning, Adaptive Networks' *International Journal of Innovation Management*, vol. 5, pp. 149–80.

[9] J. Gillies (2000) 'A Complex Systems Model of the Adaptability of Industrial Networks', PhD Thesis, Cranfield University, Bedfordshire, UK.

Table 6.1   The successive assumptions needed to produce a mechanistic description of a natural system

Number	Assumption made	Resulting model
1	Boundary Assumed	Some local sense-making possible – no structure supposed
2	Classification Assumed	Strategic, open-ended, Evolutionary – structural, qualitative change occurs, successive systems, successive structural attractors
3	Average Types	Operational, probabilistic, non-linear equations – assumed structurally stable, allows calculation of resilience and robustness
4	Average Events	Operational mechanical equations, deterministic – assumed structurally stable
5	Stationarity	Equilibrium model

of the environment, the underlying entities of the underlying entities, and so on in an irreversible cascade outwards and inwards that makes everything essentially irreversible.

6.4   The emergence of free will

The picture of complexity given above provides us with a new basis for thinking about our own evolution and beliefs and for all reflexions on justice or on religion. Traditional science at the scale of our normal experience was dominated by a fundamental paradigm that explained things in terms of mechanical systems operating according to unchanging natural laws. In other words, determinism was at the heart of science and if it could have been carried through to include the biological and human domains would have left no room for free will or choice and, therefore, would eliminate any ideas of praise or blame with regard to human behaviour.

Complexity showed that this mechanical model is wrong. When Poincaré studied the dynamics of as few as three bodies colliding, he showed that the long-term trajectory was in fact impossible to predict, owing to the gradual amplification of even the smallest micro-deviations. Of course, three bodies colliding do not really 'evolve' in that there is no emergent behaviour or properties. But when we get to the non-equilibrium chemistry of the Brusselator and then of the populations of ecosystems or of human societies, we find that the nonlinear interactions lead through instabilities to different possible futures with their own emergent structures and collective behaviours. In turn these new collective structures and modes of behaviour can also interact and lead to still higher levels of structure and emergence. Each successive set of instabilities depends on the details of what preceded it, and so we get a general view of an expanding tree of possibilities, in which reality only goes down some of the branches of those theoretically possible. Neglected pathways are soon forgotten and become inaccessible, and evolution focuses on evolving from the actual present into its possible futures. So, determinism is defeated and replaced by 'path-dependency' in non-equilibrium systems, as individual elements gain a degree of internal autonomy in which personal histories, local, internal details and momentary incidents can influence the choices made, and hence the future of the individual and of the local system it inhabits.

A degree of 'free will' emerges, as the system is 'under-determined' and does not provide information to individuals such that they can only take a single path forwards. Both choice and uncertainty characterize the system, and lead therefore to the possibility of options for the decisions of individuals. Of course, some scientists may argue that in reality individuals are still governed by the micro-details of their brains and of their upbringing and so in actuality do not have real choice, but only the appearance of freedom. Clearly, this is not a trivial matter since it leads to matters of ethics and justice, including for potentially blameless 'automata'. However, complexity does tell us that when faced with an under-determined situation at a system level, an individual element can use its own internal values and information to act and what will matter will be the collective implications of individual decisions. Free will can certainly operate for choices with no known consequences for others, but where there

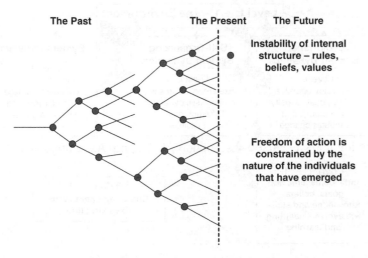

Figure 6.4 Evolution and interaction lead to the selection of individuals whose internal values, beliefs and capacities allow adequate collective behaviour

are collective implications evolution will have acted to affect these decisions in such a way as to favour the successful continuation of the social system. In this way, we see that it is not so much the evolution of 'free will' that is the question, but it is the evolution or co-evolution of individual value systems that is really crucial. Clearly, these are the defining realities of 'free will', since they limit and constrain the decisions that will be made.

Individuals may act in pursuit of their current goals and desires, according to their current beliefs and skills. Their actions however, may lead them to see either that their knowledge was inadequate to achieve their aims, or that their aims were inadequate to provide the satisfaction that they thought would arise. Their actions are therefore directed either to improve their knowledge concerning how to obtain their goals, or towards new, updated aims and goals. As their behaviour changes, so those with whom they interact take stock of this, and in their turn modify their own behaviour and knowledge. In this way systems of interacting, partially autonomous agents generate a co-evolution of ontology, epistemology and axiology (theory of values). The overall ontology is the current collective result of the current individual, diverse path-dependent epistemologies and values of the system, and individuals change their inner 'structure' and 'identity' as part of this on-going co-evolutionary process. In complex systems modelling we have at least three levels of description co-evolving, while in more traditional, mechanical models we only have two. In Figure 6.5 we see these three levels and can immediately comprehend that there is necessarily a 'problem' of identity for any individual element at the lower level.

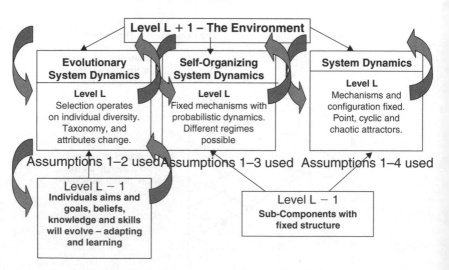

Figure 6.5   Complex system models on the left link simultaneously the co-evolution of the environment, the system and the individuals

Individuals have both an individual identity and also an identity as part of the collective structures they inhabit. So how do our goals and aims reflect this reality? The answer is – with difficulty. We can clearly see the benefits of others behaving reasonably, while potentially seeking exemptions for ourselves. Of course, societies that give rise to large numbers of individuals that only consider their own immediate requirements and ignore others will in general be unpleasant to live in, and more importantly will probably not be sustainable. There is clearly a selective advantage for societies that can act collectively and cohesively, but of course if collective success comes at too high a price at the individual level, then probably this will not be sustainable either. Sustainability comes from a balanced delivery of sufficient satisfaction at the three levels of Figure 6.5 – environmental, collective system and individual.

It would be too trivial to jump to an 'explanation' of the remarkable geographical spread of particular religious beliefs on the basis of selective advantage of a people united by a religion. Clearly, however, what matters more is the aspect of shared individual values that embrace sufficiently the collective and the environment without repressing individuals too much. An individual awareness of being part of a greater whole is certainly a step towards spirituality, and clearly complexity provides us with a conceptual framework that both allows and supports the emergence of such a thing.

6.5 Emergent economic coordination

Let us briefly consider the practical expression of some of these thoughts in our social systems and human organizations. For example, let us consider a market system and see how the successful co-evolution of the three different levels of description are involved. We shall view this as a situation involving an economic and social environment, some potential consumers who may choose to buy one of the products offered in this market, and a collective system that we call the market in which agents running firms decide on their strategy in order to capture sufficient potential demand to survive financially. The potential customers of course will see the different products according to their particular desires and needs, and in the simple case examined here, we shall simply consider that customers are differentiated by their revenue, and therefore have different sensitivities to price.

The structure of each firm that is modelled is as shown in Figure 6.6. Inputs and labour are necessary for production and the cost of these, added to the fixed and start-up costs, produce goods that are sold by sales staff who must interact with potential customers in order to turn them into actual customers. The potential market for a product is related to its qualities and price, and although in this simple case we have assumed that customers all like the same qualities, they have a different response to the price charged. The price charged is made up of the cost of production (variable cost) to which is added a mark-up. The mark-up needs to be such that it will turn out to cover the fixed and

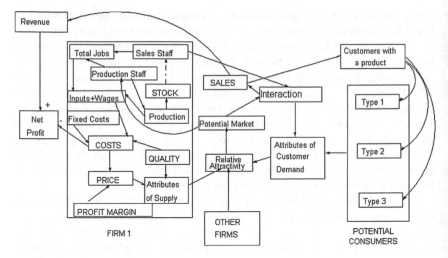

Figure 6.6   A model of six interacting firms/agents whose choices of mark-up and quality represent their strategies

start-up costs as well as the sales staff wages. Depending on the quality and price, therefore, there are differently sized potential markets coming from the different customer segments.

When customers buy a product, they cease to be potential customers for an interval that is related to the lifetime of the product. For high-quality goods this may be longer than for low quality, but of course, many goods are bought in order to follow fashion and style rather than through absolute necessity. Indeed, different strategies would be required depending on whether or not this is the case, and which is one of the many explorations that can be made with the model.

The model calculates the relative attractivity of a product (of given quality and price) for a customer of a given type (poor, medium or rich). It then calculates the 'potential market' for each firm at each moment, and the sales staff must interact with these potential customers in order to turn them into customers. When a sale is made, then the potential customer becomes a customer and disappears from the market for a time that depends on the product lifetime. The revenue from the sales of a firm are used to pay the fixed and variable costs of production, and any profit can be used either to increase production or to decrease the bank debt if there is any. In this way, the firm tries to finance its growth and to avoid going near its credit limit. If a firm exceeds its credit limit then it is declared bankrupt and closed down.

In traditional economic theories, firms are supposed to act, or to have acted, in such a way as to obtain maximum profit. But here, in a complex systems view, we find that if current profit is the driving force for increased production then the firms cannot launch a product because any new product must start by an investment – a negative profit. So, if firms do start production, and increase it, then this cannot be modelled by linking the increase in production to the profit *at that time*. Instead, we might say that it is driven by the *expected profit over some future time*. But this is clearly wrong, since their expected profits would depend on the behaviour and expectations of other firms. Whatever firms expect, in reality, clearly some of them get it wrong, because a large fraction go bankrupt. We see that launching into the market cannot be governed by 'knowledge' but must instead be based on 'belief'. Belief, that is, in the future success of the chosen strategy.

Managers in our model may be driven by a goal of future profits, but they do not know how this can be achieved. They face the uncertainty of an under-determined system and will construct the future by their collective interaction. They have an interpretive framework, but it may well prove inadequate, in which case they may seek other knowledge (evolve their epistemology) and either change their behaviour according to their adaptive rules, or they go bankrupt. In other words, the ontology will select for agents with aims and goals (axiologies) and interpretive frameworks (epistemologies) that can successfully coexist. Our model shows that it is the economies and diseconomies of production and distribution that will determine the number, size and scale of the niches that may be discovered.

We can use our model to explore the effect of different learning strategies of firms. The strategy space in view here is that of what percentage profit to charge and what quality of product to make. Obviously, a lower mark-up will provide larger market share, and lead to economies of scale, but these may not come soon enough to avoid bankruptcy. Alternatively, a firm can have a very high mark-up and make much profit on each unit it sells, but its sales may be too small to allow survival. We ran four series of simulations, and compared for different random seed-sequences the relative performance (total profits minus bankruptcy costs) of the market, with different individual behavioural strategies:

> **Darwinian Learning**: In this case we launch firms with random strategies, and if a firm goes bankrupt, we replace it with a new firm with a random strategy. In this way, in theory the performance of the market will improve as unsuccessful strategies are eliminated, and only successful ones remain after a long time. The model shows us that average market value achieved by the process, including the cost of bankruptcies, is actually negative. In other words, Darwinism applied to market evolution, using bankruptcy as the selection process, is so costly on average that the industry as a whole makes a loss. There is in fact enormous variance in the performance of the market as a whole, with some simulations showing very effective organization by chance, and others with very negative performance following a different sequence of choices.

> **All Imitate**: Here, firms are launched initially with random strategies, but firms adopt the strategy that is winning. In this way, in theory, the resulting

market should evolve to a collection of firms all using a very successful strategy. This does perform better than Darwinian learning on average, with an average final value of over 800,000 currency units compared to $-114,000$. But the strategy seems to provide the most unstable trajectories, with some examples of market crashes and severe set-backs in the general pattern of improvement.

All Learn: In this case, after being launched with random strategies, firms each explore the effects on profits of changing quality and mark up. They then move up the profit slope – if possible. In this way, they demonstrate the effect of a learning strategy. The firms here have an 'experimental' strategy of probing their 'profit' landscape and moving in the direction of increase. This works much better than the previous cases, with an average profit of 1.4 million currency units for the different computer runs.

Mixed Strategies: Here, after a random launch, we have two Darwinists, two imitators and two learners. This leads to an evolution of the market structure gradually exploring and changing as profit and loss select for the winners and losers. This actually has the highest average profit but is less consistent than the 'all learning' strategy.

The results of these simulations are shown in Figure 6.7, which illustrates the complex relationship between individual and collective behaviour and values. The model allows us to test which strategies firms should adopt for the greatest chance of success. It shows us that it is false to believe that firms can simply come to market with price/quality strategies that they believe will work, and that their success or failure in the market will effectively lead to efficient economic market structures.

The simulations could be used to examine particular cases, and could offer advice to particular firms engaged in market competition; however, here we are really more interested in investigating the general properties of evolutionary markets. Our model shows us that the basic process of 'micro-variation' and differential amplification of the emergent behaviours is the most successful process in generating a successful market structure, and is good both for the individual players and for the whole market, as well as its customers.[10,11]

The important result that emerges is that for the same potential demand, the same technology, the same strategies and the same interactions, chance can still allow great variation in the market structures that emerge. In general the Darwinian method (death and replacement) is so poor that the cost of learning

[10] J.S. Metcalfe (1998) *Evolutionary Economics and Creative Destruction*. London: Routledge.
[11] J.S. Metcalfe (1999) 'Restless Capitalism, Returns and Growth in Enterprise Economics', CRIC, University of Manchester.

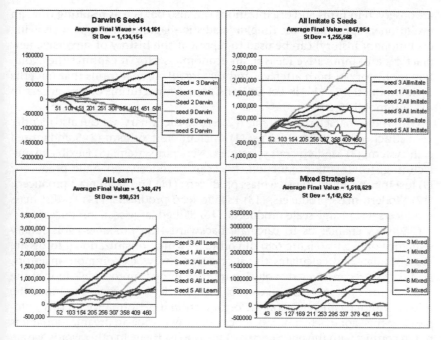

Figure 6.7   The abscissae give total profit minus total cost (including bankruptcies). Through these multiple simulations we see that Darwinian learning is very ineffective, and the best overall performance is achieved by firms with learning mechanisms

exceeds the total profits of the sector in three of the six cases! Although firms actually believe that their goal should be to beat other firms, here we see that in reality it is how to find strategies of price and quality that enable profitable coexistence. We see that what really works is something that forms a successful collective structure from the actions of individuals acting in pursuit of their own success.

Since each computer run has a different detailed outcome, what we can say overall is that evolution does lead to some collective structure that is 'good enough', but which does not mean that it is very good. This evolutionary process is one of 'satisficing' not optimizing,[12] as it operates by the elimination of behaviours that turn out not to survive, and not by the excellence of the chosen few. Individual agents may theoretically have free will, but in reality they can only continue to exist if they adopt strategies that allow them to co-evolve successfully with the other agents in the market.

Another example of the interplay of three levels of description is afforded by the evolution of organizations. The internal practices and routines that

---

[12] H. Simon (1957) *Models of Man: Social and Rational*. New York: John Wiley and Sons.

are observed in firms and organizations can also be seen as resulting from an evolutionary process. Over time, a 'cladistic diagram' (a diagram showing evolutionary history) can be used to represent the history of successive new practices and innovative ideas in an economic sector. It captures the evolutionary history of both artefacts and the organizational forms that underlie their production.[13,14,15,16] Let us consider manufacturing organizations in the automobile sector.

With these characteristics (Table 6.2) as our 'dictionary' we can also identify 16 distinct organizational forms: (1) Ancient craft system; (2) Standardized craft system; (3) Modern craft system; (4) Neocraft system; (5) Flexible manufacturing; (6) Toyota production; (7) Lean producers; (8) Agile producers; (9) Just in time; (10) Intensive mass producers; (11) European mass producers; (12) Modern mass producers; (13) Pseudo lean producers; (14) Fordist mass producers; (15) Large scale producers; (16) Skilled large scale producers.

Cladistics enables us to calculate backwards the probable evolutionary sequence of events (Figure 6.8). It considers which organizational forms are most similar, and calculates the shortest pathways to common ancestors, leading to a reconstructed evolutionary tree. In our approach we look at the pairwise interactions between each pair of practices, in order to examine the role of 'internal coherence' on the organizational performance. In this 'complex systems' approach, a new practice can only invade an organization if it is not in conflict with the practices that already exist there. In other words, we are looking at 'organizations' not in terms of simply additive features and practices, but as mutually interactive 'complexes' of constituent factors. We see that this is a more precise way of talking about the practices involved in creating 'dynamic capabilities'. In automobile manufacture, the most 'evolved' organizational form is that of agile manufacturing. This is what wins in sophisticated, mature markets, but there still can be a place for mass production and maximum economies of scale in developing markets.

From a survey of manufacturers concerning the positive or negative interactions between the different practices,[17] a matrix of pair interactions was constructed allowing us examine the 'reasons' behind the emergent organizational

---

[13] B. McKelvey (1982) *Organizational Systematics*. Berkeley: University of California Press.

[14] B. McKelvey (1994) 'Evolution and Organizational Science', in J. Baum and J. Singh (eds), *Evolutionary Dynamics of Organizations*. Oxford University Press, pp. 314–26.

[15] I. McCarthy (1995) 'Manufacturing Classifications: Lessons from Organisational Systematics and Biological Taxonomy', *Journal of Manufacturing and Technology Management – Integrated Manufacturing Systems*, vol. 6, pp. 37–49.

[16] I. McCarthy, M. Leseure, K. Ridgeway and N. Fieller (1997), 'Building a Manufacturing Cladogram', *International Journal of Technology Management*, vol. 13, pp. 2269–96.

[17] J.S. Baldwin, P.M. Allen, B. Winder and K. Ridgway, (2003) 'Simulating the Complex Cladistic Evolution of Manufacturing', *Innovation: Management, Policy and Practice*, vol. 5, pp. 144–56.

Table 6.2   53 characteristics of automobile manufacturing organizations

1	Standardization of parts	28	100% inspection sampling
2	Assembly time standards	29	U-shaped layout
3	Assembly line layout	30	Preventive maintenance
4	Reduction in craft skills	31	Individual error correction
5	Automation	32	Sequential dependency of workers
6	Pull production system	33	Line balancing
7	Reduction of lot size	34	Team policy
8	Pull procurement system	35	Toyota verification scheme
9	Operator based machine	36	Groups vs teams
	maintenance	37	Job enrichment
10	Quality circles	38	Manufacturing cells
11	Employee innovation prizes	39	Concurrent engineering
12	Job rotation	40	ABC costing
13	Large volume production	41	Excess capacity
14	Mass sub-contracting by	42	Flexible automation
	sub-bidding		of product versions
15	Exchange of workers with suppliers	43	Agile automation for
16	Training through socialization		different products
17	Pro-active training programme	44	In-sourcing
18	Product range reduction	45	Immigrant workforce
19	Automation (machine-paced shops)	46	Dedicated automation
20	Multiple sub-contracting	47	Division of labour
21	Quality systems	48	Employees are system tools
22	Quality philosophy	49	Employees are system developers
23	Open book policy with suppliers	50	Product focus
24	Flexible multi-functional workforce	51	Parallel processing
25	Set-up time reduction	52	Dependence on written rules
26	Kaizen change management	53	Further intensification of labour
27	TQM sourcing		

forms, with successful forms arising from positive mutual interactions of constituent practices. This 53×53 matrix allows the calculation of the degree of synergy, or of schizophrenia, that the internal structure of an organization may have.

We have then been able to develop an evolutionary simulation model, in which a manufacturing firm attempts to incorporate successive new practices at some characteristic rate. The 53×53 matrix provides the information about pair interactions of practices, and so it is possible to calculate the 'synergy' of the practices present in an organization and the receptivity of the organization to some new practice. Depending on the order in which practices are added an incredible range of possible structures can be tried, but only those with high levels of synergy between their practices will actually persist. Each time a new practice is adopted within an organization it changes the 'receptivity' (recettività) of the organization for any new innovations in the future. This

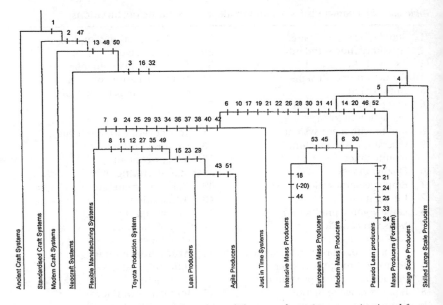

Figure 6.8   The cladistic diagram for automobile manufacturing organizational forms
Source: McCarthy *et al.* (1997)

is another illustration of the 'path-dependent evolution' that characterizes complexity science. Successful evolution is about the 'discovery' or 'creation' by individuals of highly synergetic collective structures of interacting practices.

The model starts off from a craft structure. New practices are launched at random intervals and either they decline and disappear or they grow and become an integral part of the organization, changing the receptivity to further possible innovations. The particular emergent attributes and capabilities of the organization are a function of the particular combination of practices that constitute it, and these reflect a particular culture, shared values and beliefs on the part of the participating individuals.

The model based on the opinions of the manufacturers surveyed shows us that synergy does indeed increase in the more evolved organizational forms, reaching very high values in the 'Japanese' style agile manufacturing. However it in no way asserts that in real life there are not all kinds of practices introduced, or mergers attempted, without any knowledge or understanding of the possible synergy or conflict that may be unleashed. Indeed, the purpose of the model is precisely to awaken ego-ridden CEOs to the probable failure of many suggested mergers. The model shows us what historical pathways can be successful in the long run – not what CEOs may actually do. The model is attempting to establish a real basis for the assessment of possible organizational innovations or mergers, since we know that the majority of mergers do not achieve their avowed aims.[18]

Different simulations lead to different structures, and there is a very large number of possible 'histories'. This demonstrates a key idea in complex systems thinking: the explorations/innovations that are tried out at a given time cannot be logically or rationally deduced because their overall effects cannot be known ahead of time. The impossibility of prediction gives the system 'choice'. In our simulation we mimic this by using a random number generator to select what to try out, though in reality the selection would actually be promoted by someone who believes in it, and who will be proved right or wrong by experience, or in this case by our simulation. In real life there will be debate and discussion by different people in favour of one or another choice, and each would cite their own projections about the trade-offs and the overall effect of their choice. However, the actual success that a new practice meets with is pre-determined by the 'fitness landscape' resulting from the practices already present and what the emergent attributes and capabilities encounter in the marketplace. But this landscape will be changed if a new practice does successfully invade the system. The new practice will bring with it its own set of pairwise interactions, modifying the selection criteria for further change. So, the pattern of what *could* then invade the system (if it were tried) has been changed by what *has already* invaded successfully. This is technically referred to as a 'path-dependent' process since the future evolutionary pathway is affected by that of the past – i.e. its historicity.

The evolution through the tree of forms corresponds to a gradual increase in overall 'synergy'. That is, the more modern structures related to 'lean' and to 'agile' organizations contain more 'positive' links and less 'negative' links per unit than the ancient craft systems and also the mass-producing side of the tree. Here, new aims and goals are defined within the organization, and new ways of achieving them are created and tried out. Reality selects for those aims and goals, and those practices that can successfully coexist together in a synergetic structure. Of course, some firms find particular niches that allow them to stay where they are, as for example Morgan Cars may be essentially artisanal in its organization, but it finds enough customers to keep going year after year. So, the exploration produced by the different types of emergent capability respond to the needs of different parts of the market, and this becomes visible post hoc. Obviously, the market itself is evolving, as for example the tastes of the US, Europe and Japan appears to have tipped the balance in favour of agile and lean manufacturing, but with the rise of the Chinese and Indian economies, the market for ultra-cheap, mass produced cars may well grow enormously. In this way organizational evolution and industrial

---

[18] P.M. Allen, R. Ramlogan and S. Randles (2002) 'Complex Systems and the Merger process', *Technology Analysis and Strategic Management*, vol. 14, pp. 315–31.

patterns co-evolve with the changing aims and goals of different potential customers, and with their changing circumstances. The exploration afforded by ignorance in knowing the precise order in which new ideas should be tried out leads to an ability to co-evolve and innovate new forms and new capabilities. Our work also highlights a 'problem' with the acceptance of complex systems thinking for operational use. The theory of complex systems tells us that the future is not completely predictable because the system has some internal autonomy and will undergo path-dependent learning. However, this also means that the 'present' (existing data) cannot be proven to be a *necessary* outcome of the past – but only, hopefully, a *possible* outcome. So, there are perhaps so many possible structures for organizations to discover and render functional, that the observed organizational structures (Figure 6.8) may be merely 16 out of several hundred that are possible. In traditional science the assumption was that 'only the optimal survive', and therefore that what we observe is an optimal structure with only a few temporary deviations from average. But, selection is effected through the competitive interactions of the other players, and if they are different, catering to a slightly different market, and also sub-optimal at any particular moment, then there is no selection force capable of pruning the burgeoning possibilities to a single, optimal outcome. Complexity tells us that we are freer than we thought, and that the diversity that this freedom allows is the mechanism through which sustainability, adaptability and learning occur.

This picture shows us that evolution is about the discovery and emergence of structural attractors[7,8,19] that express the natural synergies and conflicts (the nonlinearities) of underlying components. Their properties and consequences are difficult to anticipate and therefore require real, ongoing explorations and experiments, based on diversity of beliefs, views and experiences of freely acting individuals.

6.5   Conclusions

The sections above illustrate how complexity science provides us with a new basis on which to understand our world. It is remarkable therefore that one finds in the *Dao De Jing*, composed more than 2000 years ago, remarkably similar ideas. In the space available here, we can only quote some small extracts from a remarkable translation and commentary made by Ames and Hall.[20] Their commentary on Chapter 1 of the *Dao* is:

> *Experience is processual, and thus always provisional. Process requires that the*
> *formational and functional aspects of our experience are correlative and mutually*

---

[19] P.M. Allen and M. Strathern (2004) 'Evolution, Emergence and Learning in Complex Systems', Emergence, vol. 5, pp. 8–33.

[20] R. Ames and D. Hall (2003) *A Philosophical Translation of the Dao De Jing*. New York: Ballantine Books.

entailing. *Our new thoughts shape how we think and act. And how we are presently disposed to think and act disciplines our novel thoughts. While the fluid immediacy of experience precludes the possibility of exhaustive conceptualization and explanation, enduring formal structures lend the flow of experience a degree of determinacy that can be expressed productively in conceptual language. The relative persistence of formal structures permits us to parse and punctuate the ceaseless flow of experience into consummate yet never really discrete things and events.*

This seems an extraordinary recognition of the limits of language and of 'models' in describing an evolutionary world. Another short extract is also highly relevant. From Chapter 4 they explain:

It is the underdetermined nature of way-making that makes it, like a bottomless goblet, inexhaustibly capacious. The processive and fluid character of experience precludes the possibility of either initial beginning or final closure by providing within it an ongoing space for self-renewal. Within the rhythms of life, the swinging gateway opens and novelty emerges spontaneously to revitalize the world, tempering whatever has moved to an extreme, and reclaiming whatever has strayed from the path. Whatever is most enduring is ultimately overtaken in the ceaseless transformation of things.

The depth and profundity of experience lies in the inexhaustibility of its possibilities. And what makes these possibilities inexhaustible is real novelty: uncaused and inexplicable. As the creative origin of everything that happens and the locus of all relationships, experience itself is an appropriate object of awe and religious deference.

These short extracts hopefully demonstrate the remarkable similarity in views that complexity science has to some forms of ancient wisdom such as the *Dao*. In some ways the Enlightenment was such a powerful event within Western society that it has tended to overshadow these more subtle thoughts. Clearly, the emergence of modern science and the use of reason have given us incredible technological powers and an undreamed of quality of life for millions. But our science was based on the clear understanding of closed systems, and models could be calibrated and validated because repeatable experiments could be performed. Our knowledge of real life, open systems, the basis for collective behaviour and social interaction, however, remained the province of religion and philosophy until recently. Complexity science is simply the science of open systems, and is about collective structures that are the outcome of evolution, in which emergence and contextually-dependent transformations have occurred. It addresses systems for which repeatable experiments are not really possible – social systems, for example, where every situation is potentially unique. Reason has shown us the limits of reason, because instead of determinism we have an open-ended evolution with multiple possible pathways. Traditional science is contained within complexity science, as it simply requires more assumptions to be made in order to achieve the clarity required. In Figure 6.3 we have shown the assumptions that lead from a complex reality to a mechanistic representation of that reality, which appears deterministic. While this may be a good representation of reality for some short time interval, over longer times at some point a structural instability will occur in the system of which this is a reduced representation, and then the mechanical model will be wrong.

If the ancient wisdom of the *Dao* fits so well the view coming from complexity science, then we can ask – in what way does complexity science go beyond ancient wisdom? The answer is that it possibly makes more precise the courses of action suggested by wisdom, and in addition can offer models that can tell us things that wisdom cannot. For example, models of particular organizations can be used to discover how its participants could actually improve overall performance. Similarly, integrated models of systems such as global climate, cities, regions, economic markets, river basins, fisheries etc. can be used to provide information that is not otherwise available.[21,22,6] Such models do not 'predict the future', because the future is open and dependent on the decisions that will be made, but they do demonstrate the probable impacts of particular choices and policies on the overall evolution of the system studied.

In our presentation of complexity modelling, we see that evolution and emergence is about the changing constellations of interacting elements that have mutually supportive, complementary attributes – meaning that they have the possibility of emergent capabilities which can access resources from their environment. This addresses the question that underlies the theory of systems and asks 'why' any particular system exists. Systems arise by chance and persist for as long as they successfully access the resources needed for maintenance and growth. Darwin's Galapagos finches, and the different permutations of finch that inhabit differently sized islands, are illustrations of this. These are complex systems of interdependent behaviours whose attributes are on the whole synergetic. They correspond to the emergence of hypercycles in the work of Eigen and Schuster,[23] but recognize the importance of emergent collective attributes and dimensions. The sequence of successive systems that emerge and dissolve in a domain over time reflects the particular historical pathway that has occurred. It results from the particular local, idiosyncratic deviations and peculiarities that occurred to perturb the pattern of positive and negative interactions of the structural attractors that emerged. Evolutionary

[21] P.M. Allen (1997) *Cities and Regions as Self-Organizing Systems: Models of Complexity.* London: Taylor and Francis.

[22] P.M. Allen and J.M. McGlade (1987a) 'Modelling Complex Human Systems: A Fisheries Example', *European Journal of Operational Research*, vol. 30, pp. 147–67.

[23] M. Eigen and P. Schuster (1979) *The Hypercycle.* Berlin: Springer.

drive describes how underlying micro-diversity drives systems forward through successive structural attractors.[24,25]

Throughout the economy, and indeed the social, cultural system of interacting elements and structures we see a generic picture at multiple temporal and spatial scales in which *uncertainty about the future allows* actions that are exploratory and divergent, which are then either amplified or suppressed by the way that this modifies the interaction with their environment. Essentially, this fulfils the early vision of dissipative structures,[26,27] in that their existence and amplification depend on the internal agents or elements 'learning' how to access energy and matter in their environment, and this brings intentionality, whether well-informed or not, into the dynamics of micro-diversity generation. Individual values, beliefs and actions co-evolve with others with whom they interact, and so there is a constant generation of potential diversity in these, and the wider system selects upon the emergent collective capabilities.

In effect, the successful working of the ecosystems, markets and social systems requires the constant generation of underlying heterogeneity. This can be in the aims and goals (axiologies) of the agents, in their attempted interpretive frameworks (epistemologies). The resulting heterogeneous ontology selects over time for synergy and co-operativity amongst all this. Uncertainty about the future, the admission of ignorance, leads naturally to the freedom to think and aim for different things and hence to propose different ways forward. These then compete and co-operate between themselves leading to a selection of a compatible subset. Selection from the level above leads to the retention of systems with such dynamic capabilities that allow transformation and restructuring to occur within. Evolution selects for an evolutionary capability, and so the outcome is that we live in a world for which there is no 'correct' axiology, epistemology or ontology, since this is always changing, as part of an evolving heterogeneous whole. In the words of Stacey, *'The human self-conscious mind is not an 'it' located and stored in the individuals. Rather, individual mind arises continuously and transiently in relationships between people'.*[28] We see our individual selves as emerging and evolving as part of the collective system – and so our identity is itself an expression of collective history and part of the ongoing drama.

---

[24] P.M. Allen and J.M. McGlade (1987b) 'Evolutionary Drive: The Effect of Microscopic Diversity, Error Making & Noise', *Foundations of Physics*, vol. 17, pp. 723–8.

[25] P. Allen, M. Strathern and J. Baldwin (2006) 'Evolutionary Drive: New Understandings of Change in Socio-economic Systems', *Emergence: Complexity and Organization*, vol. 8, pp. 2–19.

[26] I. Prigogine (1981) *From Being to Becoming*. New York: W.H. Freeman.

[27] I. Prigogine and I. Stengers (1987) *Order out of Chaos*. New York: Bantam Books.

[28] R. Stacey (2001) *Complex Responsive Processes in Organizations*. London and New York: Routledge.

Part II
Synthesis

7
New Thinking: A Synthesis

Jeremy Ramsden

This chapter opens on a world stage darkened by a backdrop of grim wars and daily atrocities, the relentless destruction and despoilation of our environment, endemic corruption in public service at local, national and international levels, and an unsavoury smell hanging around the boardrooms and activities of many prominent companies.

Some perceive in technology the saviour of this seemingly headlong rush towards disaster. Genetically modified organisms to provide food for the whole world, and later on personal nanofactories to provide an abundance of every imaginable artefact for the comfort and convenience of the Earth's denizens – to keep the theatrical imagery, these are the brilliant floodlights shining from high above. To be sure, high technology seems to have a universal allure. There are now more mobile telephones in Africa than in the USA. While awareness among the general population of the knowledge on which the technologies are based seems to diminish from year to year, public acceptance, albeit selective, seems to grow from year to year. I have seen it asserted that possession of a television set is now considered to be an inalienable human right (*sic*). Increasingly crowds flock to the air for the most trivial excursions – an inhabitant of Birmingham may well travel to Milan for an afternoon's shopping, for example. A corollary of that is that we now have multitudes of engineers, planners and other government officials engaged in making quieter aircraft engines, trying to work out ways of combating pollution caused by motor vehicle exhausts, etc.

On the other hand, there are equally loud voices asserting that technology without ethics is dead. Rising above this clash of opinions, however, is the incontrovertible empirical observation of the history of mankind that leads to the conclusion that knowledge about the universe and man's place in it has enormously advanced during the last three millennia, while ethics have advanced very little. This kind of comparison led the English historian Buckle to the conclusion that it is improved knowledge that has led to better behaviour, rather than the discovery of hitherto unsuspected and unrevealed ethical principles.[1] That is why, for example, human sacrifice has become a thing of the past, and one may fairly assert that (despite reports of atrocities) the conquistadors were morally superior to those they conquered, and that the basis of their superiority was superior knowledge about the world.

Yet new knowledge inevitably leads, not only apparently to better behaviour, but also to new technology. The knowledge of the society whence the conquistadors sprang also equipped them with superior weaponry, including firearms. Seen from the viewpoint of the middle of the nineteenth century, when Buckle was writing his monumental work, this would not have created any particular difficulty. The results from the waging of wars using gunpowder seemed to be less cruel than the ghastly wounds that were so characteristic of medieval warfare. Yet one wonders whether Buckle would have revised his conclusions had he lived through and observed the First World War and its successors in the twentieth and twenty-first centuries. The First World War, with its tanks and aeroplanes, was the first large-scale example of a truly mechanized war, the manner of the waging of which was a direct result of technology rooted in those very advances of knowledge that Buckle held to be responsible for improvements in human behaviour. The First World War was ghastly enough, with its millions of dead soldiers, the flower of Europe's male population slain. The link between knowledge and warfare was already perceived at the time, as expressed by that perceptive observer, Frederick Scott Oliver:

> Barbarism is not any the less barbarism because it employs weapons of precision, because it avails itself of the discoveries of science and the mechanism of finance, or because it thinks it worthwhile to hire bands of learned men to shriek paeans of praise and invectives against its victims. Barbarism is not any the less barbarism because its methods are up-to-date. It is known for what it is by the ends which it pursues and the spirit in which it pursues them. The modern spirit of Germany is materialism in its crudest form – the undistracted pursuit of wealth, and the power as a means to wealth. It is materialism, rampant and self-confident, fostered by the State – subsidized, regulated, and, where thought advisable, controlled by the State – backed in the last resort by the fleets and armies of the State. It is the most highly organized machine, the most deliberate and thorough-going system, for arriving at material ends which has ever been devised by man. It is far more efficient, but not a whit less material, than 'Manchesterism' of the Victorian era, which placed its hopes in 'free' competition, and also than that later development of trusts and syndicates – hailing from America – which aims at levying tribute on society by means of 'voluntary' cooperation. And just as the English professors, who

---

[1] See Chapter 4, footnote 7.

fell prostrate in adoration before the prosperity of cotton spinners, found no difficulty in placing self-interest upon the loftiest pedestal of morality, so German professors have succeeded in erecting for the joint worship of the Golden Calf and the War-god Wotun, high twin altars which look down with pity and contempt upon the humbler shrines of the Christian faith.[2]

The alliance between knowledge, wealth and state power is only the logical endpoint of a policy apparently first advocated by Francis Bacon in Elizabethan England – knowledge leads to technology, and technology leads to (state) power. The present practice of financing scientific research from the public purse could indeed trace its roots back to that Baconian idea. Clearly, it has been enormously successful. If perhaps in Britain it was not systematically applied in that era of the great flowering of science and engineering, i.e. the nineteenth century, perhaps it did not need to be, such was the world pre-eminence of Britain's position in industrial technology. Later, on a more crowded stage, Germany's similar aspirations needed a more systematic policy in order to be realized, and since the First World War a similar policy has been continued by the USA. There, it has been successful beyond perhaps the wildest dreams of the time when the policy was set in motion. It is perhaps hard now to realize that at the post-First World War peace conferences, the then President of the United States, Woodrow Wilson, with his credentials as the sometime President of a still rather obscure New Jersey college (that has since become one of the world's pre-eminent universities), came across as a rather narrow-minded provincial schoolmaster rather than as a world statesman. Barely two decades later, the United States would be engaged in perhaps the most remarkable example of organized science and technology that the world has ever known – the Manhattan project. That too was crowned with success. But can one really call the massacre of hundreds of thousands of civilians (many of whom died a horrible lingering death from radiation sickness) a 'success'? Of course, it served the purpose of consolidating the position of the USA as a world power, and in a narrow sense may be said to have been successful. But taking a wider view, which should properly also encompass the massacre of comparable numbers (in proportion to the total population) of civilians through almost unimaginable quantities of conventional bombs dropped on Hamburg (1943), Brunswick (admittedly a major centre for the manufacture of armaments) and Königsberg (1944), and Dresden (1945) during the same and preceding years, it would be very difficult to justify the unequivocal use of the epithet 'successful'.[3]

---

[2] F.S. Oliver, *Ordeal by Battle*, 2nd edn. London: Macmillan (1915).
[3] Even today, Europeans find it difficult to come to terms with the destruction of some of the loveliest and most historically significant sites of the Middle Ages and the Renaissance in these cities.

Nor can the Second World War in any sense be said to have been the 'war to end all wars' – one sense of that meaning being that the horrors of what happened in that war would cause humanity as a whole to decisively and resolutely repudiate such warfare for ever. Things have become worse. The most prominent contemporary example is, of course, Iraq: recent estimates of the numbers of civilian deaths since the 2003 US-led invasion show that, as a proportion of the total population, they exceed even those in the Second World War,[4] and apart from that rather prominent example there are dozens of more or less minor conflicts around the world, often almost wholly hidden from western view, that appear to be pursued with unimaginable cruelty to civilians. In these conflicts, not only is one confronted with reports of the torture of military captives, and the killing and maiming of innocent civilians, but also the reckless dispersal of unexploded ordnance, which continues to pose a cruel threat to life and limb long after the conflict has officially ceased.

I have dwelt at some length on the state of the world regarding wars, because if new thinking cannot solve that difficult problem, we shall have failed dismally in the mission with which we began this book. The only possible ground for dismissing it is that it might be postulated that it is rather a political problem, for politicians to solve, and has little to concern the businessman, to whom this book is primarily addressed. Let us, however, remember that the provision of ordnance and military logistics are very significant sectors of the global economy, and deserve attention even from a purely business perspective.

To recapitulate the arguments so far, it has been proposed that the acquisition of knowledge is the key to solving the world's problems, yet, as Oliver pointed out, 'Barbarism is not any the less barbarism because its methods are up-to-date' – knowledge is also the key to technology, and while much technology is undoubtedly beneficial, there is a lot that has disappointingly trivial applications, and much that has many deleterious consequences. Hence the role of technology needs to be scrutinized more carefully.

Another ingredient of the current situation, impossible to ignore, is the role that religion currently appears to play in fomenting conflict. Hence one cannot very well ignore religion, which has traditionally been one of the main purveyors of ethics.

One possible solution to that problem would be to strive to convert all inhabitants of the Earth to a common religion. Quite apart from the sheer impracticality of such an enterprise, such a solution would never be stable, as past schisms in Christianity and Islam demonstrate abundantly.

A more creative solution is to attempt to unite all the world's (major) religions into a new synthesis. I should like to pay tribute to the recent attempt of Cambridge theologian Don Cupitt to do precisely that.[5] The subject of

---

[4] G. Burnham et al., 'Mortality after the 2003 Invasion of Iraq: A Cross-Sectional Cluster Sample Survey', *The Lancet*, vol. 368 (2006) pp. 1421–8.

[5] D. Cupitt, *After God: the Future of Religion*. London: Weidenfeld and Nicolson, 1997.

that book is the future of religion in our modern global world. He argues that we should take the best features of each major faith – which one may presume to be major because of some attractive feature – and combine them to create a new practical synthesis. From the Christian tradition he advocates taking the eye of God as a means to grow in self-knowledge: by the 'eye of God' he means the concept that in some way we are under surveillance – not in the rather unpleasant way in which video cameras seem to have become ubiquitous, but that one somehow cultivates the ability to stand outside oneself and examines who we are and what we are doing. The second of the three strands to be woven together in Cupitt's synthesis is to learn to accept the transience and insubstantiality of ourselves and everything else – this is the blissful void, and is particularly emphasized in Buddhism (but also in the Judaeo-Christian tradition,[6] probably more in the Middle Ages than nowadays). The final strand is simply what Cupitt calls 'solar living' – to learn to say a wholehearted 'yes' to life. This is connected with the sometimes overwhelming feeling that we have very little time in life to do what we want, so we had better get on with it with all our energies, echoing the author of Ecclesiastes, 'whatsoever thy hand findeth to do, do it with all thy might; for there is no work, nor device, nor knowledge, nor wisdom, in the grave, whither thy goest.'[7]

Cupitt's erudite proposal of a world religion, set against a backdrop of commercial, financial and technological globalization, has much to commend it. In the cited publication, and elsewhere, he describes the philosophical core of this new world religion as 'a new way of feeling and living our own relationship to the world of our common experience'. His encouragement to 'feel how world-energies come welling up and support you, and in return language flows out from you to form, organize, make conscious and embellish the world of your experience' is particularly appropriate to the age of the Internet (which has continued to grow exponentially since *After God* was written), but it answers not one of Kant's three questions: What should I do? What can I know? What can I hope for?

Japan is a culture of immediacy. One of the most striking illustrations of that is the style of the mansions of the daimyo in the early Tokugawa period.[8] Unlike temple buildings, which were influenced by monumental architecture in China, these mansions were built sequentially, adding one room at a time as required without any overall plan, and brought to a close when the energies or interest of the builder were exhausted. Another example, temporal rather than spatial, is the way that traditional story books are written, for example 'Utsubo monogatori', written in the Heian period. It consists of many short stories accumulated one by one, without any clear overall context. And artistic expression generally focuses on the sophisticated perception of parts rather

---

[6] E.g. 1 Peter, chapter 1, verse 24.
[7] Ecclesiastes, chapter 9, verse 10.
[8] See Table 4.1 in Chapter 4 to put the chronology in context.

than a grand overall conception. In short, the culture is remarkably unfettered by the transcendental values that have engendered so many problems in Europe. The important thing is the present. Commitment to the present is more important than commitment to the past. In France and other European nations, year after year one still celebrates events such as the Armistice (at the end of the First World War) and victory (at the end of the Second World War). Even some Europeans think that it is now time to move on. Furthermore, commitment to this world is more important than commitment to some other world. One may call this Japanese attitude worldliness, but worldliness has an unsavoury air about it in Europe, where it quickly became an ugly manifestation of crass materialism, Mammon or plutolatry, whenever it took hold.

Cupitt comments that in some respects, Mammon has become ethically admirable, pointing out that 'Mammon is an internationalist. He wants people to be healthy and well educated. He wants peace and stability, progress and universal prosperity.' Unfortunately, that rosy viewpoint ignores the cupidity and venality that leads to endemic corruption and the wanton destruction of our environment for short-term gain. Christ uncompromisingly placed God[9] and Mammon in stark opposition, and there appear to be good reasons for doing so. Chapter 4 notes that the knight errant was typically poor; chivalry as a sublime form of secular life embodied a primitive and spontaneous asceticism, and these features are germane to those of bushido and the life of the samurai. In mediaeval times, riches had not acquired that spectral impalpability, which capitalism, founded on credit, later accorded to Mammon. The enormous concentrations of wealth (and, following it, power) made possible by the technologies of the Industrial Revolution reached their zenith in the United States of America, a nation founded on prosperity. Yet even 80 years ago Joad could write, amusingly but quite accurately, that

> the objects of American civilization are to substitute cleanliness for beauty, mechanism for men, and hypocrisy for morals. It devotes so much energy to obtaining the means to make life possible that it has none left to practise the art of living. Large, larger and ever larger hotels, fast, faster and ever faster cars, cocktails and culture, psychoanalysis and faith healing, sensual poetry and sensational sports, supported and maintained by an illiterate governing class ready to be imposed upon by any charlatan who can persuade it to take an interest in what it imagines to be its soul.[10]

Possibly after several millennia of further maturing Mammon may be able to present himself as a candidate for an ethical principle, but it seems premature at present.

---

[9] I use God in the sense made intelligible by Nicholas da Cusa, i.e. 'the absolute'.

[10] C.E.M. Joad, *Thrasymacus, or, The Future of Morals*. New York: E.P. Dutton & Co., 1926.

Another candidate deserving serious consideration as a world religion is football. According to the philosopher Erich Fromm, anything that offers (1) a person or group of persons ultimate orientation, and (2) an object to which complete devotion can be accorded, ranks as a religion. As Josef Hochstrasser pointed out recently on the occasion of the world championship, football fulfils both Fromm's criteria.[11] In Europe in June and July of 2006, one might have been forgiven for imagining that football was indeed a world religion. Only the fact that it is not especially popular or even well-known in several huge and populous areas of the world prevents it from being further discussed here.

Finally, there are the rational outlooks to be considered as foundations for a system of ethics. The oldest intelligible attempt to define such 'natural religion' was probably that made by Paul of Tarsus.[12] As he himself recognizes clearly, the difficulty is that there is no clear recipe for deriving a system of ethics from a knowledge of nature. In other words, any ethical system that might be inherent in nature is not self-revealing.

The notion of a natural system of ethics enjoyed a revival in the Renaissance in the shape of humanism, which might roughly be defined as a system in which 'man is the measure'. Since that time, it has never really died away, and indeed could be considered as a parent of 'scientific socialism', which was a sort of ethical partner of Marxism (as practised in Soviet Union) *qua* economic theory. It was, however, the events of the 1920s and the succeeding two decades that really discredited humanism. Man as the measure led directly to the eugenics programmes that reached their zenith in Nazi Germany, bolstered by a mass of anthropological and genetic data whose validity is still being debated to this day. It is extremely difficult, if not impossible, within a humanist framework to counter the arguments in favour of a eugenic policy.

Recognition that natural ethics are not self-revealing has as its corollary that a good deal of hard work is necessary in order to extract some principles from what is to hand.[13] As knowledge has advanced, through the hard work of generations of scientists, we are today in a stronger position than Paul to evaluate the possibilities of nature providing a system of ethics. Darwin's work on the origin of species and the struggle for survival was an important milestone in this development. The enormous body of investigation that has built up around the Darwinian idea has led, *inter alia*, to the notion of the 'evolutionarily stable strategy' (ESS). One important problem that has been tackled by

---

[11] J. Hochstrasser, 'Der Fussball und seine Aura des Göttlichen'. *Neue Zürcher Zeitung*, 3/4 June 2006. Illustrations of the cathedrals of football, i.e. the stadia, can be found in the *Neue Zürcher Zeitung*, 10/11 December 2005.

[12] Paul of Tarsus, 'Epistle to the Romans', chapter 1, especially verses 18 to 20.

[13] This recalls an idea put forward by Paracelsus. See J.J. Ramsden, 'Paracelsus: the Measurable and the Unmeasurable'. *Psyche: Problems, Perspectives*, vol. 4 (2004) pp. 52–88.

this approach is the paradox of the well-known Gresham's Law: bad money drives out good. Generalizing this law, one has to address the question of how to prevent something which we feel to be (or demonstrably is) intrinsically superior from being overwhelmed and eliminated by something we feel to be (or demonstrably is) inferior. In that regard, a variant of the so-called 'prisoner's dilemma' has been instructive: two prisoners can only escape if they join forces, but they have to leave their cell one after the other, and the first to escape has the possibility of reneging on his promise to help his companion, thereby making his own escape with greater facility and hence more certainty of ultimate success. Clearly if neither prisoner agrees to assist the escape of the other, both remain trapped indefinitely. If one agrees to help unconditionally, regardless of what the other will do, overall his ilk will die out (or remain trapped forever). The ESS for this situation, which perhaps adequately mimics many far more complex human situations, is for the prisoners to help each other in good faith, assuming that the other will fulfil his obligation, and only to change behaviour in direct response to an incident of recividism (clearly that will not help the prisoner in an individual case, but statistically over many cases modelling shows that it is advantageous).

ESS is, of course, none other than the old Jewish system of 'an eye for an eye and a tooth for a tooth',[14] and it is perhaps a little disappointing that millennia of work have only succeeded in demonstrating the validity and rationality of an ancient tradition. The important innovation of Christ was to invert this reciprocity and to express it as 'And as ye would that men should to you, do ye also to them likewise.'[15] This formulation of what we might call the 'principle of reciprocity' appears to be an irreducible and incontrovertibly valid foundation of ethics, and scrutiny of the entire contents of the Library of Babel would be very unlikely to find anything superior. Hence anything that is propounded needs to be compared with this principle, to which we can and should at any time return if all else fails.

Just as the foundation alone is insufficient to provide a dwelling from which one can shelter from the elements, or housing for the machinery of a factory, this irreducible foundation of ethics is insufficient to provide practical guidance in a multitude of situations actually encountered in life. It is useful to distinguish between 'spontaneous ethics' – we wake up in the morning in front of a clean white sheet of paper on which we can sketch out a plan for the day – and 'responsive ethics', when we are confronted with a situation brought about by the actions of others. Both form part of the challenges daily confronting the director of a company. What indeed motivates the director? both in the sense of what motivates him or her to do anything at

---

[14] Exodus, chapter 21, verse 24.
[15] Luke, chapter 6, verse 31. This forms part of the famous 'Sermon on the Mount'. Christ goes on to say 'If ye love them that love you, what thank have ye? If ye do good to them that do good to you, what thank have ye?'

all (as opposed to merely languishing in repose) and in the sense of what motivates a particular action. Possible answers to this question are 'to achieve maximum return to the shareholders', but this must be qualified by a subsidiary phrase 'in the next quarter', 'in the next year', or 'over the next five years'. The practical working out of the answer might be very different according to which time scale is selected. Another possible answer is 'to contribute to terrestrial well-being' (i.e. to minimize any damage to the environment), although this is likely to be insufficient on its own, since in many cases it would simply mean doing nothing and closing down production, and this answer must also be qualified by a subsidiary phrase 'in the surrounding hectare', or 'in the surrounding x hectares', where x could be any number up to that corresponding to the area of the Earth's land mass. Another possible answer, related to the previous two, is 'to ensure the survival of the company', again with qualification of the timeframe. Yet another is 'to maximize my personal gain for as long as possible'; it might be 'fulfilment of duty', in the rather dry sense expounded by Cicero in his 'De Officiis'; and it might be non-financial personal fulfilment, the attainment of tranquillity, even personal salvation: this is often an ultimate, albeit vaguely formulated, motive that could exist in parallel with any one of the others.

These are all essentially possible answers to Kant's first question, 'What shall I do?', and all are capable of giving rise to one – or more usually several – rational, practical actions. Any ethical system applied to real, as opposed to artificially constructed, situations is early on confronted by constraints that cannot all be simultaneously satisfied. This is the notion of frustration, which was for the first time explained, in the sense of being intelligibly expressed, by Philip Anderson in connexion with the so-called 'spin glasses'.[16] So our knowledge of nature, which in this case is associated with a subtle manifestation

[16] P.W. Anderson, 'The Concept of Frustration in Spin Glasses'. *Journal of the Less-common Metals*, vol. 62 (1978) pp. 291–4. See also G. Toulouse, 'Theory of the Frustration Effect in Spin Glasses', *Communications on Physics*, vol. 2 (1977), pp. 115–19. The explanation in its most concise form is unfortunately rather technical, but may be sketched out as follows: suppose we have an initial sample of the solid (a spin glass, which consists of magnetic atoms characterized by their spin embedded in a much larger number of non-magnetic, i.e. spinless, ones) that is subdividable into small blocks. It should be noted that the system, like any physical system, strives to reach a state in which it has the lowest possible energy, and that the energy of a spin glass comes from the spins of the magnetic atoms interacting with each other: the lowest energy state would be reached if they were all aligned with one another. The point is that the blocks into which the solid as a whole is subdivided can individually reach their lowest energy states if the interactions between blocks are artificially cut off, but the mutual bonds between pairs of blocks have random sign when the blocks are separately set in their optimal internal structure. Another way of expressing this is to say that no arrangement of spins will allow every one to be optimally oriented to yield the lowest minimum global energy.

of magnetism in artificially made condensed matter that could not even have been experimentally investigated until comparatively recently, illumines ethics, in this case in a rather negative sense by making it clear that typically no action can be ethically unexceptionable in all respects. At present this rather negative result is practically all that is available; the richness of the theories of spin glasses have barely begun to be exploited regarding their potential in terms of ethical implications. Suffice it to say here that one can already perceive possible ways forward: concepts such as the sequential minimization of entropy loss,[17] which have been so powerful in inspiring practical algorithms for computing the confirmations of biopolymers such as proteins and polynucleic acids (RNA), have almost obvious implications for deciding what to do, in response to Kant's first question.

Permitting ourselves to run practically to the end through what could be at this point a very lengthy exposition, I want only to bring out the point that emerges from the earlier Chapter 6, namely that the world is inherently complex and hence extraordinarily difficult to predict and foresee in any circumstance other than a highly artificial one. It is in this context that we see the tremendous value of the Japanese culture of immediacy. The contrasts between this culture and the western norm are elaborated upon more fully in the following Chapter 8; here I only want to emphasize that in a constantly evolving and unstable world, the most successful ethics (i.e. principles governing conduct) are those rooted in the immediate here and now. As I have pointed out elsewhere, far-sighted western thinkers such as Clausewitz have made this point in the past, but otherwise it has not been deeply embedded in western consciousness. In Europe we have preferred to invoke mysterious and possibly transcendental forces such as von Reichenbach's od, or simply sheltered under the umbrella of tychism, in order to preserve the credibility of grand plans. Whether in business or in politics, grand strategic plans are very much expected, and their absence is seen as a sign of unforgivable weakness and unfitness for office. In reality, however, although no one wishes to admit it, these grand plans are thoroughly futile; only a truly transcendental being, i.e. God, would have any use for them. In contrast, they are not at all expected in Japan, and as far as business is concerned the lack of the necessity of being fettered by a grand plan is doubtless the main reason for the extraordinary success of the Japanese industrial corporation. In politics, this absence on one side sometimes makes for difficulties in negotiations between Japanese and western politicians. In fact, it should come as no surprise to any European acquainted with Japanese art, especially the picture scrolls so popular since around the thirteenth century. They are hung on walls, and only one part of a lengthy, unfolding story is visible at any one

---

[17] A. Fernández and H. Cendra, '*In vitro* RNA Folding: the Principle of Sequential Minimization of Entropy Loss at Work'. *Biophysical Chemistry*, vol. 58 (1996), pp. 335–9.

time. Scenes that have been seen and absorbed are rolled up, and the future, as yet unknown, remains hidden for the time being. This mode of representation contrasts strikingly with the paintings of mediaeval Europe, in which all the incidents happening over a very long interval are placed on the same picture, all to be viewed at the same time. The picture scroll epitomizes life as a sequence of unpredictable surprises. In contrast, the West is obsessed with the idea of finding shortcuts and predictions. In the terminology of cellular automata,[18] life is a 'class IV' automaton (capable of universal computation) which admits of no shortcuts and whose evolution can only be explored by explicit simulation.[19]

This mode of living is, of course, the heart and soul of bushido, the Way of the 'bushi'. As Shinagawa has pointed out in Chapter 2, one is not born a 'bushi', one becomes a 'bushi'. Hence it is accessible to all. And here we see a striking similarity to the ideal of the English gentleman. As Keyserling has pointed out, it is a democratic ideal, in that everyone can, should, and wants to be a gentleman (which incidentally enables an acceptable compromise to be made between the demands of personal sovereignty and social equality).[20] His instincts are trained; it is a state in principle attainable by all, which is of course the first prerequisite for anything claiming to be universal.

In conclusion, I should like to say a few words about the relationship between bushido and knowledge (science). Essentially, the samurai as a man of action was only interested in science if it was of practical use. He did not concern himself with striving for objective truth, over which dozens of generations of European philosophers and scientists have racked their brains. Rather, he strove for good writing, the way to express important ideas with maximal economy. In one sentence, the tripod on which the bushi's ethics stand are wisdom (chi), benevolence (jin) and courage (yu). Science is therefore only important if it can contribute to deepening wisdom. This is essentially the same as the last of Francis Bacon's three reasons for devoting time to science: delight (i.e. enjoyment), ornament (i.e. embellishment of our surroundings, in the same way as a beautiful garden or painting) and ability (usefulness in the judgment and disposition of business). In a not too dissimilar vein, Goethe also insisted that science should explain what we notice, not (as it is all too wont to do) notice only what it can explain (which is often quite uninteresting).

---

[18] S. Wolfram, 'The Statistical Mechanics of Cellular Automata', *Reviews of Modern Physics*, vol. 55 (1983), pp. 601–44.

[19] The same love of ordered structure in Europe could also be illustrated by the clock, whose importance as a symbol in post-Renaissance life is too well known to require elaboration here.

H. Keyserling, *Das Spektrum Europas*. Heidelberg: Niels Kampmann Verlag, 1928.

8
Bushido in the IT Era: Enduring Features of the Spiritual Character of Japan

Kaneyuki Hamada and Yutaka Ujiie

After the Second World War, the Japanese economy recovered and developed almost from scratch to become an economic giant in Asia over a period of just 25 years. During the 1960s and 1970s, studies on that period of rapid recovery and comparisons between Japanese and US business methods were very popular in the USA. Typical subjects of the studies were improvements in 'QC Circle' and 'Just-in-Time Methodologies', exemplified by 'The Toyota Way' or the 'Toyota Production System'. However, this was never intended as a methodology to provide a management tool (or for cash flow management), but rather it originated in the ideas and philosophies that emerged from the chaos of the 1950s. It was a management philosophy based on people-centred survival and individual enthusiasm derived from the universal life and death struggle, and persistent efforts of organization. Since then Japan has focused on and has been following the notions of competitive strategy during the 1980s, and on re-engineering or the IT revolution in the 1990s. These are operational methods that originated in the USA, but the Enron scandal has raised doubts and shown the limits of prioritizing for profit. Now we are entering a new era that requires the establishment of new management principles for the twenty-first century.

The authors, as baby boomers, are in a position to draw implicit wisdom from the pioneers who led the recovery of Japan and to present it to the current management arena as explicit wisdom. We believe that the essential part of company management lies in people. The words 'Keiten Aijin: Revere Heaven, Love Man', uttered by Saigo Takamori, one of the last samurai leaders who led the Edo Shogunate to a modern democratic society, contain the so-called Seven Spirits of Bushido: in other words, 'Love society, people, country, and heaven and earth'.

The differences between Japanese and US enterprises, and between the Japanese and the American people, focusing in particularly on their merits and demerits, have been often discussed. Numerous authors have tried to extract the backgrounds behind these differences, and what they portend for the future. In this chapter, we cut through these often sterile comparisons and eschew the often contrived and artificial links to imagined background from which they are supposed to be derived. Instead, we shall take a direct look at the Japanese 'spirit' as manifested by the range of experience of the Japanese businessman of the 'baby boom' and post- 'baby boom' generations. Ever since the Meiji restoration these businessmen have had a weak connextion to the spirit of bushido, but this connexion is by now so attenuated that although it might be felt in some vague way, unless it is expressed in explicit terms – and that is our purpose in this chapter – it is scarcely perceptible. In other words, the more-or-less direct connection with that bushido spirit traceable by the economic historian has in reality by now almost completely disappeared, and with it the chance of the businessman to directly experience and consider such things personally, in daily life.

Today, the first reaction invoked in many people, especially in the USA, upon hearing the words 'spiritual motivation' is (and we say this without irony) 'stock options'. Let us explain this. Long extolled as the typical labour motivation technique of Silicon Valley and its imitators, it is the method whereby willingness to work is driven by allocating the company's own stock (this especially applies to the new venture company) to the core directors as well as the rank-and-file employees, at the stage before that stock is offered to the public through the so-called initial public offering (IPO). It is usual that at the IPO the stock price rapidly rises, hence this arrangement is economically especially advantageous for the employees receiving the stock options offered by the company. This method is also known as 'placing the carrot in front of the cart'.

It is beyond the scope of this chapter to begin a discussion of the problems and weaknesses of this method (whose effectiveness is anyway very much dependent on the premiss that stock prices will indeed rise at the IPO). That it was necessary at all is something of a poor reflexion on the mental state of the employees and their personal commitment to the enterprise. Be that as it may, there are numerous verifiable stories about people, including receptionists, employed by venture companies in Silicon Valley who became millionaires or even (US) billionaires through this 'carrot'. Indeed, the creation of such millionaires was almost a daily occurrence during the peak of the 'bubble' period, and such occurrences continue to be made known by the success stories of the enterprises through which such millionaires were created.

Yet no matter how many times one hears such stories, they fail to strike an emotional chord. Beyond the confines of the microcosm of Silicon Valley, in a world with a wider range of emotional and spiritual experience, they are heard simply as fantastic fictional stories, and if any credence at all is attached to them, they would be associated with the Japanese term *abuku-zeni* ('easy money') and all that that implies in terms of losing sight both of the importance of money and of human respect for, and the joy of, honest work.

Thinking now somewhat seriously from a managerial point of view, we want to draw attention to an alternative motivational model, namely, to allot work that 'suits the image of the businessperson, who stands considering the work that he or she truly wants to do', or, in other words, the content of the research and development (if one wishes to retain the Silicon Valley context) that he or she wants to carry out, and the state in which he or she 'wants things to be', as determined by each individual person. Even nowadays, the personnel or human resources department in the typical corporation in Japan tends to execute their strategy based on that policy as much as possible. We wish to emphasize that the potential of this strategy is far from exhausted as it is currently realized in the typical corporation. On the contrary, it should be possible to create an increasingly perfect database that would enable this strategy of personnel utilization to be realized more and more objectively, and with which the matching of ideal and reality would become closer and closer. Tellingly, even during the height of the bubble period in Silicon Valley, we often heard people say, 'if it's for hundreds of millions of dollars I'll do it, otherwise it depends on the content of the work'. Since then, the importance of spiritual motivation corresponding to the notion of the 'will to work' has not abated. It is perhaps a particularity of Silicon Valley that some kind of true spiritual motivation model suits the development-oriented people working there, who perhaps have purer technological intentions than elsewhere (compare with for example the strong volition toward business embedded in life on the USA's east coast). Backing that up, it appears to be the case that certain top software business administrators who have impetuously accumulated technology while garnering great profit because of skilful business development abilities are always treated as natural enemies in Silicon Valley, perhaps because of that 'pure' technological development orientation there.

The strength of Toyota

When comparing this Japanese-style spiritual motivation with the US-style motivation model that has also in recent times flowed increasingly into Japan, it is natural to take a look first of all at a striking example of the success case within Japan – the Toyota Motor Corporation. In what follows, we are indebted to the earlier work of Takahiro Fujimoto.[1]

While living on the West Coast of United States, we have ourselves experienced the remarkably comfortable ride to be had in Japanese automobiles, especially those of Toyota. Nor is it is a mere personal observation: the great number of Toyota cars that are in general use in California is proof of that comfort, so, where does that good quality come from? Fujimoto uses Table 8.1 as an explanation of this excellence, common to many Japanese companies. The horizontal axis shows the ease of copying information, or, in other words, the ease with which business information is shared with others, standardized, and set down in a written manual. The further to the left one goes, the

---

[1] Takahiro Fujimoto, *Capability-Building Competition – Why is Japan's Automobile Sector Strong?* Tokyo: Chuokoron Shinsha, 2003.

Table 8.1 A diagrammatic representation of Japanese and US working styles. After *Fujimoto*

	Information difficult to write down	Information easy to write down
Integral/closed (more towards manufacturing)	**Area of specialty of Japanese companies** (matching and creating) Example: automobiles	
Modular/open (more towards service)		**Area of specialty of American companies** (combining and writing) Example: digital information assets

greater the necessity of matching and creating, something that cannot be achieved by the mere combining and writing down of information. The vertical axis on the other hand shows how easily copied information deteriorates. In the upper part of the table, it is more difficult for information to deteriorate, but at the same time correction is also more difficult. This corresponds to the manufacturing environment. Lower down in the table, service industries and information trading businesses that deteriorate more easily are favoured. The product-making industry in Japan (i.e. manufacturing industry) belongs to the former 'manufacturing' group: this indicates greater organizational abilities, more concentrated communications, and better cooperative adjustment abilities – collectively we can label these mixing and matching. The Toyota Motor Corporation is a very good representative of a mixed and matched manufacturing company. In contrast, the software industry is characterized by facility of combining and writing, and what is primarily demanded there are original ideas.

Having established that, the question then arises, what causes such differences? Americans clearly have an abundance of diversity, and we propose that this is a source of the oft-mentioned strength of the United States of America. On the other hand, this can have some negative consequences with respect to interpersonal relationships. First of all, an American may feel that another person is someone who may not understand him and thus might even be an adversary. Hence, in terms of information transfer in business, business simply cannot move forward if information is not given in a common expressive language that can be understood at all times by both sides. In practice, each party makes an effort to communicate in English, often of a somewhat standardized and even stereotyped form (especially since the group may have diverse origins and hence have a diversity of native languages), which might be considered as being rather limited in expressive power, but it is a necessity if general solutions are to be sought. This stereotyping can greatly vitiate the advantages potentially accruing from the creativity inherent in the original information asset, and it is a possible limitation in the US working environment.[2]

On the other hand, in Japan one's coworkers are basically Japanese. As is well illustrated by the terms *Anmoku no ryokai* (an implied consent or understanding) and *Aun no kokyu* (the mental and physical harmonizing of two parties), it is fairly unlikely that others are significantly different from oneself in their level of basic situational understanding, or in methodology. Hence, dealings can be rather confidently advanced under such an assumption, and indeed in practice major problems arising from misunderstanding are extremely rare. In the American view, there is, however, a negative side to this way of working. A frequently-quoted example is that of software development. When developing new software, Americans (and, we note, Indians as well) only begin work after first stringently creating the development specifications based on requirements, a process that often simply doesn't exist in Japan.[3] (For huge software projects, the existence of stringent specifications really is a necessity since the product is well beyond the ken of any individual, but for smaller projects its value is somewhat dubious and may be questioned.)

When considering manufacturing work and the creation of products, the working characteristics of the Japanese becomes a definite strength even for the largest projects. That is because the transmission of information that is difficult to write down – in other words, techniques that are not easily explained – resides in the tacit knowledge of the so-called artisans, and can be shared much more certainly and effectively in this Japanese way (i.e. as characterized by *anmoku no ryokai* and *aun no kokyu*). For instance, strict matching of work becomes possible even between the workers of a major contracting company and affiliated subcontracting enterprises. It is moreover said that a further strong point of the Toyota Motor Corporation goes beyond that, to achieve a union of effective product-making techniques and state-of-the-art high technology. That ease in essence unites the respective strengths of Japanese and US corporations, i.e. in some way succeeding in combining and writing features that are essentially represented by the matching and creating approach.

---

[2] A similar argument applies to the joint European projects somewhat artificially assembled as a consequence of the policy of the European Union – in principle they unite great diversity of ideas and hence should stimulate creativity, but in practice the relatively primitive language available for communication between the participants generally ensures a mediocre outcome.

[3] Nor, one might add, in Switzerland, where there is also a rather homogeneous workforce, particularly in small companies. This lack of the need to create stringent development specifications enormously accelerates software development and ensures that there is sufficient flexibility for the product to remain close to the client's wishes until completion. That is why Swiss software companies find it much more cost-effective to develop code in-house, rather than outsourcing it to, say, India, for which indeed the stringent specifications would have to be written.

What is it that the Japanese mutually share?

Even at this point, after having given it some consideration, the secret of the strength of Japanese management, especially of manufacturing-based companies, is still unclear. It seems to be connected with the mutual sympathy possessed by all Japanese. Here again, a remarkable difference appears when comparing Japan culturally with the USA. For instance, in the normal US lifestyle there exists a fragile relationship between a company and its individual employees, and between individuals; firings are sudden, and there are a large number of divorces among the workforce. If one wishes to persist with concepts such as self-responsibility and individualism (which, we note, is different from egoism), it is necessary to ensure that a standard form of expression accepted even by third parties, such as that represented by firm, solid contracts, is in place. That is a kind of minimum requirement, which is essentially a self-defence mechanism available for periods when things do not go well. This way of thinking applies no less in the business realm than it does in the personal realm. And here we return to the assertion that in a production process, the existence of essential features that cannot be readily standardized and set down in a manual make it impossible to effectively transmit skills between individuals. This impossibility is very possibly connected with the fact that the volume of manufacturing in the USA has decreased and continues to do so.

Are we now closer to identifying what it is that the Japanese mutually share between themselves? In some ways the argument has been privative: we arrived at where we are now by looking at some of the unfavourable features of US society.

So, exactly what it is that the Japanese mutually share between themselves just might arise out of such a comparative look at the current state of the US Finally, we have reached the core subject of this book. Certainly, it is interesting that there are considerable common points between the chivalry of Britain and Japan's bushido chivalry. And one would be especially surprised by the possibilities of resemblance that emerge when relating, in English, the spiritual objects that both sides value.

What can be said from the considerations we have adumbrated up to this point is that there is something latent internally in the Japanese, that this is not at all standardized or set down as in a manual, and that it seems to be somewhat different from something that descends formally or as a pressured type of reasoning from management to employees. In short, it is the 'information difficult to write down' and 'integral/open' items within product-making, the area of greatest specialty and strength of the Japanese, and something that the Japanese originally and naturally sometimes just seem to happen to have, intensely and even to the point of weakness. That might match the methodology in management of 'drawing out what lurks internally in the employee'.

Two highly pertinent questions are: (1) What are the realities of the content that is drawn out? and (2) What is an effective means of 'drawing it out'? We are seriously delving into the area of managerial practices here.

1   Japanese spirituality, inherent subjectivity, ambition and self-reliant normativity

When considering this 'thing that lurks internally', again we use the United States as a point of comparison, with one clear phenomenon appearing in the MBA courses in the United States. Such courses ideally attempt to turn tacit knowledge into wisdom and to set down that content in written form in a manual in order to share it with others, a truly American-style idea and technique. Following along those lines, it is the accumulation of a period of apprenticeship, silently mimicking the master's skills, and then stealing that which is Japanese-like. It goes without saying that this resembles the 'meister' system of Europe, a vestige of which lingers on in the apprenticeships offered by companies to youngsters in Switzerland and elsewhere. Incidentally, right in line with the chivalry of Britain, the fact that Japan and Europe, with their same training ideas and techniques as the 'meister' system, are keeping in step within this management principles project is something that can be considered as being absolutely inevitable.

Whether it is the bushido chivalry that consists of seven keywords, or the way of Zen, what lies unadulterated therein is the Japanese spirituality. That spirituality is close to ethics as well and, at times, also constitutes a universal outlook. And, when it appears in business, it becomes both the code of conduct for each individual and the corporation's very own ethics. To give one example, we have the recent 'Livedoor' economic scandal in Japan. If seen from the standpoint of those related to the market, this and other events seem to be a sort of 'payment on account' for the mistaken attempt to forcefully mimic merger and acquisition (M&A) and initial public offering (IPO) techniques as a US style here in Japan, where the fertile ground for such actions simply doesn't exist (in other words, we have no experience in this at all). It was 'payment on account' inasmuch as that only the surface of that US standard was forcefully employed in the service industry field, the weakest point of the Japanese. Such a series of acts may capture the young generation's sympathy on the one hand, but in perceiving that, on the other hand, it concretely and consequentially ended up misfiring, one can feel both the danger that Japan clearly embraces today and the 'self-reliant normativity' that even now much of the general public may still possess. Indeed the very issue of corporate compliance itself makes the greatest noise now. And it connects to the spiritual climate related to business intentions. To state this in somewhat universalized terms, it is expressible by Japanese spirituality, inherent subjectivity and ambition, and self-reliant normativity.

2   The formation of spiritual motivation

How does a manager draw out that latent Japanese spirit from his or her employees? The concept of the formation of the spiritual motivation briefly described at the beginning of this chapter makes its appearance here. In a phrase, it is 'a model that matches the living sense of values of each individual employee and the significance and purpose of existence of the enterprise'. It is also a strong response to what all employees ask of themselves and answer. And that is, 'What existence can I find in this enterprise socially and for myself?, and therein, what level of significance and desire to work can I find in what I am doing right now?' To what degree that answer can be ardently presented to employees in the form of financial rewards 'plus something extra' is the thing that is continually asked of management. And actually, this is a common point regardless of whether it is a Japanese, a US or a European enterprise.

In essence, it is presenting the value of work in a way that would perk up employees to the point of them even considering the level of pay as being of secondary importance – to strategically present to each employee the work that they would really enjoy doing. You, dear readers, are probably saying, 'That's easier said than done.' Hence, in order to execute this strategy, first of all we want at the very least to fully equip it with an 'Employee Consideration Database'. But, more than that, to truly fill it with detail. It is preferable that this includes a theory on how the future of the company should be, so that it will also be a reference for those people who don't quite understand when they are told that this is not simply a matter of being asked to 'select the three types and content of work that you want to do in the future' on a purely question-naire level, but rather the profounder consideration for an ingeniously planned corporate value and sense of values.

Essentially, this way of doing things is the IBM way. It is, *inter alia*, a technique for presenting employees' own ideas in question and answer form (e.g. What do you think?) to their marketing department, drawing out that other party's thoughts, and quite naturally conveying their own intentions to that party. Actually, in Japan as well, this is a method used by a lot of successful managers in daily communication with employees as the 'art of employee control', but we probably can't say that it is necessarily fully established as organized behaviour. More and more, such daily give-and-take bridges the gap between the company's purpose and the employees' desires. This is a next-generation motivation formation methodology that has still not been achieved, even in advanced model enterprises and regions in the world. So, what do you think?

Updated bushido chivalry

There has, incidentally, been an unpardonable loss of confidence in Japan and the Japanese people during the last ten years or so, and I do feel that we have created a structural, or to slightly exaggerate it, almost completely social, anthropological depth from which we cannot return. And this has reached the point that, for example, bad bank loans have been cancelled. Such wounds do not seem to heal easily. So now let us undertake what we have hitherto deferred – an analysis of Japan's strengths and weaknesses.

First of all, let us consider the weaknesses. In brief, as noted above, if we do a comparative analysis of Japan and the US, haven't we Japanese on a daily basis seriously become able to only sense those lucid 'differences' as being 'differences that can't be helped'? Consider, for instance, the Chinese. A great many Chinese are very active in the United States, including in Silicon Valley. They return to their motherland with that same energy and try to execute the technology and business experience that they have acquired in the United States as though it were a matter of course in their new 'old' environment. The management technique in China's new companies, and especially the sense of their rapid growth, particularly those in the coastal regions, does not involve 'imports' or 'imitations' from the United States, but is the unadulterated Silicon Valley style itself. We have seen this in the example of their 'metal mould factory' management, something that should be the specialty of Japan. While this is originally the typical business style of the 'Information difficult to write down' and 'Integral/closed' concepts mentioned earlier, the Chinese interestingly take basic technology and techniques from Japan, and then wherever possible implement those parts that it seems can be enumerated, standardized and set down in a manual in the 'US style', with the scariest thing (perceived as an economic threat to Japan and the rest of the world) being that the result is then used for employee training. When we saw an introductory video on that training, we honestly felt that it might just be a matter of time before they catch up with Japan. But why is China able to accomplish such a thing? The answer is simply because they are able to recognize the 'differences' from the United States style, can objectively bring the necessary measures into operation, and can then premeditatedly execute them.

However, the story in that introductory video did not end there. Its final comment was that this method works up to 99 per cent accuracy, but in pursuit of the last 1 per cent, or rather of the last 0.1 per cent, Japanese-made is simply second to none. The Chinese manager in the video admitted this undeniable fact. Pertinently, it reveals the current foundation of an unlimited sense of reliance on 'made-in-Japan', as represented by Toyota (as mentioned above). As also noted before, this is where the strong point of Japan exists, at least in the manufacturing field.

On top of that, the shortage of confidence that exists in the IT service provider field, represented in particular within software development, as well as in other high-technology service provider fields, still seems structurally likely to be considerably prolonged. However, this weakness is actually surmountable, provided it is self-recognized as a clear weak point, and if it is also recognized by one's periphery. And that, in fact, is the US style; this aspect is recognized as the area in which the United States style considerably excels – that is to say, actually emphasizing one's own strong points to their utmost by clearly admitting one's own limitations and weak points. Furthermore, the open indication of a weak point naturally suggests the best partner candidate for others who see that same point as their strength. Of course, if your weak point is left untouched, you will not be able to answer the needs of the market, but more often than not a partnership of mutual benefit is established on that basis.

These points all imply economic rationalities. If the Japanese people and Japanese corporations can, more than ever before, shake off the negative aspects of a self-sufficient creed (specifically Integral/Closed) and if, in addition, they can acquire the above-mentioned character of partnership (which corresponds to Modular/open) and is the positive aspect of the United States, then what has tended to be a weakness will become a strength. Strong points such as the spirituality and sympathies of the Japanese will be at their strongest at that time. This matches exquisitely with the actual situation at the Toyota Motor Corporation that is becoming its most powerful through the 'union of the techniques of product-making with state-of-the-art technology'. It is in such areas that we look for the future of the spiritual character of Japan, a character that it seems could be considered as updated bushido chivalry in terms of enterprise management, a character that is modern, and a character that is worthy of being passed down in perpetuity.

Part III

A Spiritual Method Based on Bushido

9
The Road to the Spiritual Mind for Entrepreneurs[1]

Masayuki Koyanagi

9.1 Introduction

In recent years the strong interrelationship between body and mind has become known and the intense influence of the mind on the body has become clearer.[2] When one feels pleasure, all functions of the body reach their maximum potential. On the contrary, when one feels sorrow or anguish, all functions of the body deteriorate. When we are healthy, we can bear any mental anguish; conversely when we are not in good condition, we become timid and suffer from trivial matters and get lost in the maze.

What we, ordinary persons, are seeking is not lofty teachings and a high level of training but a plain teaching with a concrete and plain method of managing our minds. I used to think that the discovery of such a method would be worthy of a Nobel Prize. In fact, there lived a person who became aware by himself, who practised and taught such a method concretely and plainly. It was really amazing for me to come across that person since I had never dreamed that there could really be an effective practical method of managing our minds. It is no exaggeration to say that my coming across that person was a remarkable stroke of luck.

9.2 A brief history of Nakamura Tempu

Nakamura Tempu (1876–1968, see next chapter) was born in Oji, in the northern part of Tokyo, a member of the aristocratic Tachibana family, and part of the Yanagawa clan of Kyushu. From the age of six Nakamura's mother and father enrolled him in judo and kendo (a sword-based martial sport)

---

[1] The sources for this chapter are material provided by Toshiro Ono and *Kokoru no Kenko ho* ('The road to a healthy mind') by Masayuki Koyanagi, published by HABA Laboratories, Inc., Tokyo, in 1994.
[2] See, for example, J.J. Ramsden, 'Conceptual Aspects of Consciousness', *Psyche: Problems, Perspectives*, vol. 1 (2001) pp. 93–100.

classes. He excelled in both. He also studied *Zuihen Ryu batto-jutsu*, classical systems of swordsmanship, for many years. Always interested in things of a spiritual nature, the young Nakamura practiced a variety of native Japanese ways (*do*), and he investigated traditional Japanese healing arts. He would remain interested in both of these throughout his life.

After completing his primary school education, he attended a fairly prestigious school, renowned for its instruction in English, in Kyushu, the birthplace of his father. Despite his active participation in various *do* forms, young Nakamura had a violent temper that worried his family. Hoping to curb his behaviour, his parents encouraged his involvement in the *Genyosha*, a political organization. As a result of this association, Tempu went to China to engage in Japanese reconnaissance just before the outbreak of the Sino-Japanese War in 1894. He went on another reconnaissance sortie in Manchuria just before the onset of the Russo-Japanese War of 1904. Due to his earlier training in Japanese swordsmanship, the agent Tempu earned quite a reputation for fearlessness in battle.

On a later trip to China, he contracted tuberculosis, which in those days was frequently a fatal disease; the army doctor who made the diagnosis gave him only six months to live. He frequently coughed up blood, though receiving western-style medical treatment, which had impressed him with its effectiveness.

Despite his past training in various Japanese spiritual paths, he had over the years become almost totally preoccupied with the body – his body in particular. Realizing this, and perhaps feeling that he had gone as far as he could with different 'body-oriented cures', he decided to explore the mind as a possible means of curing his illness. This made him start detailed research work on the relationship between mind, body and spirit.

He renewed his study of different Japanese spiritual paths. Yet after his medical training in America, he felt that the truth was not limited to Japan. He began to read a variety of what are known today as 'self-help books,' including *How to Get What You Want* by Orison Swett Marden.[3] There was, however, no change in him. He tried a health improvement system called Motion Motive with little result. He heard of a philosopher who had successfully treated an illness that had befallen Thomas Alva Edison, using psychosomatic medicine. Through this philosophy, Tempu formulated a theory of spiritual transformation and non-materialism that would stay with him for the rest of his life, but he was still plagued by a life-threatening illness.

Tempu even travelled to England to study with H. Addington Bruce, who had developed his own form of personal growth. Bruce encouraged him to transcend worry and forget useless things. It was, again, something that he would later transmit to his own students, but he was still coughing up blood.

In London, Tempu attended a lecture on the subject of 'Mental activities and the nervous system' by Dr Bruce. The doctor told him, 'You are better off

---

[3] New York: T. Y. Crowell Co. (1917).

not thinking about something if the more you think about it the more nervous you become, it would be better if we you can just forget about it.' If we could live without thinking about negative things we would suffer less in consequence. But we do not seem able to do so.

Later, he learned the power of suggestion using a mirror from Lindler at Lyons University and, notwithstanding the further deterioration of his condition, he went to Germany to meet Dr Hans Driesch, then considered to be one of Europe's leading philosophers. The doctor told him that we can't control our minds, and if we could, neither philosophy nor religion would be needed in this world. Searching for the person who can teach us how is an absurdity – like searching for a seawater fish in a forest.

9.3   Tempu's encounter with yoga

While Tempu was in Europe, he decided to explore the newly developing field of psychology, and later he would also use the general concepts he had learned through teaching Japanese yoga. His study of psychology spanned France, Germany and Belgium, but he still could not shake off the tuberculosis. Despite believing even more strongly in the possibility of a psychosomatic cure, Tempu met with no success. Despondent, he decided to return to Japan.

In this state of despair, Tempu embarked on a ship at Marseilles bound for Japan, perceiving that there was no way of being delivered from his mental agonies since even the one of the world's leading scholars had confirmed it, but as the ship was anchoring en route in Egypt he made the acquaintance of a great master of yoga, Kaliapa, who was also on board the same ship, and they subsequently disembarked together. Around 1916, he was taken to a mountain village in the Himalayas, where he spent slightly more than two years practicing asceticism. He finally set out on a path to nirvana (religious awakening) and his illness quickly improved.

Kaliapa taught him various methods, but most importantly he created an environment in which Tempu ceased to look for answers in books, theories, or the belief systems of other people. Kaliapa, using psychological techniques that Tempu later recalled as being harsh and demanding, encouraged his student to search for first-hand understanding that was not dependent upon any authority or system.

While in the environs of Mount Kanchenjunga, Tempu learned much about the fundamental concepts of yoga from Kaliapa. To summarize Kaliapa's position is fairly simple: we are one with the universe, we are therefore imbued with the energy of the universe (*ki* in Japan, *purana* in India), and as a result we can learn directly from the universe itself. This learning and experience constitute the fundamental background of Tempu's methods for dynamic meditation.

By this time Tempu had attained the age of thirty-seven. The master who became the first Japanese to be taught directly by a great master of yoga subsequently devoted the rest of his life to teaching and saving people until he died at the age of ninety-two.

His teachings are something along the lines of how to settle worries pressing on our minds, and plainly explained how it is possible to be released from this weight that we cannot settle by ourselves. It was the ultimate way of keeping our minds healthy, which is what we are seeking.

As a result a great many people were indeed saved, and this has been attested to by a large number of his followers. Among them were many distinguished medical doctors. Taking it the other way round, because they are medical doctors they could understand how amazing the effect of controlling our mind is, what our mind should be, and its importance to our well-being.

9.4   Fundamental conditions for the unification of mind and body

Here I summarize the Tempu method from the mass of literature about him. If I can express his teachings in one phrase, I believe it would be 'establishing how to unify mind and body'. It is very important to have a full appreciation of the decisive influence of the mind on the body. Mind and body should be in unison and securing life's power can be accomplished by working both mind and body so as not to disobey natural laws.

First of all, with respect to mind, it should be positive at all times. Having a positive attitude will always lead to a noble, right, pure, and strong life. Nothing is more important than having positive attitude towards one's life. One may accept this as a matter of course, but it refers to a great truth. A positive mental attitude is indeed the most important thing for the mind.

If we put into practice this fundamental condition for the unification of mind and body, our minds and bodies can be united and unified, and as a result our life force will be strengthened, even our fate may change for the better as well as our health, and we can accrue the benefits of a happy and fruitful life.

If the mind remains positive, life becomes bright, lively and one is possessed of greater energy, so that even what formerly seemed to be impossible upon close inspection can be achieved.

What I would like to emphasize is that anybody can positively strengthen the mind through conscious and systematic practice, even though having a positive mind itself seems not to be a natural state. In what follows, I would like to give some indication of this practice.

- Try to maintain a positive mind and attitude. Do not think that you cannot do this or that you are of no value and so forth. A positive mind is latent in every person at birth.
- Check calmly whether or not your mind is positive by always putting yourself in another's shoes. Do not try to excuse yourself and your actions, have the courage to drive out negative thoughts.
- Do not let yourself be adversely affected and dragged under by the negative words or behaviour of others.

- Many are not aware of just how much of their life is affected by anxiety. You must absolutely not let this affect you. It is the equivalent of bringing about your own ruin. Though lots of people may not notice, they are likely to meet troubles halfway and feel stress over that which has not yet and may not ever become a problem.
- Do not say or do anything that your conscience speaks out against. Your mind power shrinks with a guilty conscience and unintentionally you become negative.
- Even though there may be something dark hovering in your mind, try to feel light at heart and behave as cheerfully as you can.

Words are important in order for us to practise these matters and we should not use negative phrases conveying concepts such as, 'I am in trouble', 'This is a disaster', 'I am miserable', 'It cannot be helped', 'I'm angry', 'I'm going nowhere', and so on. Avoid using negative phrases, do not complain or grumble about your circumstances and try to work hard.

To begin with, just think about the cause of the illness or bad luck. Those would not have come to you unless you were at fault or to blame in some way. All effects have their own causes. The way you are living was wrong and that's why the disease or bad luck came to you so that you could become well aware of your faults or wrongdoings. You should think this way and then these things can turn out to be great gifts.

If you have time to mourn or lament or otherwise weaken yourself you should turn towards the positive and healthy side of your mind, this is your birthright. After all, it depends on where your mind is.

There are simple and plain techniques we can practice to make our minds completely positive. These involve methods for 'Removal of obsessions in the subconscious', 'Neuroreflex modulation', and 'Unification of mind and body', and I will explain them in order.

Tempu was harassed by worldly passions, suffered greatly from pain and, finally, obtained wakening. What is the method by which we can control the mind through our own efforts?

9.5 A practical way of unifying mind and body

Tempu was harassed by worldly passions, suffered great pain and studied desperately under the great master of yoga for more than two years. He kept searching for the answer to the question: what is the nature of the ego and for what purpose am I born into this world? Finally he understood the greatness of the mind, which was given only to human beings by the Creator of the cosmos. And further he understood that disease of the body is only of the body and not of the mind. Even though bad luck comes to you, your mind need not be sickened or afflicted by this bad luck.

Tempu taxed his brain for a further eight years and finally understood how we can control our own minds. His understanding can be summarized in the following three points:

- Removal of the obsessions lying in one's subconscious, i.e. how to clean up one's mind, thereby removing the negative accumulated in one's subconscious and further cultivating a positive mind.
- Neuroreflex modulation, i.e. how to stabilize and strengthen one's mind by means of autosuggestion or *Kumbbahaka*, a technique of yoga performed in order to keep the nervous system and the vital functions that control life and normal living intact when we are in a situation of shock or great stress or otherwise in a negative environment.
- Completion of the unification of mind and body through an understanding of the ego.

9.6   Tempu method for unification of mind and body

If a stone is cast into a pond it makes a ripple that heads towards the bank and then returns to the point of origin. As in the principle of the conservation of energy, the ripple caused by a stone would, in a certain sense, exist forever in this world even after we cannot see it.

9.6.1   How to clean one's mind

People are unconsciously likely to have a negative way of thinking, and inputs to the senses accumulate in one's subconscious just like the sediments in a pond. All negative experiences and behaviours are accumulated deep in the well of one's heart and become unconscious stress. As a result, one becomes oversensitive, everything one sees and hears becomes a source of anxiety and irritation, and then one becomes unaware of one's happiness even though one is happy. Those who are oversensitive are the ones who cannot put up with what has to be put up with. They may think as follows, 'How can I stand this life?', or 'This is a burden I have to carry myself and I must worry about it.'

It is indeed foolish to think this way. It requires cleaning up one's way of thinking and removing the sediments accumulated up to the present in order for one to put up with what has to be put up with.

The Master said that even he himself did not know that for a long time. He is quoted as saying, 'I believed myself to be unequalled in courage, however as I thought about my physical disorder night after night, I became miserable and overly anxious. I did not understand that it is no good to bring to the bed what happened in the daytime no matter how irritating or painful it was . . . I didn't understand anything while I was lying at rest.' Even when we are lying in bed at night and seemingly unaware, the infinite power of the Creator of the cosmos comes into us. There are hints that power comes to us through the middle of the forehead, then moves to the cerebrum and then to that important part the solar plexus in the pit of the stomach along the nervous systems via the pineal body and then from there it is distributed to every part of our body.

'Word' is originally *kotodama* in Japanese, which means the soul of word. If you say something negative or passive, then the negative implied suggestion within those words remains. As long as you are using positive words, without knowing it, all aspects of life become very good and reach an ideal state. Tempu said, 'If one speaks ill of others, the words spoken with ill and unpleasant intent remain in one's subconscious and this leaves a negative effect upon the person who spoke them.' If you take the trouble to clean up your mind at night, accordingly you must not contaminate it during the day. You should use only bright and positive words in the daytime. If you can improve your subconscious by the above process, your powers will increase immensely.

9.6.2 How to stabilize and strengthen one's mind

The vital functions of the nervous system are the foundations of our well-being. What we think or feel reflects upon our bodies through this nervous system and we have to endeavour to adjust this properly. Modern life, with its multitude of troubles and stress, would almost inevitably lead us toward a state of oversensitiveness unless we are able to adjust our nervous system accordingly. Nothing is more saddening than being oversensitive.

Once we become oversensitive, a subtle sense or a shock or emotional stress is transmitted to our minds traumatically. If we receive an impact on our mind, our bodies soon react. If we are engaged, our faces may turn pale. If we are surprised, we may quiver. If we are joyful, we laugh. If we are ashamed, we blush. We should consider that if such big changes appear on the visible part of our bodies, then how significantly may such feelings cause changes to our internal organs.

On the face of it, we can get influenza, dizziness, and headache without any apparent cause. Dr Hans Selye of Canada advanced his theory of stress, claiming that humans can live to 150 or even 200 years of age if they have no stress, but can die younger than 50 due to stress and there is no way of otherwise preventing it.

Tempu found the way to adjust and mitigate the effects of stress. When he reached the summit of yoga philosophy called Raja and Karma, spiritual aspects of yoga, he noticed that the method intensified *Kumbbahaka*, which is an esoteric method of yoga, and would function as a shock absorber whenever we receive a great mental shock. It requires a very strong mind and body to practice yoga austerities, and there are various austerities constituting the foundation of *Kumbbahaka*. Below I would like to quote Tempu's remarks about his own way of *Kumbbahaka*, which he deepened and sought to apply with those various austerities into a practical form for stabilizing and strengthening the mind.

The most important thing to maintain as a habit is the contraction of the anal region at all times. With our anal region contracted even when we are walking, thinking, and talking like this for a long time, we can attain a strong state in which we can cope with anything that may occur. Only contracting the anal region, putting your whole strength in the abdomen, and loosening your shoulders makes a difference in the resisting power available to the organization of our body.

9.6.3   A practice *Kumbbahaka* (see also the next chapter)

For example, the most vital point of the human body is the pit of the stomach. If we suffer a sufficiently strong impact against this part of our body, we will die. However, if we practice *Kumbbahaka* we can keep cool, even in the case of a rather strong impact. Here is a good path to forming good habits with the benefits of both techniques. Train for deep breathing at various times throughout the day as well as practicing the austerity described above. Exhalation is more important than inhalation in deep breathing. The essence of deep breathing is exhalation only. In the first place, it is important to send out bad gas from the lungs. As the Japanese word for breath suggests, exhale first whilst practicing *Kumbbahaka*.

We can't understand anything about the method the Master has taught us unless we actually practise it. If you practise it, then you can appreciate that it would be easier to sit straight with your legs apart rather than with your legs placed together and so the way of sitting characteristic of yoga makes it much easier to contract the anal region. If you contract the abdomen, then it will help you to straighten the spinal column and take a good posture. Try to let the sacred bone stand right above the coccyx.

Within this posture, release the tension from the shoulder and set the strength in the upper part of the body to zero. If you meditate thus, you may find yourself different from before. As for me, I come to feel like I have become two with another self that grew much bigger looking down upon me meditating. From time to time it is as if I see a smaller myself, or even the very earth on which we live, far below, and I also feel another me assimilated into the universe. And then I come to see the essence of each of my worries together with the solutions for them.

Here are the words of the Master himself introducing *Kumbbahaka* according to his method:

> The method of releasing tension from the shoulders simultaneously with placing the body's strength in the abdomen and contracting the anal region is a practical way of recovering from a difficult situation rapidly. As a matter of fact, this posture is very similar to that recommended in sports and military arts, and releasing tension from the shoulders is a common and important point.

The importance of focusing the chi on the lower part of the abdomen is widely recommended by practitioners. T'ai chi, Japanese fencing, judo, karate and so on all adopt the same posture. I think this should be the strongest position physically. And the Master noticed that such a posture could protect our mind as well. When we have a great shock or are in pain, we indeed need this *Kumbbahaka*. If you are in the habit of practising it regularly, you can call on this technique quickly in times of extreme stress. The Master said, this is the best and simplest way for anyone to strengthen one's mind. If you habitually exhale calmly and slowly whilst taking this posture over and over again each day (it can be effective especially when you wake up or fall asleep), the body as well as the mind is strengthened and your quality of life will improve.

9.6.4 Attaining concentration of the mind by means of the *Anjo Daza* method

I will introduce the *Anjo Daza* method (see also the next chapter), which leads to a state of samadhi, an ultimate method of meditation. Like *shaka-muni*, attaining a spiritual awakening through meditation, yoga or Zen is aimed at achieving a spiritual state of selflessness and awakening through meditation. When we reach a state free from all worldly thoughts, when we no longer have worldly thoughts or worries, we, thereby released from any stress, can exercise life's power and tap its capacity to effect natural healing to the utmost and attain such a state of mind and body with which even a so-called incurable disease can be cured.

This state is the state in which the universe and human life are completely unified. One day the Master found himself in a state where he could no longer hear the roaring sound of water nor anything else while meditating in front of a waterfall in the Himalayas. From the time that he reached this state of awakening and started devoting himself to this state he no longer had a fever associated with the 'incurable' disease from which he had suffered for eight years, nor had haemoptysis, and his health started to improve. How wonderful are the life forces of people!

This world in which sound is absent is the spiritual state of samadhi in Zen. And a world without any sound is indeed the actual existence of the universe, the state in which the energy of the universe is omnipresent. There is neither sense, nor conscious reaction. If you get used to it, you will be able to transfer your mind quickly to the soundless world – no matter how noisy your surroundings are. Therefore no matter what kind of disease you may contract or what kind of pain you may have in your mind, you can transfer yourself with ease, noting however that the attainment of such proficiency requires time and practice.

Accordingly, we can enter this vacant world at any time depending upon how we use our minds. Reviving power is abundant in the vacant world. It is a natural principle that if our mind is pulled in there, our entire life is combined into the infinite power.

Tempu expanded further teachings but I hope that you, dear reader, have understood these three basic practical methods that will be expanded on in the next chapter.

9.7   Positive self-improvement for entrepreneurs according to the Tempu method

What I want you to practice is a suggestion method in addition to the basic method of unification of mind and body, Tempu improved himself constantly using this method. Just face a mirror and gaze at yourself and say, 'I will be a man of strong faith tomorrow morning' before you fall asleep at night, when the suggestion is most likely to be accepted. You may say it with a small voice but say it. Next morning when you wake up, say 'I have become a man of strong faith.' In this case you don't have to speak it out loud but to say it firmly to yourself in your mind. If you practise this everyday method of autosuggestion you can change your character for the better.

Tempu and I need this kind of autosuggestion, but it might be good for you to suggest to yourself other variants, such as 'I will be bright and cheerful'. I think there are many, e.g., 'I will have a broad mind and won't be prejudiced', 'I will have a strong will and won't eat between meals', or 'I will always be relaxed and won't get nervous in public', etc.

Tempu further recommended we say something like, 'Today was my day, thank you', before we fall asleep, and 'It is a wonderful morning, deliver me from all evils today' when we get up. As for me, I would try to make myself strong when I faced difficulties and couldn't sleep at night. Sometimes I forgot to do so and went to bed. Then I calmed myself in the bed and suggested it to my mind.

He himself decided to purge himself of the three poisons – anger, complaint and envy – and kept on reciting, 'Do not get angry', 'Do not grumble', 'Do not be envious', three to five times each to make his mind empty when he woke up and before falling asleep.

If one uses a mirror, I think it is even more effective. Regarding timescales, it is typically necessary to continue the practice for at least six months. Then one can actually feel one is changing. Before long one will be a new person able to begin a new and fruitful life.

Tempu looked for the root of human existence in attitude of the mind and declared that our life is under control of the mind. He remarked, 'Be a person who does not feel lonely even if you are alone', and if you can do it, you would emanate an aura that will attract many friends. This is what is called being your natural self.[4] It has something in common with Musashi's 'strategics'

---

[4] Cf. Hohenheim (Paracelsus)'s dictum, 'Alteris non sit, qui suus esse potest' (editors' note

introduced elsewhere in this book and it makes a spiritual symbol for corporate management. Professor Toshiro Ono will further explain 'unification of mind and body' according to Tempu in the next chapter. That chapter begins with some examples of Tempu's way of thinking that are often quoted for entrepreneurs to help them to understand the Tempu Method.

Tempu thinks it important to recognize the almost magical power of the human mind as follows, and accept the synonymity of 'high concentration' and 'utilization of subconscious power':

> You certainly shouldn't forget that thoughts in the human mind have effectively magical power. By giving good stimulation to the mechanism of your mind with its limitless imagination, and by keeping it well-focused, the power of your belief will become strong and will realize everything. It means that a very effective way to utilize the subconscious is constantly keeping an image in your mind.

The subconscious is defined as 'latent conscious deep in the mind of which one is unaware'. However, it has great power and one's ideal can be realized by applying the effect of subconsciousness. Tempu also remarked in his work 'Greatness of Ideals' or *Riso no Maka*:

> Ideals need belief. Without belief, your power to drive yourself toward the accomplishment of the ideal by eliminating all the difficulties will be broken apart. With belief the power to push your mind vigorously to the accomplishment of the ideal will follow rather than emerge. Therefore you always have to have a clear image of the ideal in your mind and never change it. Moreover, the ideal should be as sublime as possible because it will become your driving force that could lead you to greatness.

Tempu says that alongside positive thinking one should also maintain a sense of humour. In 'Real Positive Thinking', or *Shin no Sekkyoku*, he asserted:

> Don't forget to feel grateful first. In an extreme case, no matter what illness or bad luck you may have, you should transform it to appreciation and pleasure. In the first place, please think of the cause of illness and bad luck. Illness or bad luck cannot happen without your fault. Where there's a cause, there's a result. That's why if you are given illness or bad luck to promote your awareness that your way of life has faults, it should be a great blessing. Looking at it this way, what you need most is to transfer it to appreciation to correct your errors with pleasure rather than having a grudge.

Since ancient times, Japanese culture has believed that words have quasi-magical effects on the world. The Japanese call it *kotodama*, which means the soul or power of language. Similarly in Tempu's philosophy words are not considered as a mere communication vehicle but as something with power. Tempu again:

> Once spoken, seemingly words will lose their sound but the undulation will in some sense stay. Thinking of it in that way, don't you feel that you shouldn't curse someone's happiness with your words, or should impair other's joy, even in fun? Why don't we utter encouraging words, words to share happiness or pleasing words with each other when we start our day? Words, you see, have power because words are outcries coming from your soul.

Corporate management means continuous decision making. The same thing can also be said about individual life. The range of influence of individual decisions on individual life is limited, but corporate decision making has a social nature and the range of its impact may be enormous. Tempu asserts that 'a human has potentially a sincere conscience or spiritual mind'. Decisions should be made based on that sincere conscience or spiritual mind. To the question of how to exert this 'spiritual mind', Tempu gave this answer in his lecture 'Rational Mind and Spiritual Mind':

> Spiritual mind is the easiest one to exert. But as you get it wrong and think the easiest one is the hardest one to exert, you end up wavering or suffering in life when you don't have to. What should we do to exert it? It's quite easy. Try not to carry distracted or evil thoughts in your mind. Try to reduce the frequency of having negative thoughts in your mind. Spiritual mind emerges when your mind is pure.

> Once you get rid of distracted or evil mind, your good spiritual mind or inspiration will appear. When a spiritual mind belongs to your life, you will get a totally different brain. You will always get clear and liberating feelings, like a pearl just after being polished and wrapped with thin silk.

The points described above are the most important factors for start-up managers drawn from the Tempu method. Each of them is not a sufficient condition but just a prerequisite. Then, to what degree should we observe them? The answer is 'to our limit'. You cannot succeed without self-sacrifice. Putting a start-up company onto a sustainably profitable path is exceedingly difficult.

> It is unprofitable imagination, to be rejected, to imagine only satisfying earthly desire in your life after creating wealth and status. Instead, have a picture of yourself being healthy, or think of working for people in the world with the money you have made, that should be the real thing. Otherwise, however much money you earned, the money would not make you feel secure and happy.

Before concluding this part, I would like to introduce one more part of Tempu's lecture to encourage managers and businessmen who are faced with big problems in business:

> I have something to say to the people who run businesses for providing useful information. When I was young, a man called Hibiya Heizaemon lived in Horidome, Nippon Bashi. He was a roustabout whose job was unloading light packages from the ships and carrying them in a basket. He was famous as a hard worker and accumulated more than 500 million yen. He purchased cotton in India and a fire broke out on the ship that was carrying the cotton he bought and all of it burned. The damage amounted to about 200 million yen. 200 million yen in those days! That would be astronomical amount of money now. It even caused a sudden fall in the stock market in Kabuto-Cho.

What impressed me was the indescribable light in Hibiya Heizaemon's mind, which in a way exceed his power. At that time he was 65 years of age. At such a stage ordinary people would usually only have thoughts about life after retirement with no big dreams still to be fulfilled. When I said to him, 'A really bad thing happened to you,' he replied, 'No, no. That sort of thing happens all the time in business. I just got a big motivation to earn more again.' Astonished, I said. 'What? I have heard you suffered damage of 200 million yen.' He answered, 'Well, I don't think of it as damage. I think that in a sense God made the capital of 200 million yen and I hope that several times the amount of that capital will come back to me, so I'm really looking forward to it.'

I became amazed by him and I realized that I had taught a great guy. Within three years, he indeed recovered from the damage and had moreover accumulated a surplus of 500 million yen. He was just an upstart roustabout with little education, but he didn't turn a hair at that devastating shock.

9.8 Concluding remarks

On the contrary, look at entrepreneurs these days. Typically they soon crack up from receiving a dishonoured bill or some small damage. The reason why a lot of them who had grown up under the postwar booming economy fell down one after another like dominoes is that they don't have belief at all, but just avarice. In a nutshell, they are not well-rounded or decent as a human being.

MBA graduates are not always successful in corporate management and we have seen many examples of that. I would go so far as to assert that the number of MBA graduates who are not successful exceeds the number that succeed. The entire course work for MBA study typically covers nothing but 'necessary' conditions as a management technique. However, we need to get hold of 'sufficient conditions' like the spiritual motivation that we advocate. That really is where the significance of introducing the Tempu Method, based on the concepts of *The Book of Five Rings* by Miyamoto Musashi, lies.

10
'Shin-shin-toitsu-ho' for Dynamic Meditation

Toshiro Ono

This chapter is devoted to the essence of *Shin-shin-toitsu-ho*,[1] the Tempu method for dynamic meditation,[2] whose purpose is to teach how to construct a human life worth living (see the summary in Table 10.1). The core curriculum for *Shin-shin-toitsu-ho* is divided into the following fundamental disciplines:

Ia. Basic principle of unification of our mind and body
Ib. Reformation of held notions to induce positive ideas in our minds
Ic. Training methods for concentrating our positive ideas
Id. Method of brightening up our feelings (*Kumbbahaka*, a method for self-control of our nervous systems)
Ie. Method of using our spirit ('*An-jo-daza-ho*', the Tempu method of Zen sitting meditation).

Table 10.1 Seven recommended steps to construct a human life worth living

1. Learning the methods for the unification of mind and body
2. Practising the methods for the unification of mind and body in our daily lives
3. Transforming the attitudes of our minds to be positive
4. Pulling out our reserve power to activate our human potential
5. Strengthening of our minds and bodies
6. Enhancement of our human potential power (life power)
7. Building up a worthwhile life stage-by-stage

---

[1] T. Nakamura: '*Shin-jinsei-no tankyu*', or the Profound Research for a True Human Life, *Kokumin-kyouiku-fukyuukai*, Tokyo (1947) (in Japanese); revised version of '*Shin-jinsei-no tankyu*', published by Nakamura Tempu Foundation, Tokyo (1994); 'Ways for Unification of Mind and Body', an English translation of '*Shin-shin-toitsu-ho*', has been privately published by Prof. Tetsuichi Hashimoto in Tokyo (n.d.).

[2] H.E. Davey, *Japanese Yoga: the Way of Dynamic Meditation*. Berkeley, California: Stone Bridge Press (2001).

The fundamental discipline course is followed by a summer training course mainly devoted to the application of the disciplines lectured on during the fundamental course:

IIa. *Kumbbahaka*, a method for the self-control of our nervous systems, with practical applications

IIb. '*An-jo-daza-ho*', Tempu's method of Zen sitting meditation, with practical applications

In accordance with the seminar courses (standard curricula) described above, we will describe the essential points of *Shin-shin-toitsu-ho* in the following sections.

Basic principle of the unification of mind and body

The Tempu method for dynamic meditation can be traced back to the oriental philosophy of recognizing human life power as a part of the universal energy source, the very Original Spirit of the Universe, *Sen-ten-no-ikki*, from which all phenomena in the universe are considered to emanate.

The very principle of sustaining our existence using life power is that we can only really live our daily life in accordance with natural (universal) law. Under the assumption that a positive way of feeling and thinking makes it possible to activate our life power, the Tempu method, the *Shin-shin-toitsu-ho*, is a unique system for dynamic meditation. Careful observation of natural phenomena reveals that the universe continues to change and reform in order to evolve and elevate in a universal sense. Accordingly, the life power of ourselves as human beings could potentially also be activated by the power of universal energy if – and only if – we try to keep the attitudes of our mind positive in order to cooperate with the creative mind (spirit) of the universe.

What is human potential power?

Human potential power consists of six fundamental components of vitality, namely physical strength, courage, judgment, power for decisive implementation, energy and ability. It is referred to as reserve power by Tempu in his book (see footnote 1).

Figure 10.1 illustrates how to evaluate our human power, which is necessary for enjoying a positive human life. The procedure to follow is:

1. Evaluate a score with respect to each potential component of human power
2. Plot the six score points to construct a polygon and draw an inner circle tangential to the polygon
3. The area of the inner circle symbolizes the level of one's human potential power, with which one could accomplish something by oneself.

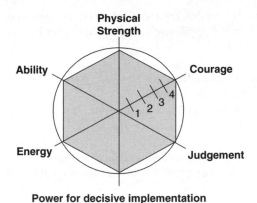

Figure 10.1   Evaluation diagram for human potential power

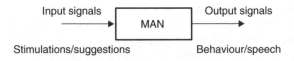

Figure 10.2   Input and output of man as a system

The relation between spirit, mind and body: the basis of the Tempu method for dynamic meditation

It hardly needs to be stated that we encounter various kinds of physical stimulations and suggestions throughout everyday life. So, we can consider a man as the system illustrated in Figure 10.2, in which environmental stimulations and suggestions are the inputs and our behaviour and speech are the outputs. The system elements of a man consist of two subsystems – mind and body. It is reasonable to consider that these subsystems are objects controlled by our spirit, the controller. In order to explain this interpretation, we shall consider the function of our mind in a little bit more detail in the next section.

The object of *Shin-shin-Toitsu-ho* is to cultivate and upgrade the score of each of these vital components of our human potential power.

From our many years of life experience, we are very much familiar with the following facts, listed in Table 10.2.[3]

Using the block diagram representations familiar in control engineering, the mutual relationships between our spirit, mind and body are shown in Figure 10.3.

---

[3] Cf. J.J. Ramsden, 'Computational Aspects of Consciousness', *Psyche: Problems, Perspectives*, vol. 1 (2002) pp. 93–100.

Table 10.2   Empirical knowledge of mind and body

1. The attitudes of our mind affect our behaviour and speech
2. The physical conditions of our body reflect and influence the state of our mind
3. Our spiritual power, force of will, governs the present state of our mind
4. The present positive state of our mind charges up the potential level of our spiritual power, which governs the developing attitudes of our thinking and feeling

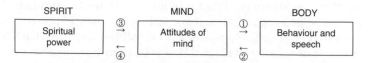

Figure 10.3   Relationship between our spirit, mind and body. The encircled numbers refer to the facts listed in Table 10.2. The direction of an arrow implies information flow from cause to effect, or the direction of control actuation.

Since we live in the midst of various kinds of suggestions (our environment), we have to learn more about the function of our subconscious, and the response characteristic of our mind that closely relates to the unconscious adoption of suggestive elements involved in words, images and behaviours of other persons, and so on (see also footnote 3).

Response characteristic of mind influences thought and feelings

One of the very important natural functions of our mind is the automatic adoption of suggestions from others. This implies that our mind always responds unconsciously to suggestive elements in our environment. There exist both positive and negative suggestive elements in broadcasting media such as radio and television programmes, printed media as books, photographs, etc. It is very important to eliminate negative elements from these suggestive media in order to maintain the attitude of our mind in a positive character. We should pay much attention to the response characteristic of our mind, the essential function of our subconscious. If its response characteristic tends to be negative, the contents of our feelings or thoughts – or both – tend to be negatively oriented. On the contrary, if it moves to be positive, the attitude of our mind then becomes positively oriented, and our thoughts and feelings change to be positive and constructive.

Since our living surroundings contain plenty of suggestive elements, we have to work actively to select the positive elements. In order to explain intuitively the sophisticated features of our mental function, especially of sensing and the response characteristics of our mind, we use the three icons in the upper part of Figure 10.4, antenna, level indicator and battery, mimicking the display panel of a cellular telephone. The antenna symbolizes the state of receiving a suggestive element – that is to say, we live in the midst of suggestions. The level indicator symbol expresses the intensity level of receiving positive suggestive elements. Finally, the battery icon implies the charged level of our human potential power, which is in a state of readiness to activate response characteristics our mind.

Figure 10.4 illustrates the existence of positive and negative elements in suggestive media. Figure 10.4(a) shows that a positive thought or feeling is induced upon stimulation from a positive suggestive element if and only if the response characteristic of our mind is of positive character. Similarly, Figure 10.4(b) shows that a negative thought or feeling is induced upon stimulation from a negative suggestive element if and only if the response characteristic of our mind is of negative character. However, even if we receive a negative suggestive element, we could continue a positive thinking or feeling as long as the response characteristic of our mind is kept positive. Figure 10.4(c) illustrates this desirable case. On the other hand, even if we receive a positive suggestive element, we may not continue a positive thought or feeling if the response characteristic of our mind is kept negative. Figure 10.4(d) corresponds to this unhappy case. Accordingly, the induced content of our thought or feeling heavily depends on this response characteristic of our mind.

Let us consider the relation between our conscious and subconscious in our thinking process and construct a rough image of our thinking processes

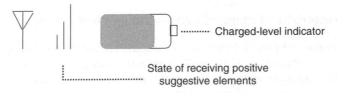

(Polar-patterns, Response characteristic of mind, Positive attitude of our mind)

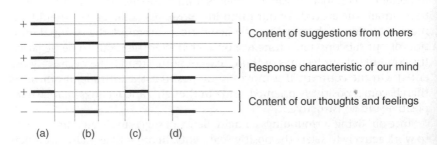

Figure 10.4　Upper part, see text, Lower part, the response characteristic of mind influences our thoughts and feelings. A positive suggestive element is marked on a plus symbol line, and a negative element on a minus symbol line. For further explanation see text.

(Figures 10.5 and 10.6). These pictures provide a visual explanation of Tempu's method of autosuggestion for the reformation of our notion factors, which are stored in our subconscious.

Control-theoretic interpretation of *Shin-shin-toitsu-ho*

Considering the relationships shown in Figure 10.3, a reasonable control-theoretic interpretation might be as follows:

Spirit is the comprehensive controller for the mind as a controlled variable; spirit actuates the state of our mind. Will power is the manipulated variable, the output from the spirit, which controls the state of mind – mentally or physically or both. Mind, the governor of the body, regulates the physical conditions of the body as a controlled variable. Rumours, evaluations by others, and so on act as disturbances that violate the states of our mind, or the coming attitudes of our mind.

On the other hand, the actual contents of thoughts and feelings are the controlled variables for the mind as a controller. Correction to the desired state of mind and/or that of our behaviour, should it be necessary, could be achieved through continuous practice of the *Shin-shin-toitsu-ho*, dynamic meditation, which was devised by Tempu.

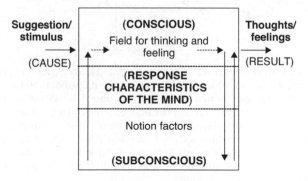

Figure 10.5   Rough image of thinking process

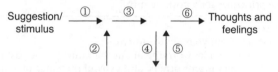

Figure 10.6   Generating process for thoughts and feelings

Mental adjustment could be accomplished via *Anjo-daza-ho,* methods of auto-suggestion, and the procedures implied by the five principles for cultivating our thought and emotion in a positive and constructive way (see Table 10.3, below).

Physical adjustment could be achieved by practicing *Yo-do-ho, Kumbbahaka* breathing, and so on. These methods are more-or-less applications of *Kumbbahaka-ho,* which regulates and maintains a balanced condition in the nervous system. An illustrative explanation of this is made in Figure 10.7 by means of a block diagram of dynamic control, which is a familiar method of representation in engineering science.

Five principles for a positive mind

Tempu instructed us that we should pay a great deal of attention to cultivating a positive mind, in other words to keep our state of mind positive during our daily life by making the best use of our spiritual power. His five principles are summarized in Table 10.3.

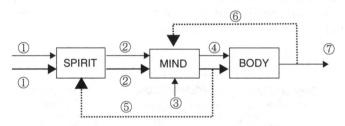

Figure 10.7   Unified control concept of the mind and body. Arrows express flows of information to control a variable physically and/or mentally. Bold solid arrows emphasize the flow of mental and spiritual information to control the state of the mind, a vital controlled variable. Thin lines represent the flow of an open-loop control concept. The dotted lines express the signal flow of feedback control, which represents the effect of practising the comprehensive methods of *Shin-shin-toitsu-ho.* Key to numbers: 1, ideal behaviour and attitudes of our mind; 2, power of our will; 3, disturbances (rumours and evaluations by others); 4, attitudes of mind in thinking and feeling; 5,6, correction by *Shin-shin-toitsu-ho;* 7, real behaviour

Table 10.3   Five principles for a positive mind

1. Examine the self
2. Analyse suggestions from your environment
3. Discover the present, and let worrying about the future or the past fall away
4. Examine your attitude towards others, and expand the range of your friendships through positive words and acts, brightening up your feelings
5. Experience the universal mind

Kumbbahaka according to the Tempu method, to regulate the function of the nervous reflex

Innate harmony exists between our mind and body, which is conducted by the joint work of the central, autonomous and peripheral nervous systems. This harmony, however, may be weakened by the inefficient use of mind and body. Our bodies must be strong, relaxed, and healthy in order to respond to the commands of our mind, the governor of our body (qua the controlled object).

Kumbbahaka in the Tempu method refers to two things: a posture of self-harmony that settles the body weight in the lower abdomen, unites mind and body, and regulates the autonomous nervous system; and a breathing method to focus *ki*, the vital power of life, at the *hara* even during moments of serious stress.

Let us briefly describe the *Kumbbahaka* posture, a correct and natural posture leading to the coordination of mind and body. Through it, it is possible to maintain our autonomous nervous system in a balanced and ordered condition. Essential points of *Kumbbahaka*, as summarized by Tempu, are given in Table 10.4.

How to manage our mental activities

The best way of managing our mental activities is stated in the following two points:

1. Do all things with full concentration of the mind, without disordering its stable condition;
2. Make a timely switching on and off of the conscious with respect to the items before us (just like the time-sharing use of an electronic digital computer).

Tempu taught five further principles in order to help us not to falter from our concentration of mind. They are summarized in Table 10.5.

Anjo-daza-ho according to the Tempu method

Anjo-daza-ho is a method for concentrating our mind by means of the sound of a buzzer or a bell. It should be emphasized that the method is considered

Table 10.4 Essential points of *Kumbbahaka* according to the Tempu method

1. Relax and drop the shoulders
2. Concentrate conscious and potential power to a point in the lower abdomen
3. Do not let any part of the body, including the anus, fall limp
4. Stop breathing for an instant

Table 10.5 Five principles for augmenting concentration

1. Concentrate on matters with which one is familiar
2. Concentrate on matters one wishes to accomplish in a hurry
3. Concentrate on matters one believes are uninteresting
4. Concentrate on matters one believes are of no value
5. Concentrate on matters one had once failed to accomplish

as effective for resetting our state of mind to a zero initial condition, just like the inchoate state of a baby's mind, without any prejudice.

We have two ways of exercising *Anjo-dazo-ho*. The essence of the method is described as follows:

A, in the case of using a buzzer:

1. Sit with mind and body unified.
2. Focus on the sound of a buzzer, which is switched on.
3. Continue listening to the sound and mentally follow the sound immediately after the buzzer is switched off.
4. Let your listening expand, so that your mind becomes one with the silence (see Figure. 8a).

B, in the case of using a bell:

1. Sit with mind and body unified.
2. Focus on the sound of the bell.

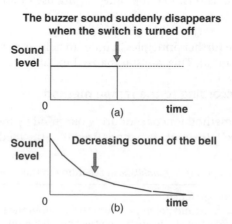

Figure 10.8 Illustration for the essence of *Anjo-daza-ho*: 'Listen to the soundless sound with your mental ears'

3. Listen to the decreasing sound waves of the bell.
4. Continue listening and mentally follow the decreasing sound of the bell.
5. As the sound waves become infinitely small, continue listening to the 'soundless sound' (see Figure 10.8b).
6. Let your listening expand, so that your mind becomes one with the silence.

Tempu suggests that the essential points of *Anjo-daza-ho* can be perceived in terms of three classical Japanese *Waka* poems:[4]

Listen to the soundless sound with your mental ears.

Put your mind out of the space and do not mind your sense.

Keep your mind still and clear in the soundless world.

Concluding and summarizing remarks

In this chapter we have introduced the Tempu method, and the essential topic of '*Shin-shin-toitsu-ho*' has also been described (Tempu's dynamic method for unification of mind and body [dynamic meditation]).

The essence of *Shin-shin-toitsu-ho* can be summarized in the following three points:

1. Training to reveal the nature of positivity.
2. Reformation of the subconscious.
3. Regulating and maintaining a balanced condition in the nervous system.

As a concluding remark, I would emphasize that a life worth living is a fruit of the unification of our mind and body – just like a masterpiece of art. It could be realized gradually through continuous practice of any part of *Shin-shin-toitsu-ho* in our everyday life. This continuous practice makes it possible to enjoy the true value and strength of a human life with peace and love. And it also results in a happy, healthy and prosperous life.

---

[4] Cf. John Keats' poem 'Ode on a Grecian Urn' (editors' note).

Part IV
Practical Applications

11
EcoDesign and Human Media

Shuhei Aida

EcoDesign is a method of environmental management that is based on consideration of the whole life cycle of products or services or both at every phase of development and use, from the design process, through the procurement of raw materials, production of the commodity, its use and final disposal. EcoDesign, based on the concept of Ecotechnology proposed by the author in 1972, aims to maximize the lifetime performance of the product and/or service while minimizing its overall environmental impact. However, a more fundamental approach would be to consider EcoDesign in terms of the way in which required functions or services are fulfilled, so that function rather than product becomes the starting point for development and innovation. Consequently, it is desirable to consider the system level rather than the product level during the early, innovative stages of an EcoDesign process.

11.1 The concept and significance of EcoDesign

In the twenty-first century we are being forced to re-evaluate the conventional forms of industry on a global scale, and to design a new civilized society in a comprehensive way. In essence, this renewal will start from answering 'questions from nature' about the civil activities of human beings, or 'questions from a sound spirit of the human', with sincerity. In order to do that, we need to have the sensitivity to understand these questions properly. In other words, we should stave off a rise of 'specialists without spirit' in international society as Max Weber once warned, and which tendency is already disturbingly apparent, for example in the Commission of the European Communities.

The goal of EcoDesign is to realize a civilized society that eliminates sources of pollution at root and maintains a harmony with all ecosystems. Specifically, it means building up a social system for the next generation, integrating the research results of diversification, distribution and efficiency with a view to the operational management of various kinds of energy, including natural energy, the networking of energy and information systems, the application of radiation and convection systems, and research and development of fuel cells. The concept of EcoDesign can be defined as follows:

EcoDesign is a philosophy that aims to develop social systems with a holistic awareness that humans are linked both materially and spiritually to the *shinrabansho.*[1] It is only through recognition of this link that humanity can succeed in exploiting the planet's resources in an efficient manner with regard to the needs of future generations.

The practice of EcoDesign begins with a total understanding and evaluation not only of production processes but also of energy use, materials, products, distribution, sales, service and collection of waste materials in terms of the global social system.

Consider the metaphor of a big tree trunk supported by numerous roots that extend steadily into the earth, extending all sizes of boughs, branches and leaves out from the trunk, and a natural environment that nurtures them holistically; we need to aim to create a 'civilization with good boughs and branches', thinking of the expansive world of the tree. In that sense it is highly desirable for us to have a solid, philosophical framework in order to return to the starting point.

11.2   Human media, the humane use of IT systems[2]

Human media can be achieved based on the philosophy of EcoDesign. 'Human Media' is a typical twenty-first-century term and is aimed at the realization of 'human + IT and robot as tools = pleasant society'. Recently, a Japanese newspaper company promulgated a journalist's declaration entitled 'word power'. I feel now the dawn of a new era that will again see the appearance of the importance of words in mass media. The spirit of the term 'human media' is filled with phil-osophy to open a new era with appropriate ideals and beliefs for this backdrop.

Miyamoto Musashi, a prominent samurai whose fame has spread posthumously, clothes thoughts with words in his *Book of Five Rings*. He provides a clear picture of the relation between tools by comparing a general of samurai to a master carpenter and emphasies the utilitarian aspects. He considers the strategics relevant to the course of daily life and suggests that the samurai's body should be together with his weapon in harmony with natural behaviour.

Although the work is called *The Book of Five Rings*, it has nothing to do with the now rather tarnished symbol of the Olympic Games, although it may enable one to win gold medals, because the book explains the tactics for winning competitions. Actually, it is said that it was originally named after the five elements in the universe according to a Buddhist idea: earth, water, fire, wind and emptiness.

When one uses a tool, it becomes an independent entity, quite possibly far from the intention of the manufacturer, without limits. Especially after it has been used for a long time, the tool's function is likely to have been repeatedly renewed, according to the user's ingenuity. The tool's range of applications would have been expanded and its function would have become

---

[1] A Japanese word meaning the entire planet and its ecosystems.
[2] S. Aida and H. Zaidan (eds), *The Humane Use of Human Ideas: The Discoveries Prohject and Eco-Technology*. Oxford: Peragmon, 1983.

polyvalent, leading to a fuller utilization. In other words the tool's function and characteristics evolve due to the various uses more or less distant from its original purpose. When one uses a tool, one will work together with the stage upon which one will use it by making use of the tool's good points and characteristics. Under the circumstances, the user, tool and stage would be integrated according to the scenario. The tool for a martial artist would be weapons including swords and the stage would be the place for fighting against the enemy. Musashi, who found the law relating the three entities by understanding the compound dynamic relations between samurai and sword on the stage, called it Musashi's *hyoho niten ichi-ryu*.

Information technology (IT) and robots are our tools. Here I would like to elaborate a scenario for the development of a new civilized society in order to realize the dream of a 'pleasant society', in line with the principles espoused by Musashi.

It is a striking characteristic of the strategics expounded in Musashi's *Book of Five Rings* that the concept of complementarity found in modern quantum physics, i.e. that two complementary entities can fully exist simultaneously, can be applied. In a fight with real swords, when your enemy's sword is light, you should move together with it like its shadow. In other words, the basic idea is to accommodate your mind and body movements to those of your opponents such that they become one. This is exactly the root principle of the 'Stance/No stance' concept in Musashi's strategics: the free and flexible way.

Musashi's notion can be applied to the solution of many social issues, including recent international conflicts. Specifically, he advocates that an institution beyond winning or losing should be created from the process in which your enemy and you move like light and shadow. Winning your enemy's heart and mind can be used in the creation of the new institution in a highly effective way, and we should incorporate it into our strategic thoughts. It should not be the strategy to force your opponent down and under, but could be called democratization – you read your opponent's mind and seek that system which enables you to live side-by-side.

Space does not permit the exhaustive elaboration of this idea here, but we emphasize that the content of Musashi's *Book of Five Rings* is an excellent basis for human media, being filled with the descriptions and explanations of important scenarios for us to learn optimal and appropriate, even adapted, ways of 'mind and body' in order to live in modern society.

No matter who will read this book, he or she will be able to feel that it was written for them because it discusses the intrinsic spirit required to deal with the various challenges that one encounters in life, without a limit to the complexity of the challenges that can be tackled. It is in this sense that I wish to make this little book known throughout international society as a vital and effective source of life philosophy for leaders throughout the world.

Translated by Kieko
Mombayashi

12
Eco-design and Sustainability

W.J. Batty

12.1 Introduction

During the 1960s the rapid growth of the world's population was a cause of great concern. How could this burgeoning population be supported, fed and watered? At that time, many considered that scientific and technological developments could provide the solution. It was believed that increased agricultural output could be achieved by utilizing more land for farming and also through the development and export of new agricultural techniques and technologies throughout the world. Although the successes achieved by these means have been considerable, they have not been without cost. These gains have been achieved largely through the use of agricultural machinery, and consequently fossil fuel-based energy use, to replace human and animal labour, and also through the increased application of fertilizers and agrochemicals such as weedkillers and insecticides.

The oil crises of the late 1970s and early 1980s made both industry and the public aware that the fuel resources that were essential to maintain current lifestyles were finite. New ideas and concepts were presented to the public, but not always communicated very successfully. For example, 'Energy Conservation' was a commonly used term in the 1970s and 1980s. To engineers and scientists it had a well-defined meaning, but to the public it came to mean 'doing without energy'. Using less meant poorer conditions; colder rooms in winter, hot and humid rooms in summer. Consequently, it became difficult to promote the notion of 'Energy Conservation' because people equated it with poorer service or conditions. Concepts and ideas had to be more meaningful and 'marketed' more carefully.

While much of the doom mongering of the 1970s has been shown to be excessively pessimistic, a public awareness has developed that at some time in the future these resources will become very limited and consequently expensive. It was in the context of this growing awareness that notions such as ecotechnology, eco-design and sustainable development evolved.

12.2 Sustainable economic development

12.2.1 Sustainability

Since the publication of the Brundtland report (1987) and the Rio Conference of 1987 sustainability has been a major topic of discussion. Essentially, the sustainability debate relates to the view that present human behaviour in terms of utilizing the Earth's resources is not sustainable. The consequences of these behaviours are claimed to be ecological and environmental degradation and climate changes that will further upset the balance of the existing ecosystems. Most of the world's governments were able to agree with the basic notion of sustainability and sustainable development as defined by the Brundtland report: 'development that meets the needs of the present without compromising the ability of future generations to meet their own needs'. However, as the political machinations required to achieve the Kyoto Agreement have shown, self-interest and the interpretation of responses to sustainability in terms of political ideology have made globally agreed and co-ordinated actions extremely difficult to achieve.

The key principles involved in the definition of sustainable development are summarized in the diagram of Figure 12.1. (Palmer et al., 1996). These principles have overt political implications and so will be interpreted differently by those of different political persuasions. If this is the case is it realistic to

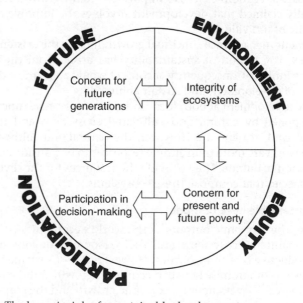

Figure 12.1 The key principles for sustainable development
Source: Palmer *et al.* (1996).

expect a wide degree of agreement about the nature of the problems involved and the strategies adopted to solve them?

Much of the disagreement regarding the extent and speed of action required arises from different perceptions as to the degree of change that will occur – and even the desirability of maintaining the current equilibrium state of the world's various ecosystems. While simple definitions of sustainable development can engender general agreement among all those involved, the multidisciplinary nature of the problem makes agreed, holistic and practical responses more difficult. Consequently, the temptation exists to consider the different aspects of the sustainability debate separately and so ecology becomes divorced from economy and the two notions come to be considered as irreconcilable. If the practical application of the notion of sustainability through integrated and coordinated global actions is going to be difficult, it may be that local actions need to be developed and assessed in terms of their contribution to the global requirement. The acceptance of differences in cultural and political interpretations of sustainability is important for the development of a global strategy.

12.2.2   Development

At the most basic level development involves the transformation of resources into productive economic output. Development implies change and in terms of classical economics it also implies economic growth. Additionally, it is generally claimed that development involves the improvement of the quality of life of individuals.

Development that assumes continual growth implies the existence of infinite resources. The notion of sustainability has arisen from the belief that resources are limited. Consequently, a conflict would appear to exist between the notions of development and sustainability.

Economic development at both local and global scales relies upon resources that are supplied by natural and cultivated ecosystems and the mineral resources of land, sea and air. However, the natural and cultivated ecosystems of the world are more than simple resources to be transformed into productive economic output. They provide the resources for the diverse animal and plant species that comprise these ecosystems.

12.2.3   Sustainable development

Wisely used, the economic outputs of the world's economies could support actions to maintain ecosystems and their resources for long-term use as input to productive economic output. However, at best sustainable development suggests a compromise between economic growth and the husbanding of finite resources. Development, economic growth and the conservation of resources are linked and so should not be considered in isolation.

Sustainable development could be perceived as an attempt to create a balance between economic development and resource management. It implies that a long-term view should be taken when examining development decisions, seeking to provide equity between the rich and poor within current generations and across generations in terms of present populations and those yet to exist. This means that current human populations have to live within the limits of available resources rather than borrowing resources from the future. For economic activities to be sustainable they must neither degrade nor deplete natural resources, and nor should they have serious impacts on the local or the global environments that are to be inherited by future generations. How feasible is such a notion? Where should the baseline be set?

By most definitions the achievement of sustainable development is probably impossible during the current stage of human development. Rather it is something that we should strive to achieve. Development projects should promote both economic and social progress while simultaneously minimizing impact on resources in particular and the environment in general. In terms of economics, financial return from such projects will be assessed with objective goals such as maximizing profit; however, environmental and social goals are more subjective and, consequently, more difficult to assess.

While it is probably true that most development projects in the foreseeable future will continue to consume more resources than they create, the notion of sustainable development can be used to provide a set of goals to ensure that project outcomes are closer to sustainable ideals.

12.3   Productive output and eco-design

A major consequence of the oil crises of the late 1970s and early 1980s has been the introduction of increasingly demanding energy and environmental legislation at both national and regional levels. The legislation and information campaigns led by governments have caused many manufacturing companies to realize that cost savings could be made by introducing more energy-efficient and less wasteful manufacturing processes. Generally, industry and commerce adopted technical responses to environmental problems that removed pollution and wastes after they had already been produced; for example, by equipping cars with catalytic converters to remove the pollutants produced by the combustion of petrol.

In the late 1980s some companies began to consider how waste and pollutant production could be reduced during the manufacturing process itself and more efficient use made of energy and materials. A growing understanding developed that environmental impacts are generated not only during the manufacturing process, but also when products were used during their lifetime and when they were disposed of. Consequently, attention began to turn to the design of products that attempted to take account of all the environmental impacts that would occur throughout a product's life cycle, from initial manufacture through to its final disposal. Consequently, the productive economic output of development has been connected to the notion of minimizing resource use and environmental impact. This provides the basis for eco-design.

Eco-design can be defined as 'design that addresses the resources utilized together with all the environmental impacts of a product throughout its complete life cycle without unduly compromising other product parameters such as function, quality, cost or appearance' (ECO2-IRN, 1995). In this context eco-design is more than a design methodology and becomes a method of environmental management that is based on consideration of the whole life cycle of products and/or services at every phase of their development, from the design process, through the procurement of raw materials, production of the commodity, its use and its final disposal. Eco-design aims to maximize the lifetime functionality and performance of the product and/or service while minimizing its overall environmental impact.

In terms of the development of sustainable products, manufacturing companies are being challenged to reduce the environmental impacts of their current ways of doing business. This means reducing the quantity of natural resources utilized, and the rates of energy consumption and toxic emissions generated related to the manufacture, use and disposal of their products and services. Targets have been proposed, often referred to as 'Factor X', for reductions in global resource and energy consumption. These targets range from reduction by a factor of 4 [4] to as much as a factor of 20 [5], i.e. providing the same function or service while only using 25 to 5 per cent respectively of the resources that are currently used. At present, the exact level for the factor of improvement required is debatable and the changes that are required are unclear.

If manufacturing industries, for example, are to achieve these 'Factor X' levels of reductions of resource and energy consumption, the balance between retaining existing products and extending their product lives and the development of new products or services that consume new fuel resources or require the extraction of new materials will need to be examined. Antiques provide a good example of the link perceived by many between the 'economic price' of a commodity and the 'psychological value' of ownership. Where a perceived value of ownership of an artefact exists it generates an economic value. The value of an artefact is rarely perceived in terms of price alone. Within the sustainability context, there is a need to generate a conceptual understanding of the environmental value of products amongst both producers and consumers.

12.4   The design process and eco-design

12.4.1   Design

Much has been written about design, ranging from the philosophical to the practical. Definitions of design and the processes involved depend upon the viewpoint from which it is being explored. However, in the context of designing objects that are to be manufactured as saleable products a useful definition was that put forward by Jonas (1993): 'a process transforming a verbally-formulated 'problem' situation into a detailed plan for a tangible, usable product'. He considers design to be 'an action process aiming at predetermined goals'. In terms of manufactured products the goal is mostly an artefact providing a required function(s) at a price that customers are willing to pay. As such, product design always exists within a societal context, while the price that customers are willing to pay may comprise broader considerations than money alone. The description of design as 'problem solving' is widely accepted in industrial and engineering design. However, where the boundaries of the problem are deemed to lie is an interesting point of discussion.

Pugh (1991) introduces the notion of 'total design' where he states that any product, be it 'bridge or bulldozer', requires inputs from many disciplines, both engineering and non-engineering, in a combination that is unique for the particular product under consideration. Total design perceives design as a systematic activity that arises from the identification of a market/user need and the consequent design of a product that will successfully satisfy that need. A typical product is assembled from many different components, which range from the individual parts of the artefact itself to the manner in which it is packaged for sale. Pugh (1991) states that the distinction between 'total design' and the 'partial design' that is involved with the components that comprise the complete artefact is important and should be understood. Many specialisms may be employed to solve the design 'problem' and may include materials science, mechanical engineering, electronics, ergonomics and aspects of aesthetics such as shape, colour or texture. Manufacturing industry is generally well equipped to deal with the organizational requirements for the integration of the partial design inputs into the total design for a product.

In the fields of architecture and building services design, environmental concerns have acted as a creative spur to reduce the quantity and cost of energy and, more recently, to consider the choice of materials used and where possible the recycling of building structural and system components. Since the 1970s a number of different design descriptors have been developed to provide labels for particular design approaches. Some of these labels encompass a number of design methodologies; for example, passive solar techniques could be an aspect of Energy Conscious Design, Bio-climatic Architecture, Low Energy Design and more recently Zero Energy Design. These labels have attempted to encompass design philosophies that take more regard of the energy and resource issues when constructing buildings and building systems, and try to make them easier to understand. However, this profusion of labels, each with their own 'champions', has probably caused more public confusion than clarity. It is worth asking – what do these labels have in common? What are the key drivers of the processes that they describe?

'Energy and Environmental Efficiencies' are key concepts involved in all of these methodologies. Efficiency implies that the level of service or the

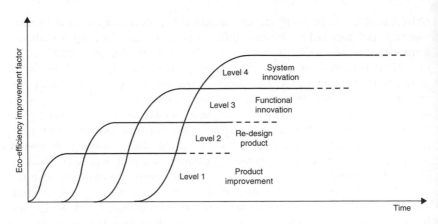

Figure 12.2 The four stages model for eco-design

condition supplied should be as high as that expected previously, or even improved, but that it should be provided with less resource expenditure. It certainly should not imply reduced levels of service. Experience suggests that people will tolerate unusual conditions or demands, or accept lower standards of service only for short periods. If people are to use less resources then they have to be provided with more resource-efficient and energy-efficient commodities and services.

Definitions of eco-design, such as that given previously, have mostly been interpreted to date in terms of product improvement or product redesign. However, the four stages model for eco-design (Brezet *et al.*, 1995) illustrated in Figure 12.2 shows a hierarchy illustrating that four stages or levels of environmental improvements can be considered to exist. With each ascending level the degree of innovation required in the design process and the potential environmental benefits of eco-efficiency that can accrue increases (van der Zwan and Bhamra, 2003). The graph is indicative only and suggests that the later levels, 3 and 4, are likely to become more dominant in the future.

The four stages can be explained as follows (Brezet *et al.*, 1995; van der Zwan and Bhamra, 2003):

Level 1:   **Product improvement** that improves the environmental performance of aspects of products that already exist in the marketplace.

Level 2:   **Product redesign or eco-redesign** that optimizes the environmental quality of existing or newly developed products.

Level 3:   **Function innovation or alternative function fulfilment (AFF)** where change is no longer confined to the existing product concept but considers changing the manner in which the required function is fulfilled.

Level 4:   Sustainable systems innovation where whole product systems are replaced by more eco-efficient systems that require less energy, materials and space-intensive infrastructure.

As experience in utilizing the concepts of eco-design increases so is academic and industrial thinking moving towards utilizing the more advanced stages of eco-design; advancing from product improvement and product redesign to consider the more holistic approaches implied by function and system innovation.

Levels 3 and 4 require a more fundamental approach to the development and provision of required functions or services. The function to be fulfilled rather than the notion of a product becomes the starting point for development and innovation. It has been suggested that levels 1 and 2 of the eco-design hierarchy, illustrated in Figure 12.2, are essentially eco-design but its more advanced levels 3 and 4 can be considered as 'eco-innovation' (van der Zwan and Bhamra, 2003).

Eco-innovation has been summarized by three main points (van der Zwan and Bhamra, 2003):

(i)   A function or need is the starting point for new development rather than product optimization or redesign;

(ii) Initially an 'innovation process' is used rather than a product design process;

(iii) The innovation process considers the system level rather than the product level during the early stages of the eco-design process.

Designers in many fields often use archetypes as starting points in the design process, i.e. existing and accepted responses to a design problem. Consequently, it is often difficult to introduce new ideas or use new routines. Existing starting points based on these archetypal solutions need to be discussed and, if necessary, abandoned. In principle, designers have the freedom to determine the way in which a specific need is fulfilled, and the outcome of a design process does not necessarily arise explicitly from the description of the desired function. The function or service need not necessarily be defined in terms of the product that needs to be designed but rather in terms of the desired functional result. Generally, alternative solutions are always possible and so the notion of alternative function fulfilment is relevant. The functional innovation required at Level 3 implies a strategy of 'alternative function fulfilment', which requires critical analysis of the function, the underlying needs for its existence, and the ways in which specific needs are fulfilled in order to generate innovative solutions to the function fulfilment. Consequently, functional innovation focuses on the initial stages of the product/service development process.

Buildings and their services systems present considerable challenges for the application of eco-design principles (Batty, 2004). Unlike product manufacture for mass consumption, many buildings are single products and any additional costs for design process can only be defrayed against the cost for that single entity. However, it is not always true that the design of energy-efficient buildings or system needs to cost more. Life cycle costing (LCC) is a technique used in quantity surveying to assess the initial financial investment of a project in terms of the anticipated future cost in use over the lifetime of the investment. This concept is not new, but it is rarely applied intelligently to the appraisal of elements of project costs. When care is taken to evaluate design ideas both in terms of their functional and financial viabilities the real costs are often reduced. For example, when services equipment such as air conditioning is sized accurately it usually has a lower capacity and is consequently smaller; therefore, it is generally cheaper to buy and more efficient in operation, leading to reduced running costs.

Life cycle analysis (LCA) is a relatively recent conceptual addition to design considerations. However, it is an important evaluation tool. Many so-called 'energy saving' schemes actually use more energy when considered over the lifetime of the investment. This is not identified because insufficient or no evaluation is carried out during the design phase. This method of analysis is still relatively new and has introduced the notion of embodied energy into design considerations. The necessary information required for evaluation may be difficult to obtain. However, when sufficient information is available such analysis can expose important effects of design decisions.

The Engineering Academy of Japan (EAJ) has proposed a Life Cycle Value (LCV) index that attempts to integrate the quantitative assessments of LCC and LCA with qualitative aspects of performance (Hiromatsu *et al.*, 2000). A case study considered housing development to test this notion and considered that four criteria could be applied as significant aspects for the LCV index in this context:

   (i) Adaptability and exchangeability performance of fittings and equipment in the dwelling units, and of the dwelling units themselves;
  (ii) The long-term performance of the building skeleton and the infrastructure of the building services;
 (iii) Development of amenities over time generated by the architectural and social composition of housing estates;
 (iv) Ergonomic performance of the building operation and maintenance management over time.

The LCV attempts to include the potential to adapt the building and its systems with time in relation to changing social needs and technical innovations and develop the notion that building designs can include the potential for the buildings to be adapted and customized in response to unpredictable future demands.

More advanced notions of eco-design, levels 3 and 4 of Figure 12.2, consider the concepts of function innovation and sustainable systems innovation. These concepts require innovative responses to the design of a product in terms of the underlying needs that it satisfies and the manner in which those needs could be fulfilled. How can such notions be related to the design and future functioning of buildings? Would they affect the way in which building components are utilized or the adoption of services such as solar and wind energy use?

A key aspect of fulfilling customer or client needs relates to the issue of ownership. When considering buildings at a systems level both constructional and service systems elements could be leased rather than owned by building owners (Hiromatsu *et al.*, 2000). This notion is illustrated in Figures 12.3 and 12.4. However, it is by no means certain that customers would easily accept such notions of ownership.

The supply and inverse leasing supply chain, Figure 12.3(b), considers the supply of building element components in terms of a service rather than a commodity to be purchased and owned. This innovative response to the building as a system allows more opportunity and flexibility for component re-use and may increase the useful lifetime of individual components considerably. A similar approach could be taken for constructional elements of the building, as demonstrated in Figure 12.4. These examples demonstrate

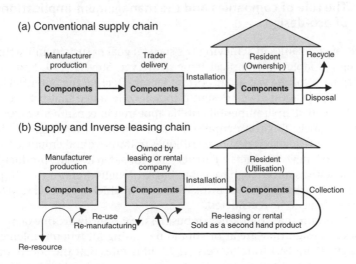

Figure 12.3 Conventional and supply and inverse leasing supply chains for building element components
Source: Hiromatsu *et al.* (2000).

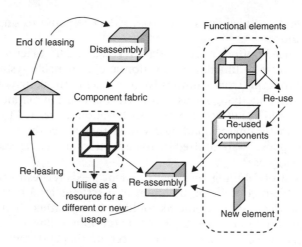

Figure 12.4   Schematic diagram of the possible chain of use of leased modules and components for a building construction
Source: Hiromatsu *et al.* (2000).

that alternatives to the traditional methods exist for fulfilling functions by re-examining the notion of ownership and service. Similar reasoning could be applied to the supply and use of energy and energy services equipment in buildings.

12.5   The role of companies and the management implications of eco-design

The role of companies in achieving the societal goal of sustainability through eco-design is largely a technical issue. However, Stevels (1997) considered that corporate culture was an important factor affecting the potential for the successful application of eco-design principles. He stated that between 1991 and 1994 the first environmental criteria appeared in consumer product tests and in eco-labels. Environmentally aware companies then began to implement product-related eco-design techniques to improve and enhance the eco-efficiency of new products. Further he considered that product-based eco-efficiency was not enough to realize breakthroughs or innovative improvements and that the systems or infrastructures in which a product functioned would also have to be considered.

It is important that companies or business units are aware of exactly what level of eco-design they are at or should be aiming for when implementing eco-design. Table 12.1 from Stevels (1997) illustrates that the choice of level has considerable consequences for the type of information required, the environmental validation techniques that need to be applied, financial costing aspects, and the possible assumptions about and consequences for consumer

Table 12.1 Some implications for product design related to eco-design levels

Level	Purpose	Environmental validation	Investment level	Implied change of consumer lifestyle	Social infrastructure change required
4	System innovation, functionality fitted to the needs of a sustainable society	Extended life cycle analysis Complete life cycle cash flow	+++++	+++++	+++++
3	Alternative fulfilment of required function, i.e. functional innovation	Life cycle analysis Life cycle cost	+++	+++	++++
2	Complete re-design utilizing existing concepts	Eco-indicator Life cycle cost	+	+	+
1	Incremental improvement	Common sense Checklists	−	−	−

Source: Based on Stevels (1997).

lifestyle and infrastructure. The notions illustrated in Table 12.1 suggest that activities within levels 1 and 2 are well within the capabilities and the control of individual companies. However, for success at levels 3 and 4, consumer lifestyle and function infrastructure changes may play major roles as inputs to the eco-design process.

Beard and Hartmann (1997) considered that a scientific mindset dominates the environmental agenda and that, consequently, design programmes are driven by compliance, legal and technical requirements and environmental management systems rather than by innovation and opportunity. He suggested that scientists and engineers tend to lead many of the environmental units in companies and that their thinking patterns are more likely to be associated with environmental damage limitation rather than eco-design. Performance assessments of products and services are often concentrated on lifecycle assessment with limited connexion to the lifestyle changes that might be implied or required. He considered that scientists might thus be spending time re-designing the wrong products with efficiency and impact reduction dominating over product or service effectiveness and true sustainable design.

Experience indicates that even at level 1 the successful application of eco-design principles generates environmental improvements and cost reductions, which contradicts the well-established prejudice that consideration of environmental impact of products only increases the cost of production (Stevels 1997). The process of bringing together relevant market needs, and environmental and financial information almost automatically leads to the generation of improvements in the projected eco-efficiency of the proposed product and may, in addition, lead to improvements outside the purely environmental boundaries of the original design problem statement. Eco-design by its nature must be an interdisciplinary activity and this links well to the complexity of today's products and suggests the need to break down the usual organized boundaries of specialized departments focusing on particular parts of the total product concept.

Stevels (1997) considered that it is more difficult to derive market advantages from level 1 eco-design activities because:

(i) both private and original equipment manufacturers customers expect that quality companies will continuously introduce environmental improvements in their new product generations; and

(ii) level 1 eco-design improvements are straightforward and easy for competitors to follow, so commercial advantages will be short-lived.

Table 12.1 suggests that level 2 eco-design activities require environmental validations such as life cycle assessment and that life cycle cost calculations are needed to ascertain the best options. Stevels considered that it was possible to design products utilizing level 2 at approximately the same cost as current products. However, a major barrier for such a development would be the investment that might have to be made to transform the present production facilities into suitable facilities for the new product (Stevels 1997). This transformation would also have consequences for suppliers, as they would have to change their production facilities and would have to learn to work with new and perhaps recycled materials. Consequently, he suggested that the development of such re-designed products could only be implemented in stages over a longer period of time.

For product development at level 3 function innovation or alternative function fulfilment design strategies would be used. This implies that major changes in consumer lifestyle and infrastructure may be needed. Generally, these implications go beyond the competencies of individual companies. The risks involved are greater than those involved in the preceding levels of eco-design and may require major investments in production systems, possible changes within the supplier base, consumer acceptance, and the need for an infrastructure that might not yet be in place. Consequently, companies involved in product or service development at level 3 would have to approach their environmental product strategy from a much wider perspective. To achieve this, environmental product strategy would need to be linked to corporate and business strategy development. From a design perspective it becomes difficult, if not impossible to apply rules of thumb at the product development level; rather, the function innovation strategy should promote and enhance design team discussions of the ways in which the product system fulfils the particular needs of society, as identified in the design problem statement or design brief. Such discussions could even cause a company to reconsider and redefine the type of business in which it is involved. This may require cultural, organizational and structural changes to be made in the company.

One of the key outcomes of applying the principles of eco-design at level 3 would be a design strategy development to consider the 'function that needs to be satisfied' as a starting point for innovation or design, rather than an 'existing product'. A potential consequence of this approach is to move from the concept of selling products to one of selling services. This notion of a move from selling products to providing services has existed in the business world for the past few decades. However, in recent years this notion has attracted renewed interest because of its potential to expand business opportunities while at the same time reducing environmental impacts. A number of critical factors are promoting this shift towards service provision, but barriers also exist that are slowing this change. Important external influences are notions such as Corporate Social Responsibility (cf. Chapter 13) and legislation that includes principles such as extended producer responsibility for the environmental impacts of the commodities that companies manufacture. Internal drivers may include a desire for improved resource efficiency and management support. Some companies are beginning to perceive providing services as a growing sector and would expect to enjoy growing revenues from high volume leasing and remanufacturing operations.

The notions of sustainability and the 'Cradle to Grave' concept for commodities and commodity components leads to the closing of product cycles. Potentially, this allows companies to control a constant flow of raw materials for new production from the recycling and re-use of existing products. However, many companies still have a perception of low demand for service-oriented solutions. Customers generally lack knowledge of life cycle costs and often perceive the prices of service-oriented functions to be prohibitively high. To gain customer acceptance, companies will have to provide attractive offers of service with at least the same level of function and comfort that existing products provide. However, it should not be assumed that customers are necessarily more interested in the product function than ownership of the actual product itself. The psychological value of ownership should not be underestimated (cf. Chapter 15).

The emergence of the notion of Corporate Social Responsibility has broadened perceptions of the societal role and responsibilities of companies. To date, however, sustainable manufacturing consumption of resources and sustainable products have not featured prominently in definitions of Corporate Social Responsibility. In future, the manner in which companies will ensure improvements in the environmental efficiency of their products and services to reduce environmental impact and enhance the development of a sustainable society are likely to be seen as fundamental requirements of good corporate practice. Companies will be expected to account for and be responsible for the environmental effects of their products in the same way that currently they account for their operations. A concern for the lifetime impact of manufactured products or services will become important aspects of the notions of social and ethical responsibility.

12.6   Development of management skills

If companies are to take advantage of the business opportunities that may emerge from a more sustainable development, then new expertise and skills need to be developed. This means that new forms of organizations, processes, products and/or the functional satisfaction of service needs will have to be created.

Products and/or services are the strategic core of activity of most companies. However, eco-design skills have not been considered as a core competence required by company employees. A number of factors contribute to this situation:

  (i)   a lack of a perceived business need;
 (ii)   poor understanding of financial arguments; and
(iii)   a weak commitment to the integration of eco-design principles into the product creation process. (Charter 1999)

Currently eco-design projects tend to be managed on an unplanned basis and so access to relevant information and the development of related databases tends to be uncoordinated. The organizational structures required to manage the interdisciplinary inputs to the eco-design process need to be defined and implemented. As in all design processes, the knowledge of team members and access to information are key components. Consequently, database development is required to provide pertinent information to decision makers throughout a company's structure involved in the eco-design process. Such information systems are required to provide design evaluation tools and to promote understanding of the technicalities of eco-design itself and to facilitate the management of eco-design systems and processes. Such knowledge transfer structures are important to enhance the development of a truly interdisciplinary approach to product development.

The development of an appropriate organizational infrastructure for the higher levels of eco-design implied in eco-innovation may mean changing the existing engineering-based perspective of product design to a broader, more outward-orientated strategic focus. This suggests that a corporate information network is required that will capture, process, store and disseminate pertinent information, which will primarily relate to environmental and financial aspects of eco-efficiency in the short term, but social and ethical aspects could become important inputs to the eco-design process in the future.

Generally, the experience and skills in eco-design are not widely available. Suitably qualified or experienced managers who can take on the responsibility for the 'eco-design brief' are rare at present. Consequently, if the employees with such expertise leave a company then their knowledge leaves with them. This may mean that competitive advantage is lost. Eco-design information systems should enable companies to retain the knowledge and expertise gained from each new eco-design project undertaken. Within companies intranets can be used to disseminate eco-design knowledge more widely. Developing, retaining and building eco-design competencies and information systems will become a key element of successful environmental and business performance and will provide strategic advantage.

References

1   Batty, W.J. (2004) 'Applying the Principles of Eco-Design to Building Design', Proceedings of JSES/JWEA Joint Conference, November.
2   Beard, C. and R. Hartmann (1997) 'Sustainable Design: Rethinking Future Business Products', *Journal of Sustainable Product Design*, vol. 3, pp. 18–27.
3   Brezet, J.C., J.M. Cramer and A.L.N Stevels (1995) *From Waste Management to Environmental Innovation*. The Hague, Netherlands: Rathnau Institute.
4   Charter, M. (1999) 'Editorial – Ecodesign: A New Core Competence', *Journal of Sustainable Product Design*, vol. 10, pp. 5–6.
5   ECO2-IRN (Ecologically and Economically Sound Design and Manufacture – Interdisciplinary Research Network) (1995) 'Defining Ecodesign, Workshop: Economically and Ecologically Sound Design and Manufacture', Third Forum, Manchester Metropolitan University, UK.
6   Hiromatsu, T., T. Murata and K. Yamaji (2000) Life Cycle Value Index of Assembled Houses. Society of the Engineering Academy of Japan, Information Paper No. 109.
7   Jonas, W. (1993) 'Design as Problem Solving? Or: Here is the Solution – What was the Problem?', *Design Studies*, vol. 14, pp. 157–70.
8   Palmer, J., I. Cooper and R. van der Vorst (1996) 'Mapping out Fuzzy Buzzwords – Who Sits Where on Sustainability and Sustainable Development', Proceedings of the Sustainable Development Research Conference, Manchester Conference Centre, pp. 181–8.

9   Pugh, S. (1991) *Total Design: Integrated Methods for Successful Product Engineering*, Workingham: Addison Wesley.

10   Reijnders, L. (1998) 'The Factor X Debate: Setting Targets for Ecoefficiency', *Journal of Industrial Ecology*, vol. 2, pp. 13–22.

11   Stevels, A.L.N. (1997) 'Moving Companies Towards Sustainability Through Ecodesign: Conditions for Success', *Journal of Sustainable Product Design*, vol. 3, pp. 47–55.

12   van der Zwan, F. and T. Bhamra (2003) 'Alternative Function Fulfilment: Incorporating Environmental Considerations into Increased Design Space', *Journal of Cleaner Production*, vol. 11, pp. 897–903.

13   von Weizsäcker, E., A.B. Lovins and L.H. Lovins (1997) *Factor Four – Doubling Wealth, Halving Resource Use*. London, UK: Earthscan.

14   World Commission on Environment and Development (1997) *Our Common Future*. Oxford: Oxford University Press.

13
Corporate Social Responsibility and Business Decision Making
Simon Knox

The rise of corporate social responsibility

For Chinese consumers, the hallmark of a socially responsible company is safe, high-quality products. For Germans, it is secure employment. In South Africa, what matters most is a company's contribution to social needs such as health care and education. Public expectations of companies are rising everywhere, but these expectations can vary substantially from country to country and region to region. However, there do seem to be some common threads: in the US, France, Italy, Switzerland, the Philippines and much of South America, consumers agree that the most important thing a company must do – if it wants to be regarded as socially responsible – is to treat its employees in a fair manner. According to GlobeScan,[1] an international opinion research company, these rising expectations among consumers are not being met by advances in the Corporate Social Responsibility (CSR) practices of most companies. In fact, GlobeScan reports that company ratings on social performance have fallen in recent years. In a similar vein, at a recent London conference John Elkington, the CEO of Sustainability and a widely-respected authority on CSR, offered a stark critique of management practices of CSR. His research suggests that although the number of firms engaged in social reporting is increasing, with a widening recognition among business leaders of the need to accept broader responsibilities than short-term profits, the quality of their company's CSR reporting has improved little in the last few years. At the same conference, Simon Zadek of Accountability concurred with Elkington's view and argues that these social reports are not having a significant impact on managerial decision making.

In this chapter, the CSR policy and practices of a number of leading multi-nationals are reported, which sheds light on some of the underlying reasons why CSR reporting seems to have evolved with such low impact on business decision making. During this study, a framework that clearly links CSR

---

[1] www.globescan.com.

programmes to both business and social outcomes was also developed. This framework is presented here and is used as a method to order the findings and to help structure the discussion of the managerial implications.

In concluding the chapter, attention is drawn to some of the policy and practice issues that need to be resolved if the general perception of CSR reporting is to change from being seen as an expensive exercise in compliance or, indeed, as another form of PR used in an attempt to satisfy ethical investors and the public in general. In the next section, the limitation of free-market ideology is explored as businesses respond to the growing pressures of differing stakeholder groups to develop sustainable business practices.

Free-market ideology alone is no longer enough to sustain business growth

More than thirty years ago, Milton Friedman (1970)[2] wrote in the *New York Times* that the social responsibility of a business was to increase its profits. Any diversion of company resources to social programmes, charity and other non-profit-generating activities, the Nobel Laureate argued, represents a tax on consumers and investors. Such a tax reduces society's total wealth and satisfaction. His position, based upon sound free-market ideology, has come under increasing attack since the time of writing and can no longer provide the business leader with an erudite means of avoiding the issue. A series of recent corporate scandals (e.g. Enron, Worldcom, Vivendi and Parmalat) clearly suggest that many companies have failed to take care of various stakeholder interests, and that some have actively neglected stakeholder interests over a number of years. These businesses would appear not to believe in CSR and their duty to satisfy various stakeholder requirements at some level.

Corporate Social Responsibility is something that every board must now address in some form or other. Ironically, it is arguably the triumph of free-market ideology over regulated economies that has foisted new responsibilities on increasingly powerful multinational companies. Globalization strategies provide businesses with unprecedented access to markets and ever-lower production costs; it has also brought closer to reality the concept of the global village first discussed in the 1960s. Business practices, even those conducted a very long way from their home markets, can be subject to intense scrutiny and comment by customers, employees, suppliers, shareholders and governments, as well as other groups on whose support the business relies. One such group, non-governmental organizations (NGOs), have become more and more powerful in recent years, calling business to account for policies in the areas of fair trade, human rights, workers' rights, environmental impact, financial

---

[2] M. Friedman, 'The Social Responsibility of Business is to Increase its Profits'. *New York Times Magazine* 13 September 1970, 32–3 and 122–6.

probity and corporate governance. In an increasingly cynical world, where the public are much less inclined to trust their governments and businesses, NGOs retain high levels of trust across a broad spectrum of society. Whilst it is true that in certain circumstances powerful multinational companies can impose trading conditions on the less powerful, such as non-unionized workers, commodity producers in developing countries and third world labourers, the idea that modern companies must commit themselves to effectively address poverty and environmental degradation must also be an overstatement. The discussion between advocates of Milton Friedman's position, limiting responsibility to maximizing profit, and NGO activists who regard firms being primarily instruments of social policy, represents the extremes of the debate. Many academics writing in the field of CSR are cognizant of these extremes and seek to establish a middle ground.

Wood (1991)[3] suggests that the public responsibility of business is divided into areas of social involvement directly related to their business activities and competencies, with secondary areas of involvement relating to its primary activities. For example, an automobile maker might reasonably be expected to deal with vehicle safety and the environment but not low-income housing or adult illiteracy. Clarkson's long-term study (1995)[4] of corporate behaviour indicates that companies deal with stakeholders, not society, and that CSR must distinguish between stakeholder needs and social issues; managers can address stakeholder requirements but not abstract social policy. Carroll (1979)[5] suggests corporate responsibility has different layers: economic, legal, ethical and discretionary categories of business performance and that business leaders must decide the layer at which they choose to operate. Similarly, the UK government wishes to establish a middle ground in this debate, with Prime Minister Tony Blair suggesting that 'We must ensure that economic growth contributes to our quality of life, rather than degrading it. And we can all share the benefits.'

Finally, although business leaders themselves acknowledge that their firms are socially created and 'licensed', most would argue they were created primarily as economic agents to provide the goods and services society wants at the right price, quality and availability. As such, their firms' competencies are built around their commercial activities. For example, 1,000 software firms tackling global poverty through a myriad of small initiatives is laudable, but likely to be ineffective. With the exception of a handful of businesses, such as Body Shop and the Co-op Bank, who have developed strong CSR policies

---

[3] D. Wood, 'Corporate Social Performance Revisited'. *Academy of Management Review,* 16(4) (1991), 691–718.

[4] M. Clarkson, 'A Stakeholder Framework for Analyzing and Evaluating Corporate Social Performance', *Academy of Management Review,* 20(1) (1998), 92–117.

[5] A. Carroll, 'A Three-Dimensional Model of Corporate Performance', *Academy of Management Review,* 4(4) (1979), 497–505.

as a basis for growth, it would, arguably, be more effective, and efficient, for governments to tax these firms and give the money to multinational agencies that are competent in the field.

On balance, it would be most unlikely to find a consensus between the various stakeholders, particularly as CSR is a relatively new and emergent business responsibility. So, in preparation for research across a number of multinationals, I sought to identify received wisdom about the business case for CSR activities in general, and linkages between these activities and business or social outcomes in particular. In both instances, the arguments presented and claims made about the positive impact of CSR on business were found to be both highly assumptive and lacking in empiricism. These assumptions are presented next and the questioning of these beliefs led directly to the development of the research agenda reported here.

Assertions and beliefs about the business case for CSR

In reviewing the arguments that 'you do well by doing good', five commonly-held beliefs can be readily identified; they seem to be largely anecdotal and, as such, highly questionable:

- Consumer preferences will increasingly favour products and services from socially responsible, transparent and trustworthy firms.
  - *The assertion that consumer behaviour will shift to reward social responsibility is grounded in surveys of attitudes and trade-off analysis, not observed behaviour. Attitude–behaviour correspondence seems to lack empirical grounding and is not obviously evident when researched.*
- Investors will increasingly favour responsible companies and irresponsible companies will find their cost of borrowing rises.
  - *Zadek[6] acknowledges that only 4 per cent of the total funds available for stock market investment are governed by CSR principles, therefore, most firms judged not to be socially responsible still have full access to equity funding.*
- Potential employees will be attracted only to responsible companies and others risk skill shortages.
  - *Arguments about competing for talent also appear to be based upon stated intention and not observed behaviour. Studies frequently cited were concluded during the last long period of uninterrupted economic growth and the phenomenon may be cyclical. This link between employee motivations, customer retention and shareholder value has been made separately from CSR theory.*

---

[6] S. Zadek, *3rd Generation Corporate Citizenship* (2002), http://www.accountability.org.uk/uploadstore/cms/docs/3rdGenCorpCitizenship.pdf

- Engaging with stakeholders encourages innovation.
  - *Von Hippel[7] has been presenting these arguments and case-studies for over 20 years without reference to CSR practices.*
- Being trusted by stakeholders and pursuing socially responsible policies reduces risks arising from safety issues (consumer, employee and community), potential boycotts and loss of corporate reputation.
  - *Clearly, concern for safety and building trust is paramount to the firm's reputation management and future sales but cannot be exclusively associated with CSR policies. In fact, it's just good business practice to pursue both with vigour.*

In essence, whilst the above arguments for CSR are intuitively appealing, many researchers admit that the links between business performance and the implementation of CSR policy are difficult, if not impossible, to prove. It is against this background that the research objectives, design and protocol for the research reported here were developed. These are discussed in the following section.

Research objectives, design and protocol

Since the research objectives set out below are essentially exploratory in nature, the study was designed to contribute to the development of CSR as an instrumental theory. The three specific research objectives are:

- To explore how and how strongly CSR investment is linked to business and social outcomes among mainstream business.
- To develop a framework for linking CSR to performance.
- To identify the consistencies (and inconsistencies) among CSR policy makers and how their CSR programmes are implemented.

Clarkson identified numerous problems encountered by researchers working towards similar objectives. In his landmark, ten-year study mentioned earlier (see footnote 4), he concludes that researchers should concentrate on how firms actually manage their stakeholders rather than upon empirically validating inherently untestable frameworks of social responsiveness. Consequently, it was felt necessary to look at CSR practice in developing a framework for linking CSR investments to performance.

Research design and protocol

Content analysis of the CSR, customer and reputation management literature identified the assertions made about the link between CSR and business

---

[7] E. Von Hippel, 'New Product Ideas from Lead Users'. *Research Technology Management*, 32(3) (1989), 24–8.

and social outcomes. These relationships are illustrated in the prototype framework (Figure 13.1) and suggest that CSR programmes affect stakeholders' cognitions which then change their behaviours in ways sympathetic to the company's commercial interests. To understand if firms do conceive of the linkage between CSR and performance in this manner, I interviewed the CSR leaders of six multinational companies who are among the global market leaders in their fields. Purposeful sampling was employed to eliminate firms facing acute CSR issues, such as extraction or tobacco companies, which are judged to be unrepresentative of typical businesses.

The selected firms were: Orange (UK), Diageo PLC, Pilkington PLC, Unisys, Company X and Company Y. (Both Company X and Company Y opted to remain anonymous by name but I can mention they are a global software vendor and an IT service provider respectively.) All six firms had a readily identifiable executive responsible for CSR. This person normally reported into the Main Board of their companies through the Corporate Affairs function. Two of the interviewees, Diageo and Pilkington, are responsible for their firm's global CSR policies, one (Unisys) is responsible for Europe-Middle East-Africa and the other three are responsible for the UK. However, the true power of these individuals within their firm and, hence, their ability to provide accurate data as to how CSR policy influences decision-making, cannot readily be assessed by the researcher.

Empirical evidence was gathered in semi-structured interviews with these CSR leaders and, whilst the literature identifies a wide variety of definitions of 'CSR investments', the participating companies were allowed to determine how they defined CSR rather than imposing a definition upon them.

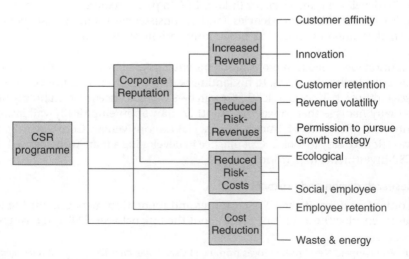

Figure 13.1   CSR link to corporate reputation and business performance

Towards the end of the interview and before sighting the prototype framework (Figure 13.1), interviewees were asked to create their own framework illustrating the links between their CSR programmes and outcomes. They were then asked to assess this prototype framework and contrast this with what they had just drawn. The framework was modified through successive interviews and, after two or three iterations, the revised framework remained largely unaltered and could be used in the final interviews to guide discussions. Interviews lasted between two and three hours and each of the respondents agreed to clarify any remaining issues as necessary, post interview. Next, this framework is reported along with key findings.

Research framework and findings

Since the CSR framework has been validated by each of our six respondents on behalf of their respective companies, it is both convenient and instructive to present our research findings against this framework (see Figure 13.2).

Most respondents agree that the common starting point of their CSR programmes was the company's vision and values which had usually developed on a normative basis. Whilst none of the respondents would claim to have such a formalized or, indeed, instrumental framework as the one above, each recognized that their corporate vision and values co-evolved with corporate reputation (sometimes referred to as brand) and the behaviours of its employees. At the same time, there was full agreement that CSR programmes favourably enhance corporate reputation and to some extent could influence

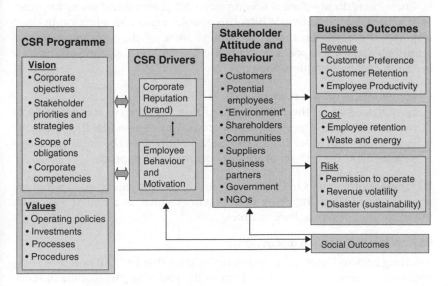

Figure 13.2 Framework linking CSR with outcomes

employee behaviour. Thus, it was felt that once CSR is 'embedded' in their employees' attitudes to stakeholders, and through listening and responding to stakeholder concerns, their business would automatically act more responsibly, have a greater understanding of the risks in its environment, and strengthen its corporate reputation:

' . . . CSR drives good corporate governance. It comes before the paraphernalia of good governance, and is more integral to the way we operate, the way we behave, the way we treat other people, the way the company is protected.'

Orange CSR spokesperson

'Every employee is empowered to do the right, responsive thing and their performance is reviewed in terms of what was achieved and how, based upon our values of integrity, honesty, being open and respectful with others.'

Company X CSR spokesperson

With the exception of Diageo which does adopt a shareholder value approach to its CSR policies and practices (i.e. programmes lead to outcomes directly [Figure 13.2]), the remaining companies tend to focus on the left-hand side of Figure 13.2; setting CSR objectives, identifying their primary stakeholder(s), scoping obligations and, perhaps, developing some measure of employee awareness and their buy-in to such programmes.

With such strong normative positions linking CSR programmes to the company vision, values and reputation, it is understandable why 'hard-edged' business cases do not always accompany CSR programmes since, for most, embracing CSR is intuitive. Whilst this enables rapid CSR adoption in these respondent companies, it fails to address some of the more fundamental questions about their policy and practices regarding CSR programmes; for instance, such policy questions as:

* For what and to whom are we to be held responsible?
* How do we manage the conflicting demands amongst our stakeholders and how should our CSR programmes reflect the way we prioritize their interests?
* How much should we invest in CSR and how does the company assess successful outcomes so that we can continuously improve?

It is these shortcomings in CSR policy among our sample companies that are reported next before discussing their practices which, in a similar way, seem to fall short of best practice examples.

CSR policy: findings and discussion

Referring back to Figure 13.2, it became evident that the CSR policy of these respondent companies in relation to both the visioning (the scoping of social obligations and the challenge of prioritizing stakeholders) and the assessment of social outcomes generally lacked detail and cohesion. Turning first to the scoping of social obligations:

- **Companies feel responsible for communities impacted by their core business operations.**

All respondents interviewed felt that their companies should comply fully both with regulatory (and legislative) demands as well as with industry norms and expectations. The key reference point for most companies was their industry, rather than an idealized gold standard of corporate responsibility:

"We are proud of our brands, and proud of how we lead our industry in social responsibility."

Diageo CSR spokesperson

"We are an increasingly grown-up business. . . we understand our impact on the industry, our customers and partners. . . all stakeholders. We must provide responsible leadership commensurate with our position."

Company X CSR spokesperson

Those with the most articulated positions on what they wish to be held accountable for used the following criteria for this assessment:

- Their social responsibilities should leverage their unique core competencies so as to make a contribution others cannot match.

For instance, Company X's policy goal is to empower the digitally disadvantaged; addressing the 'digital divide' between the IT haves and have-nots.

- Their investment should have a great impact on society.

"We are world leaders in glass, with manufacturing operations in 25 countries and are major contributors to the local communities where we are located."

Pilkington CEO

- Their social programmes should have a direct relationship to the industry in which they operate.

For instance, responsible alcohol consumption has been central to Diageo's CSR programme since it was formed out of United Distillers and Grand Metropolitan about ten years ago. Its central corporate citizenship group manages a number of global initiatives as well as providing seed capital and management expertise to local business units engaged in 'alcohol in society' initiatives.

Orange, in addition to consulting and responding to stakeholders regarding mobile masts, invests in the promotion of better communication between people. It believes the cause is relevant to its business, leverages its corporate competencies and is of importance to its employees.

What is evident from these findings is that each company has clearly scoped out its CSR policy around the impact of its operations or brands and seems to conform to Wood's (1991)[8] view about engaging in social involvement directly related to business activities and competencies. By adopting such a normative approach, the unanswered questions here are:

> How do these companies know how much to invest in CSR versus the other demands for resources?

> What is the extent of their CSR obligations and should they be conditioned by market position?

- **Companies are clear about their most important stakeholders, but are less able to set priorities among the rest.**

In response to the question posed earlier 'To whom are we to be held responsible?' most respondent firms have a flat list of stakeholders beyond their priority stakeholders (normally customers). These include: governments, NGOs, suppliers, employees and communities. There is no consistent approach to prioritizing their secondary stakeholders. Three possible explanations for this are offered:

1. Companies tend to treat all secondary stakeholders equally.
2. They do not manage secondary stakeholders actively.
3. Most likely, stakeholder differentiation needs to be developed further.

The research identifies a mechanism for this differentiation based upon Mitchell, Agle and Wood's model[9] which classifies stakeholders into one of seven types according to the urgency, power and legitimacy of their claims over the company. This issue of stakeholder prioritization is of vital importance to the effective management of CSR and seems to be largely absent in policy decision making amongst the firms interviewed.

- **Social outcomes need more formal assessment.**

Social outcomes in the context of this research mean the results of CSR programmes, such as the value of the philanthropy (e.g. curing a disease), positive

---

[8] D. Wood, 'Corporate Social Performance Revisited'. *Academy of Management Review*, 16(4) (1991), 691–718.

[9] R. Mitchell, B. Agle, and D. Wood, 'Toward a Theory of Stakeholder Identification and Salience: Defining the Principle of Who and What Really Counts'. *Academy of Management Review*, 22(4) (1997), 853–86.

impact on entire eco-systems, reduction in poverty and the increased participation in society by socially disadvantaged groups.

Diageo stands alone in publishing an analysis of social outcomes as well as
calculating the Economic Value Added (EVA) it creates in local markets
through its activities and the tax revenue generated for host governments.
The other firms face commercially difficult choices against their policy decision making discussed above since, without a mechanism for prioritizing
stakeholders for CSR purposes and with no substantive means of measuring
successful outcomes, how do senior management make these choices? Is a
philanthropic investment decision or scheme born out of an appreciation of
areas of employees' concern a legitimate CSR programme? Whilst vision and
values drive CSR policy-making in the framework (Figure 13.2), social outcomes
linked to a particular CSR programme need to have clear metrics established,
as does any area of business investment that is predicated by the achievement
of targeted outcomes such as brand share, profit and revenue growth.

CSR practices: findings and discussion

Of the three main findings reported here as CSR practices, both risk and
stakeholder behaviours are highlighted in the framework (Figure 13.2).
However, attitudes to CSR reporting are outside the framework and, in presenting this finding, a major paradox is highlighted. First, business risk is
considered:

* **Risk management is not fully integrated with business activities.**

A consistent theme throughout the management literature and these interviews was the belief that effective CSR programmes reduce a firm's exposure
to the rare, but catastrophic, risk of the magnitude of the Brent Spar, Bhopal
and Anderson Consulting events:

> "If you truly engage all stakeholders in policy making, then the chances
> of being blind-sided by a Brent Spar must be greatly reduced."
>
> Unisys CSR spokesperson

Whilst such corporate disasters are very rare events, each respondent confirmed that their companies had a risk management practice that attempts
to identify all potential risks (events) to the business through a systematic and
transparent process. This process generally involves assessing the potential
impact of each event and assigning a probability of occurrence. Summing up
the risks as a weighted average of events and outcomes provides some measure
of the total risk facing the company.

In Diageo, the External Affairs function applies this process for the firm
and has been able to correlate positively its evolving CSR programme with
a year-on-year reduction in weighted average risk facing the company.

This has been achieved by better assessment of the risks, improved contingency planning and stronger relationships with relevant stakeholders through their CSR programmes.

However, in most of the respondent companies, risk is managed separately by finance and is not fully integrated with CSR. Each respondent confirmed that finance undertakes formal risk assessment and that neither the process nor the management actions arising from it are managed within the CSR function.

It is likely, therefore, that there may be a mismatch between where the process for risk assessment resides (Finance) and where the competency for risk management exists (CSR function).

- **Stakeholder behaviours, not only attitudes, count to drive revenue and costs.**

Companies appear to be managing the left-hand side of Figure 13.2 more than the right hand side. Generally, respondents confirmed that their firms develop CSR programmes that are consistent with their core vision and values and that they are managed through their employees to support their corporate branding and to positively influence measures of stakeholder perceptions of the business. They also confirmed that this does not usually carry through to a robust analysis of stakeholder behaviours and business outcomes.

Firms are measuring what is relatively easy for them to measure, i.e. attitudes. As discussed earlier, attitude–behaviour correspondence is often difficult to reconcile. However, it is not for lack of effort or awareness that this situation exists:

> "We have been involved with benchmarking groups trying to isolate the impact of CSR upon behaviour from everything else going on . . . but it does not seem possible"
>
> Diageo CSR spokesperson

The problem of measuring behaviours transfers into problems of measuring business outcomes, as discussed previously, and attributing some portion of these outcomes to CSR investments and programmes.

The business case logic outlined in the flow of Figure 13.2 is based upon responsibility leading to increased customer expenditure, higher productivity, improved contribution from suppliers and reduced employee turnover. With the exception of risk, they all require some understanding of behaviours – and not just attitudes. If firms do not overtly link CSR to changing stakeholder behaviours (and to business outcomes), expenditures on CSR are likely to become more and more vulnerable to criticism over time.

- **Business attitude to CSR reporting is paradoxical.**

All respondent companies claim to have conducted a broad and deep scan of the NGO and stakeholder environment relevant to their business operations.

Most engage stakeholders and NGOs formally in order to understand and assess the claims being made upon them. Equally, all are comfortable with their understanding of CSR reporting, yet are fierce in their criticisms. Each respondent totally rejects the ideas of standardized reporting as not being suitable to their own industry (or firm). They listen to the points of view of NGOs and social auditors but reserve the right to report on what they feel is most relevant to their situation. CSR and financial managers feel inundated with requests for information from NGOs and ethical investment analysts, each addressing similar issues with different information demands. One respondent referred to 'questionnaire fatigue' in reference to this proliferation of social and environmental assessments. They consider these demands difficult to meet as the data are not always at hand or accumulated according to the definitions of the particular requester. Many respondents were very wary of *de facto* social and environmental legislation being made through NGOs and international humanitarian organizations. One respondent referred to this as 'mission creep'.

Across all the firms interviewed (except Pilkington), social and environmental reporting was managed and communicated to stakeholders separately from their financial reports.

Herein lies the real paradox: companies wanting standardization of the information required from them but vociferously rejecting a 'one-size-fits-all' approach to CSR measurement and reporting. If the core idea of the triple bottom line of company reporting (improved financial, social and environmental transparency) is to be achieved, then an integrated approach to such reporting and communications across the three areas is required.

The future of CSR

If this research is any guideline, it seems as if many businesses are facing a number of challenges in their approach to CSR. The argument that a firm has social responsibilities has been accepted. However, it is the researcher's contention that the lack of a systematic framework linking investment in these responsibilities to social or business outcomes could well be inhibiting the development of CSR.

In essence, the framework proposed here calls for a number of CSR policy matters and practices to be fundamentally re-evaluated. From a policy perspective, CSR leaders and other management need to build a consensus behind a CSR vision of with what and to whom they wish to be responsible and how they wish to measure and report on their performance against the vision. That process will force senior management to consider their company's unique competences and determine how they can be leveraged to differing social and financial ends. Implementation of that vision through best practices requires measurement of stakeholder behaviours, more integrated risk management and formal assessment of social outcomes.

Recent scandals have demonstrated that the reporting of financial results is problematic, despite standard reports and external verification. Social reporting is even more problematic as it requires verifiable assessments of complex social processes, such as stakeholder dialogue, responsiveness and attitudes. The campaign for global standards is led by a limited number of groups with strong links to the social responsibility community.

If business is unhappy with the plethora of reporting demanded by NGOs, then it will have to find a collective voice and create implementable reporting structures that can secure broad social support.

14
The Need for Spirituality in the Public Sphere

Nada K. Kakabadse, Paul Collins[1] and Andrew P. Kakabadse

14.1 Introduction

Religions have provided comfort, community and moral guidance to generations of people and today guide the lives of millions. Although much good has been done in the name of religion, so has much malevolence (Ayer, 1976). Through history, numerous examples of religious intolerance and persecution abound. Religious hierarchies have sided on occasions with the oppressors rather than the oppressed. Equally, many non-religious people have led very decent lives (Ayer, 1976). In the third millennium, such contradictions still abound. Alongside the advent of new threats such as ecological and nuclear disaster, people around the world violate the most basic tenets of their own creeds in promoting group and state terror.

Whilst globalization may have signalled the emergence of a certain kind of new order, in reality chaos and inequality prevails. Likewise, technology advances have made possible improved global communications but, at the same time, undermined traditional ethics and created an atmosphere of moral drift.

[1] Paul Collins wishes to thank the following: Canon Dr Edmund Newell, Director of the St Paul's Institute for his kind invitation to join in the Paternoster pilgrimage, Elizabeth Foy, Institute Secretary who with brilliant succinctness kept the monthly meeting diary and the other pilot Conference members who spoke eloquently from their hearts and who should remain anonymous. Appreciation is also due to the Rev. Dr James Hanvey SJ, Director of the Institute for Religion, Ethics and Public Life, Heythrop College, London University and to Moyra Tourlamain of the same for their key inputs into developing the conceptual and methodological aspects of Paternoster and supplying some excellent meeting questions and readings. Finally, I wish to record appreciation to Terry Armstrong, Woodstock Theological Center, Georgetown University, Washington, DC who gave his time generously on my 2004 visit in understanding better the Woodstock Business Conference. All views expressed in this paper are personal to the authors and do not represent any official view of the institutions mentioned.

In a marked depersonalization of modern life (Armstrong, 1999), there are few escapees. Even higher-level professionals involved in public sector management (national and international civil servants, state enterprise managers, consultants and policy advisers) have increasing and shared concerns amongst themselves and with private sector/corporate counterparts about many aspects of their working lives. Time pressures related to obsessions with the 'bottom line' abound – even to the point of the temptation to engage in 'risky' behaviour. Corporate, public sector and political scandals related to greed and corruption are not uncommon.

It is little wonder then that in the UK and the USA, for example, public trust has fallen from 55 per cent in 1960 to under 35 per cent in 1998 (Layard, 2005). In 1952, 50 per cent of Americans answered yes to the question whether they believed that people lead 'as good lives as they used to' but in 1998, only 25 per cent said yes (Layard, 2005). These changing attitudes are accompanied by an increase of crime rate (the economy grows but does not necessarily increase social harmony) and erosion of privacy – for example, the UK's November 2004 controversial proposals for a biometric ID card scheme.

Losses of dignity have been accompanied by 'losses of authenticity' (Namie and Namie, 2000; Antoun, 2001), which occur when our inner sense of satisfaction and wholeness wanes. The result is often addiction to consumption of either luxury goods or simply food, with consequent obesity problems. Overconsumption in turn leads to overproduction and can detract from sustainability in both environmental and human terms and implies horrendous waste problems. At the same time, child poverty in both rich and poor economies continues to rise (UNICEF, 2000).

This alienating world contains other elements. At the level of coping with increasing global conflicts, there has been institutional undermining or bypassing. This has taken the form of subordination of the development of community to the military in conflict zones to create the so-called 'development-security' complex. Such arrangements have clearly not been working in Iraq, where all humanitarian workers have had to pull out. There has been an active sidelining of UN bodies and, in the case of the World Bank, the installation of a former warmonger as president. Short-termism dominates with little long-term strategic policy thinking. Hysterical political leadership dominates major electoral fora, with fundamentalist politics on the rampage. In the US, public administration has been infected by new public management (NPM) pseudo-thinking and core value displacement.

In public administration in particular, the reduction of personnel, the need to master more complex technologies and loss of discretionary time in order to perform efficiently, has left employees demotivated if not burned out (Brandt, 1996). Public servants, untied by the ideal of disinterested public service, are increasingly being politicized (Kakabadse *et al.*, 2003). The noble ideal of a self-sacrificially public servant with qualities found in Greenleaf's (1973) 'servant leaders' has all but disappeared in an increasingly corporate, politicized and self-serving system that goes under the name of meritocracy and customer orientation. The changes we are facing in the new millennium come as much from those who reject dialogue, tolerance and humility in favour of power and fundamentalism. Scholars and practitioners call for humanistic values in leadership, but too often the values adopted are of a utilitarian nature glued to narrower goals of achieving higher efficiency and the creation of shareholder wealth (Ramsden, 1991).

Increased compartmentalization of contemporary life into distinctly separate domains, such as work, family, religion and social obligations, inevitably leads to further fragmentation and, in turn, engenders a haze around personal meaning, identity and purpose (Fairholm, 1997; Mitroff and Denton, 1999).

14.2 The relationship of spirituality and workplace

In a workplace that has become insecure and alienating, the need for development on the spiritual side has arisen in a number of contexts; the displacement of core values has thrown into relief the need for renewed search for higher purpose. Spiritual need may be seen at various levels in relation to higher purpose and core value displacement, especially to promote:

- Harmony between values and technology: dissonances between desires/ desirability and possibilities.
- Connectedness with others.
- Eco-efficiency: delivering more value with less environmental burden.

The options for dealing with spiritual need in insecure workplaces and alienating environments include a number of key elements:

- Integration of faith, family and professional life; for example, reintegration of self through engagement, by finding an appropriate way for each individual to understand the greater whole (world) and the ways in which each can contribute.
- Development of a corporate culture that reflects faith and values through, for example, an authentication process – becoming more genuine, open and non-manipulative.
- Exercise of beneficial influence on society at large. This requires will – a drive to lead a spiritual life and persistence in working towards a spiritual goal.

For those involved in or with public sector reform, the last element is particularly important as it refers to leveraging for change. An eye to 'externalities' is vital. Otherwise religion, as Cowley (2004) puts it, simply becomes a personal hobby!

It becomes an ingredient of a 'feel good' (or 'feel better') factor. In taking that step further than just feeling good, related practical issues/challenges face us:

- How do ethics and values grow and how they can be nurtured or rekindled? What is the role of spiritual dialogue in these regards?
- How to instil values in those who have no faith, or mixed heritages, to build on? How can reflexive examination of one's heritage – inward critical inquiry or spiritual journey, deciding what should be discarded and what should be grown, be encouraged?
- What is the role of Anglo-Saxon type public management and business schools in developing 'reflexive practitioners'? Should we be teaching reflexive inquiry (rather than just positivist research) and be facilitating the development of others?
- How can we practically encourage tapping into other schools of thought (e.g. the French) where there is likewise a preoccupation with how to integrate the 'dedans' and the 'dehors' – internal spiritual development with external behaviour and practice?

These are central questions in the leveraging for a spiritual betterment of society.

Spirituality in religion

There exist many spiritual and religious traditions. From a religious perspective, faith has ranged in its behavioural manifestations from fanaticism to generating humility. In Western Europe, the private–public demarcation is often cited in distinguishing religious belief and practice. Thus, spirituality can be seen as the private/individual feelings, thoughts, experiences and behaviours that arise from the search for meaning of the sacred (Schulman, 2004). Religion, on the other hand, is seen as an organized, structured set of spiritual beliefs and practices with specific symbols or ideas about divinity or divinities (Zaehner, 2001).

It is, nevertheless, both the 'inner' and 'outer' aspects of spirituality in religion that are essential to its survival as an institution and social organizer, especially in its Judaean-Christian and Islamic varieties (Table 14.1). To appreciate a religion one has to pay equal attention to its inner, less visible aspect (i.e. ideas, beliefs, hopes and expectations) and to the outer or more visible side (e.g. life and practice-customs, morals and ritual). Appreciation of other religions has not often been the case in a world where religion remains a potentially divisive force and fuel for disharmony and misunderstanding. In this connexion, there is also a clear contrast between illuminating faith and blinding faith. We argue for the need to reconceptualize religion to make it more inclusive and more disposed to inter-faith dialogue. In the UK, many workplaces are multicultural and multi-religious, accommodating both employees and management. This can of itself create tension – for example, Quakers,

Table 14.1 Spirituality vs religion

Spirituality	Religion
Feeling (of *connectedness* with a divine or large universe) or a state of mind or openness to things which are not verifiable	The way that spiritual thoughts (state of mind) are codified into religious/social law
Personal	Institutionalized
Intuitive contemplation	Dogmatic contemplation
Awareness of self and impact made on others	Obedience to religious laws (i.e. liturgy) and rituals
Inherited genetically or evolutionary (i.e. nature vs nurture)	Socially and culturally constructed
Uplifting	Uplifting but open to institutionalized corruption and potentially dangerous

Source: Compiled by the authors.

Buddhists, Jesuits and Islamists alike stress group religion and belonging. At the same time, there are also some negatives in, say, the Protestant extremes. Calvinist positions in particular reinforce very individualist and competitive work ethics.

Some of these dynamics are important to the development of ways forward. In terms of more integrated approaches to the search for meaning, we introduce the Woodstock/Paternoster approach, a method combining meditation and study: of the written word (Gospel) for guidance on understanding and dealing with situations in everyday life. The journey to becoming and willingness to explore oneself is key – as is subsequent institutional support for the same through group mechanisms. Collaborative inquiry, dialogue and engagement are essential elements in building spiritual community.

As a group phenomenon, religion shares similarities with other social groupings of belief or faith, belonging and salvation (Figure 14.1). Religious groupings are guided by their beliefs of the truth or divine. Faith means either belief in the mission of a certain individual such as prophet, incarnate god or religious group or assent to a particular interpretation of existence, which enjoys the authority of antiquity or of one or more human sages (Zaehner, 2001). Faith in a perennial god expresses itself in practical worship, or in a given interpretation of experience found in its practical application in the schooling of mind and body, all in an effort to realize the spiritual state that according to this interpretation of existence is man's spiritual goal (Zaehner, 2001). In Eastern religions, this effort is called 'realization' or 'emancipation', and by this is meant enjoyment of an eternal mode of existence here and now (Zaehner, 2001).

The desire to 'belong' is present to a greater or lesser degree in all religions and may manifest itself in varying ways (Zaehner, 2001). In its simplest form, belonging involves being an integral member of a religious society (Figure 14.1).

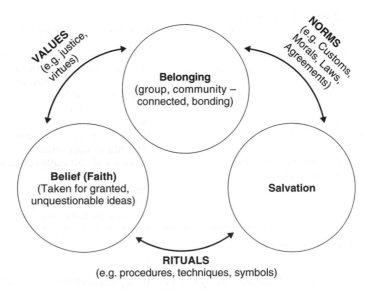

Figure 14.1 Principles of theological philosophy: religion
Source: Kakabadse and Kakabadse, 2004.

A further universal desire is that for salvation (or deliverance/escape), present in all religions but strongest within Indian Hindu traditions and least prominent in Islam (Zaehner, 2001). It is on this matter, namely the realization of salvation, that religious groupings so profoundly disagree. For example, Christians seek salvation from the bondage of initial sin. The essence of Christian salvation is to enter into a life of unity with God and with one's fellows – a life chartered by a sense of freedom from the domination of sin and by a certainty of resurrection to eternal life (Zaehner, 2001). The Buddhist, on the other hand, seeks to free himself from the suffering of egocentric existence (*samsara*), whilst through Islam (meaning 'to surrender' to God's will), Sufis seek unification with the divine (Zaehner, 2001; Bayat and Jamnia, 2001). Thus Islamic practices for attaining salvation through different forms of prayers prescribed by Divine Law (Shari'ah) can significantly differ in Sufi practice for attaining salvation through complete devotion to God and the abandonment of earthly pleasures (Bayat and Jamnia, 2001). In Cabbalist Judaism, salvation is envisaged through unification with the Divine.

Religious institutionalization and opportunity for abuse

Organized religion has the ability to either enhance or taint its epiphany. Depending on the strictness of rituals and strength of its beliefs, religion can take on either of two perspectives. First, it can be fundamentalist (i.e. rigid,

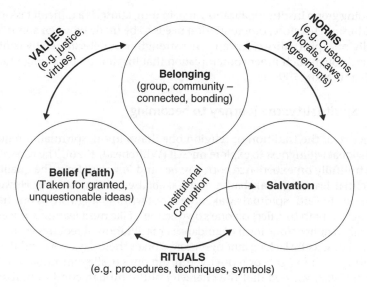

Figure 14.2   Principles of theological philosophy/religion: institutional corruption
Source: Kakabadse and Kakabadse, 2004.

dogmatic) where literal doctrines are not open to interpretation, where 'right' and 'wrong' are clearly defined and individual behaviour is viewed as 'good' or 'evil'. Second, it can take a more 'reasonable' or interpretative approach (e.g. 'Talmudic', 'Anglican', 'Episcopal') or viewpoint. From the fundamentalist perspective (often in response to a sense of embattled alienation in the midst of the prevailing culture), the fundamental and unchanging founding principles of the religion provide a certain 'wall of virtue'. This is felt to protect identity. As such, this wall can be erected against alien religions, especially those seen as 'liberal' and 'modernized'. Where used to harness innate spirituality for such organizational purposes, religion is clearly open to misuse (Chu *et al.*, 2004). Perils indeed abound. Through ritual, religion builds boundaries around 'us', namely the religious community and 'them', those outside the community (Figure 14.2). This, in turn, leads to the 'exclusion' of others or their 'colonization', and attempts to convert everyone who does not share the groups' religious belief. Intolerant misuse of religion can also fuel wars (e.g. those initiated by 'born-again' Protestants, Haredi Judaists, Jama'at Islamists). Despite their doctrinal and ritualistic differences, fundamentalists in Judaism, Christianity, Islam and other religions are united by a common worldview that anchors all of life in the authority of the sacred and a shared ethos that expresses itself through outrage at the pace and extent of modern secularization, which may take effect through violent protectionism (Antoun, 2001).

Avoiding group institutionalization and, in turn, abuse, is a difficult task, even in Buddhism. Therefore, differentiation needs to be made between spirituality and religion. Spirituality offers an inner strength not determined by context, and it is through such inner contemplation that inspiration for change can be provided (Brandt, 1996).

14.3   Spirituality: the journey to becoming

Irrespective of the tradition or religion one draws upon, spirituality requires an individual willingness to explore oneself (Whitehead, 1926). The capacity to reflect fruitfully on experience both *post hoc* and *in vivo* defines the quality of experiential learning (Kakabadse and Kakabadse, 2003a, 2003b). However, the journey towards spiritual awakening is not without anguish, as one has to find inner strength to reflect on one's own actions. Like most learning processes, it typically requires some form of guidance or facilitation. It requires creation of space and time sadly lacking amongst professionals these days as a condition for generating fresh insights or rediscovering old ones (Csikszentmihalyi, 1990).

Tillich (1963) warned that the character of the human condition, like the character of all life, is ambiguous and that a person or a nation, or both, that is not aware of these ambiguities lacks maturity. The need for understanding oneself is necessary in order to deal with ambiguity. In comparing early Roman and Greek religious rituals, Mommsen (1958) noted that when Romans worshipped, they raised their eyes to Heaven during prayers in contemplation, whilst Greeks veiled their heads, as their prayers were centred on reflexion (i.e. reflexion 'on action' and 'in action', which requires reflexivity). The truly spiritual journey requires both reflexivity and contemplation. Through reflexivity one gains insights into one's own motivation, and the impact made on others, as well as an awareness of the impact others have made on oneself. Through reflexivity and contemplation one can learn and discern from previous experiences, develop the capacity to rethink boundaries and actions that have an impact on others and self, and in so doing minimize deleterious prejudices and closed thinking.

Sense making: building spiritual community

Because of associations with mysticism (i.e. more esoteric religious varieties) – Kabbalist (or 'inherited tradition') in Judaism and Sufism in Islam, amongst others – the application of techniques of self-awareness needs careful attention. Less helpful are the purely mechanical or nihilistic. It is necessary to examine oneself in a continuous fashion. Applied to workplace issues, this implies the need for a platform for exploration and integration of self within the workplace, which in turn requires meaningful and purposive community.

Alienation in the workplace has long been recognised in modern times, including issues of values – leading to both self and organizational destructiveness (Jaques, 1965). Buber (1937) sees the need for establishment of authentic community as a process – combining individual spiritual growth with the building of spiritual community. It is a 'between', involving mutual correction of interactions between individuals and groups and a consequent enrichment of diverse overlapping spiritual perspectives (Buber, 1937). Each person will evolve in his or her own idiosyncratic way of unfolding. In spiritual engagement, each individual interacts in a mutually supportive manner. Dialogue facilitates or creates an engagement that provides the forum for complementary kinds of spiritual opening and co-creation. An example of a spiritual journey that aims to build authentic community is presented in the next section.

14.4 The need for spiritual engagement: the Paternoster Pilot Group initiative

In many countries, there is growing professional concern over roles in international public sector management, whether those of policy makers/policy advisers, administrators or consultants. Growing numbers of people employed in many sectors feel an unprecedented crisis of identity, integrity and even alienation (Donkin, 2001). In international development, institutions often find themselves subordinated to the military in ever-increasing conflict situations – the 'development–security complex' (Duffield, 2000). Locally, the global tendency is for public administration to be re-engineered on the basis of so-called market values (New Public Administration or NPA). At the same time, private sector management models are hardly exemplary. Corporate greed and scandals proliferate in a world featuring increasing poverty extremes, the resurgence of old or the advent of new diseases (e.g. HIV/Aids) and environmental degradation).

A spiritual engagement initiative is taking place on both sides of the Atlantic. Faith-based discussion groups have been formed amongst business executives and professionals in the USA (e.g. the Woodstock Business Conference promoted from Georgetown University) and more recently in the City of London at the St Paul's Cathedral Institute (the Paternoster Pilot Group). These aim to develop a more meaningful work orientation, the rediscovery of higher purpose and its relevance to restoration of ethical business and public service values, and better integration of personal and social domains.

Ideas behind Paternoster

The Paternoster Pilot Group took its inspiration from the Woodstock Business Conference in the USA,[2] which developed some fundamental questions raised by a group of business leaders in the course of three 'Business and Vocation' conferences organized in the 1990s by the Woodstock Theological Centre at

---

[2] Paternoster Business Conference, Affirming the Relevance of Religious Faith to Business Practice, St Paul's Institute, 2004, mimeo – www.stpauls.co.uk/institute

Georgetown University, Washington, DC. Two fundamental questions were raised, namely:

> *'What difference does it make and for whom, if business leadership is seen as a call for excellence, a call for God's will?*
>
> *How does a business run by a committed Christian differ from any other?'*

No easy answers were apparent, given that there are many gaps between the world of faith and the realities of the market. However, by means of regular meetings and reflexions, a path was piloted for exploring the practical day-to-day issues confronting busy executives against a background of scripture readings and with the stimulus of topical articles. A feasibility study was conducted in the UK, including interviews with industry management, and preparatory, planning and orientation meetings were held at St Paul's Cathedral with the participation of interested clergy from City-based churches and with lay members of the business community, one of whom served as facilitator at the pilot meetings.

At the Cathedral Church of the City of London, on average about 12 members of the pilot group were invited from a cross-section of City firms in law, finance and management, as well as one of the authors of this paper as an interested regular member of the congregation of the Cathedral. Perhaps unsurprisingly, in view of the social structure of the City business community, the group contained only one female participant (apart from the Institute Secretary). A facilitator was appointed from amongst the group (again male) and a preparatory workshop held with Heythrop Theology College (London University), along with clergy from other City-based Anglican churches interested in the pilot. The Chancellor of St Paul's and Director of the Institute served as Chaplain and summed up each meeting at the end, and the Institute Secretary prepared a one page diary of key learning points for circulation prior to the next meeting.

14.5 The pilot methodology: participative inquiry

Considering that spirituality in action is a dynamic process of individual engagement in a particular environment, the impact can only be assessed retrospectively. Reflexion on previous action is also useful in understanding the level of discretion available and its utilization – the scope for influence and change. Thus, in line with the study objective of accessing and understanding the meanings attached to an individual's developmental experience, the purpose here is not to replicate common sense but to explicate it (Silverman, 1992). By moving from the descriptive (albeit very rich) level to the explanatory, it is possible to throw significant light on the phenomena of spiritual development.

Meeting format

The format of each pilot meeting (organized with a breakfast from 07:45 to 08:45 every second Tuesday of each month) comprised:

- Self-introductions (to build sense of community);
- Opening prayer (by the Chaplain, acknowledging God as a source of strength);
- Reminder of the mission statement (to keep focus);
- Scripture reading by a member, followed by five minutes of silent reflexion and then a discussion;
- Summing up by the Chaplain;
- Closing prayer.

Between meetings, the Secretary circulated the diary of learning points of the last meeting along with discussion questions, bible reading and accompanying articles pertinent to the theme. These were prepared by Heythrop College (Theology Faculty of London University).

Themes

The following themes were successively addressed by the monthly pilot meetings:

- Business as vocation;
- Leadership – to unleash the human spirit;
- Creating a corporate culture consistent with Judaeo-Christian values;
- Discernment and decision;
- Wealthy business in a poor world;
- 'Morally non-negotiables'.

Approach

The emphasis through the study was on the means of awakening and developing reflexive and discerning practitioners and the kinds of spiritual resources that they may be able to be drawn upon in dealing with professional work situations in the post-modern world (Table 14.2). Attention was paid to ways in which, perhaps surprisingly for some, change management processes in public and private sectors alike can find enrichment in faith-based practices and texts.

The approach taken was to ensure consistency between categorization of the experiences analysed and the personal meanings attached to the same. Under such an 'interpretivist' approach, the emphasis is to avoid broad generalization (Miles and Huberman, 1996) and rather to tease out subjective construction of repeated situations or encounters as the basis for yielding relevant and useful insights (Prasad, 1993). Open coding for data categorization was used for data analysis (Miles and Huberman, 1996). Six broad themes emerged as a

Table 14.2   Operationalization of Paternoster inquiry

Characteristics	Assumption	Operationalization
Ontology	Constructivism: multiple realities emergent from participants	Ensuring consistency between categorization of experiences and real personal meanings attached to them.
Extended epistemology	Interpretative: inquirer is also a participant; meaning is value relevant	Inquirers (i.e. pilot convenors) used readings, reflection and discussion and observations to capture participants' interpretations of their experience.
Adopted paradigm	Participative	Focus on how participants of Paternoster Pilot Group perceive the experience of developing their spiritual awareness.
Inquiring logic	Inductive	Attention to the spiritual concepts used by the participants in relation to workplace encounters and situations.
Inquiry question	Open-ended questions	Use of guided in-depth reflexivity and discussions.
Inquiry focus	Uncovering principles adhered/ aspired to by participants within their practices[1]	Knowledge co-creation for change within individual practice and context.

Note: [1] On a broader scale, how are core values conceived in terms of the need to be perceived as active principles rather than passive labels?
Source: Based on Kakabadse and Kakabadse (2005) and pilot data.

result of data analysis, namely (a) group commitment; (b) enhanced perceptiveness; (c) confidence building; (d) integrative potential; (e) utility of spiritual resources; and (f) insights relative to decision making, bring influence to bear on making a difference. Such an interpretative approach was selected as being most suitable for undertaking a pilot study of this kind.

The main source of insight for this study was participant observation by one of the authors and the institute secretary's minutes of the meetings (Van Velsor, 1998). In order to obtain raised awareness, reflexivity needs to be brought into the open. It then becomes a *transparent* reflexivity, a state beyond privately held 'taken-for-granted' assumptions. It has been noted that *opaque* reflexivity, if left unattended, may become *alienated* reflexivity (Lamo de Espinosa, 1990); under the Paternoster approach, sharing of privately held assumptions was encouraged through guided readings and discussions.

14.6 Reflexion on the discussion questions and materials

Interpretation of the group's reflexive experience and learning emerged at three focal levels of contemplation and debate, namely individual, corporate and social meaning (public policy). This learning and its implication for practice is presented in Tables 14.3, 14.4 and 14.5.

At the *individual* level and in pursuit of more vocation in one's professionalism, learning from 'trying' appeared important in terms of both the example of good practice as well as the developmental impact on self.[3] At the same time, subtlety of approach to core values was required and the use of all one's gifts in a venture fraught with constraints – especially time and other pressures, and involving the dangers of escapism and short-termism and the deadweight legacy of hierarchy. Reflexion on the concepts of 'calling' and 'vocation' is tied to specific notions of service, where elders are 'servant elders' (Greenleaf, 1973). Leaders who achieve a deep internalization of noble purpose become transformational agents (Kouzes and Posner, 1993; Congar *et al.*, 1998). This can lead the way to building organizations as 'secular communities' where people of all faiths (and no faith) can flourish and achieve the full potential of their endowments in a sustainable manner. Such organizations cease to be simply a place of organized work where individuals are engaged in instrumental tasks.

Despite the pitfalls and challenges to discernment and well-founded decisions, spiritual resources available to the individual were equally, if not more abundant: daily prayer, faith-based texts, role models and, most importantly, wisdom. Responding in the 'right way' with little time to think ultimately rested on virtue and character. In his Nichomachean Ethics, Aristotle warned against personal excess and highlighted the value of temperance in human behaviour and how to enhance human virtues. Nevertheless, in knowing where and when to draw the line (the 'morally non-negotiables'), there were practical aids – learning ways of anticipating effects of actions on others, not separating work from morality, recognizing moral outcomes of one's action and the role of codes of conduct (*in extremis*, backed by whistle blowing) at both corporate and public policy and administration levels. Self-awareness and 'mindfulness' through cooperative and reflective practice are useful guides to individuals following such paths (Kakabadse and Kakabadse, 2003b).

We move now to the *corporate* level and issues of how vocationally-oriented and discerning professionals can bring influence to bear in group decision-making situations, embracing ability to influence corporate culture, practice and norms. Practical implications stand out in three areas: mindset,

---

[3]At the individual level, the pilot group felt that there was an important practical role for *mentoring* on the job, especially vis-à-vis the next generation.

Table 14.3 Meetings with a focus on the individual

Discussion topic	Learning points	Implications for practice
Business as vocation	• vocation and calling: the 'salt' and the 'light' in the search for replenishment and spiritual strengthening • work and vocation: making choices and being tested on the job, often under pressure and in alienating circumstances • visibility in one's priorities and how one treats people • time perspectives: taking a long term perspective which goes beyond the short termism of market based 'values' • occupation vs profession: the 'excellence' trap – finding ways out of professional meaninglessness	• as with all effective change management, the approach has to be subtle rather than preaching or sermonizing (light can blind) • how to find the time and resist mechanical escapism: testing the spirit with real work involving gritty choices and being informed • good practice shines in all organizations, especially public ones when featuring humanity, impartiality and explanation, as well as well informed decisions • in the absence of fundamental lack of clarity about where we are all rushing to and in common with all major religions in thinking long (and ultimate) term, the role of core values in strategic planning • the need to decompartmentalize and achieve better integration between personal values and professional practice – expressing our giftedness in the workplace for higher purpose
Discernment and decision making	• the role of wisdom: its resources • complementary resources aiding judgement • characteristics of wisdom and its creativity as a gift of God • how to bring wisdom into a consensus culture	• because of limited time for long contemplation of each decision, having trust in faith-based texts and role models when confronting conflicting factors/influences • reliance on the heart and prayer; drawing on the wisdom of elders and the community

	• its demonstrability; stress on communication, honesty, listening, consultation and boldness; and hopefulness (belief in humanity) • in group decision-making situations, enhancing ability to influence culture, practice and norms via character and conduct • role of mentoring in affecting culture, especially the next generation	
'Moral non-negotiables'	• unchallenged abuse of public office in the absence of moral ethos/structures • the big and small personal, corporate and policy choices (equally) • conflict and responsibilities: balancing duties to self, others, corporate and 'higher' levels • role of wisdom: having integrity, virtue and character to respond in right way with little time to think	• role of whistle blowing in enforcing accountability on the part of devious leaders • role of honesty and respect in policy commitments, negotiations and in treating 'juniors' • having the courage of convictions – don't leave morals outside the office door and know when to quit • developing ways of anticipating effects of actions on others: how to interpret and apply in work situations the Christian non-negotiable (the love ethic)

Table 14.4   Meetings with focus on corporations

Discussion topic	Learning points	Implications for practice
Leadership – to unleash the human spirit	• the good shepherd as a leadership model: benefits of a caring model in terms of results • sacrifice and service: good managers share risks with staff • relationships and seeing values played out: importance of being seen as genuine rather than just PR to extract output • unspoken concerns and risks of disloyalty	• role of meditation in dealing with causality of time pressures in adopting a caring approach; possible other tool kits • overcoming increasing aversion to risk as managers age • development of *mindsets* to resonate with faith-related precepts – opening up and taking time to develop staff as individuals • importance of professional collaborative networks to sustain outspoken, innovative individual managers
Creating a corporate culture consistent with *Judaeo*-Christian values	• accountability for the use of our talents in this world • role of codes of conduct/modelling values • community and public interest: *workplaces* are also communities where values are taught and lived • importance of commitment to process and action	• going the extra mile and trying to change organizations rather than just doing a 'good job' • more fundamental aspect of embedding values 'within' rather than imposing from 'without' or above (except by good example) • ensuring personal and short-term interest do not take precedence over collective interest and principles of fairness • confronting positively above challenges through placing premium on strengths/ opportunities

values and leadership of change ('to unleash the human spirit'). These areas resonate with Greenleaf's (1973) notion of 'servant leaders' in terms of values and behaviours.

In terms of mindsets, there was a recognition of the need to develop minds that resonate with faith-related precepts – opening up and taking time to develop staff as individuals. This was not easy and should be confronted positively through placing a premium on strengths and opportunities rather than otherwise. However, if the desire to transform business in order that it

Table 14.5   Meetings with focus on public policy

Discussion topic	Learning points	Implications for practice
Wealthy business in a poor world	• justice and wealth: spiritual well-being and perils – responsible wealth in a poor world and meaningful encounters • corporate and individual responsibility at different levels – from shareholders, partners, stakeholders and society – to the Creator himself • parochialism, internationalism and tsunami	• developing the giving self (rather than pursuit of (potentially corrupting) wealth *per se*, and use of gifts such as advocacy in speaking to and for the poor and voiceless in public policy processes • importance of going beyond tokenism in corporate charity (which may in fact be costless, since it is giving away others' money whilst buying political influence in public policy realms) • whilst there is poverty also in our own country, the immediate humanitarian response to the tsunami crisis as a reaffirmation of humanity's sense of goodwill and concern for others – yet the financial corporate world had to be shamed into waiving its charges on donations via credit card

Source: Compiled by the authors.

evolves in a human way whilst also effectively providing for global needs (Lakeland, 2003) is embraced, then this can be achieved.

Regarding values, adopting a more caring approach and ensuring that personal and short-term interest do not take precedence over the collective interest, and principles of fairness, were key values embedded 'within' rather than being imposed from 'without' or from above (except by example). These resonate with the notions of holistic strategy and spiritual leadership advanced by several writers (Fairholm, 1997; Mitroff and Denton, 1999; Korac-Kakabadse et al., 2002).

In respect of change to bring about all of the foregoing, it was important to overcome the well-known increasing aversion to risk as managers age, and to go the 'extra mile' in trying to change the organization rather than myopically concentrating on 'the job'. In these matters, there was a key role for professional networks (e.g. Woodstock and Paternoster) to sustain outspoken and innovative managers as well as educational institutions (Kakabadse and Kakabadse, 2003a).

Finally, at the level of *public policy and administration*, how do relatively wealthy professionals in corporate and government settings conduct themselves in a poor world – both internationally and domestically, and both materially and conceptually? In a world where the poor tend to be voiceless, development of the giving self was fundamental and called for full use of gifts such as advocacy skills vis-à-vis the voiceless in the public policy process. Just as public policy can be less than honest, so 'charitable' giving from the corporate sector is often far from genuine. Donations to charity do not usually come from the management's or partners' pockets but from the corporate coffers and with considerations and benefits of tax and political influence (Porter, 2003). Whilst there is also poverty in developed economies, the immediate humanitarian response to the 2004 tsunami crisis was a reaffirmation of humanity's sense of goodwill and concern for others – yet the financial corporate world had to be shamed into waiving its charges on donations via credit cards. It seems, therefore, that there is a strong need to realign institutions – public and corporate – with the groundswell of humanity.

An overall conclusion, particularly in terms of politics and administration, may be that we tend to compartmentalize too much – as illustrated by a divorce of policy design from implementation. The neat distinction or apparent separation between the two is highly problematic. The real issue is the use of professional resources for higher purposes, and the need for integration and overcoming the false dichotomy between public and private. This also raises uncomfortable issues: those of loyalty to firm or state versus loyalty to a higher purpose. Dealing with unethical and uncommitted politicians or unjust wars are real dilemmas at the highest levels of public administration (Kakabadse *et al.*, 2003).

How are civil servants prepared to handle difficult situations where conflicts of interest arise? Hopefully not in ways that involve government scientists apparently committing suicide over political lies perpetrated in the so-called 'war against terror'. In the public and private sectors alike, management development programmes (pre-entry and in-service) have their role in orientation (or reorientation) of staff. But again, there is the issue of risk. All organizations witness the need sometimes to give voice to unspoken concerns. However, this can involve taking risks in the perilous sea of being seen as disloyal. Civil services have a typical predilection for 'the safe pair of hands' (as the UK saying goes), when recruiting new employees.

The following lessons for public sector management facing its current challenges are particularly apposite and by no means unknown in change management:

- where resources are scarce but challenges immense; having the means to work in optimistic mode, i.e. seeing the strengths rather than the weakness or the potential rather than the limits, and ever widening the range of options;

* reflexiveness and having the ability to imagine oneself in the position of others and enter into dialogue; and
* developing the habit of drawing lessons. Although everyday decision making is typically a rushed, pressurized affair, long-term decision making at the level of policy can and should have the space to be informed by values.

As professionals in this disenfranchised world, how much is enough in terms of personal need (rather than how to have more)? How do we advance beyond vague compassion to commitment and seeing the other as a person and not as a work instrument or 'beneficiary' or 'target group'? How do we put humanity back into public services? How do we avoid forgetting that public services are especially for the poor, elderly and ill? What is the role of the spiritual retreat for workers to nurture appropriate mindsets and resources in these connexions? What is the role of reflexion, about the impact of organizations, both public and private, on society and ensuring the economy – and that the private sector is not a substitute for government responsibility?

14.7   Reflexions on the outcomes of the pilot meetings

The module on Discernment and Decision Making provided especially important insights into process – a key element in terms of practice and action. Aspects of particular interest included: the taking of tough decisions, exploring options and impacts, 'thinking the unthinkable' and the roles of judgement, experience and mentoring. Some of the readings were helpful in terms of scenario building.

Other especially insightful modules were on 'Business as Vocation' and 'Moral Non-Negotiables'. Relating work to higher purpose is all part of the search for meaning, a central underlying concern of this chapter, coupled with the issues of integration and influence or *how to make a difference in the workplace through drawing on spiritual resources*. Fundamentally, one might ask whether one is in the right job in terms of ability to be honest, tell the truth and take a stand, draw the line and blow the whistle, or to exert beneficial influence within the organization (its corporate culture) as well vis-à-vis its clients or those served or impacted. Ability to integrate the personal (spiritual) with the public sphere or workplace is a further source of enhanced meaning. Similar messages can be found in the leadership literature (Fairholm, 1997; Kakabadse and Kakabadse, 2003a, 2003b).

Many of the modules had great potential contribution to meeting the key challenge of what Tudway and Pascal (2005) see as how best to give expression to core values in the public sphere. Module 2 on Leadership raised relevant issues of style (caring and enabling), the imperatives of sacrifice and service, relationships, mindsets, risk taking, trust and codes of conduct. Indeed, there was consensus on most of the foregoing as having equal applicability across sectors. So, in the search for meaning and the vocational dimensions of professionalism, agreement on key values such as standards, honesty, humanity, equity, service and accountability was encouraging. As Tudway and Pascal (2005) also argue, the challenge is how to bring about on a broader scale a change in how such core values are conceived. They need to be perceived as active principles rather than merely passive labels, and that this can only be realized if administrators and corporate managers ponder, for instance, the process of being accountable to others and what this implies in daily activity.

To what extent did the piloting of the Paternoster Business Conference in the UK indicate a potential for dealing with the concerns expressed at the outset of this chapter? What areas were identified for strengthening and improvement? What are the next steps? This analysis also takes into account a group self-evaluation, facilitated by Heythrop College (Theology Faculty of London University), with all the pilot participants at a session at the end of the six pilots. It identified a number of positive outcomes as a result of the pilot meetings at the St Paul's Institute and these are summarized in the final section of this chapter.

Positive outcomes of pilot meetings

First, the very establishment of the group and the regular and active attendance by members was seen as an important commitment to building spiritual reflexiveness into one's life in the workplace and elsewhere (Kakabadse and Kakabadse, 2003b). Likewise, the evaluation of the pilot meetings was seen as a further milestone on the path of spiritual development.

Second, participants indicated that results were already being felt: they had begun to notice dissonances of the kind they had not clearly seen before: shortfalls in the required standards of honesty, equity, service, proper conduct and justice; frequent absence of humanity, caring, sacrifice, trust and taking responsibility.

Third, pilots had given greater confidence in ways of applying one's faith and in validating what one is doing at present. Although the time pressure factor was universally recognized as a major constraint, meetings had contributed to the development of beneficial habits, dispositions and frame of mind.

Fourth, they had also contributed in some cases to better integration on the broader spiritual front, connecting with and enriching parallel church participation in terms of helping to identify synergies with Paternoster business ethics in Sunday sermons and Bible readings. In other words, participants were enabled to discern both dissonances and resonances not apparent hitherto.

Fifth, in terms of other spiritual resources, it was felt that the biblical readings were perhaps the most effective in terms of their greater incisiveness, authoritativeness and often a more pithy and hard-hitting character. More academic supporting readings tended to be prone to the usual discounting in the hands of smart professionals.

Sixth, several insights were found to be of special value. In particular, the module on Discernment and Decision Making provided important insights into process – a key element in terms of practice and action. Aspects of particular interest included: the taking of tough decisions, exploring options and impacts, thinking the unthinkable and the roles of judgement, experience and mentoring. Some of the readings were helpful in terms of scenario building.

Lessons to be drawn, and the future

In terms of resources, a balance may need to be struck, on the one hand, between biblical reference points and, on the other, supporting (often academic) readings. At the same time, the temptation to see the groups as purely Bible study needs minimizing. Pedagogically, Paternoster groups are issue-oriented and the Bible serves as a springboard for reflexion on how to deal with for example 'non-negotiables', how to act as servant leaders, to influence change and to deal with dilemmas such as being a relatively wealthy (financially speaking) professional in a poor world.

A lesson concerns the need to enhance the environment for learning and knowledge creation. This can be done through pursuit of the full cycle of collaborative inquiry. The latter comprises four critical elements: knowledge creation – experiential, presentational, propositional, and practical. Particularly important is practical knowledge and the application of newly gained insights (Charaniya and Walsh, 2001; Kakabadse and Kakabadse, 2003b). Time permitting, the US Woodstock approach might be tried under which each meeting reflects back on the previous one and participants share about how they have tried or been unsuccessful in applying faith back at the workplace and what the reasons and results were. Such a process would, however, have to be managed well in order to avoid any 'confessional' atmospheres with negative or dampening effects (Kakabadse and Kakabadse, 2003b).

A further lesson is the need to strengthen understanding of process. It was felt that the core task was to ponder on application rather than biblical exegesis.

In terms of the future, it was felt that there were common problems and shared concerns amongst the City of London's professionals. Thus, initial impact of the Paternoster Business Conference in the UK is proving, subject to finer tuning, to be an effective instrument for collaborative inquiry, dialogue and engagement (Kakabadse and Kakabadse, 2003a, 2003b). It has brought professionals together with shared concerns and values across different sectors of the professions. As a group, it is a commitment in itself, a willingness to share and also to evaluate its sharing as a means of further spiritual development. If one adds to this the impressive display of humanity at the time of the tsunami disaster, one can indeed detect what Cowley (2004) refers to as 'areas of communality across a wide spectrum of groups'. However, as indicated in the UK by initial corporate ambiguities over tsunami, paralleled by the outstripping of public funds by individual citizen contributions, there is nevertheless some way to go at the level of the whole spectrum of public and corporate management to overcome managerial 'metaphysical blindness' (Schumacher, 1973).

The experience of the Paternoster Pilot Group represents an exemplary, if modest, first step forward in the integration of individual professionals with a religious (mainly Anglican) orientation into a broader spiritual community. The essence of the latter is to seek personal purpose and a path within the framework of a worldview, through engaging the whole person in social dealings at work and through better connexion between faith and practice thereat. Small, but profound yet subtle steps along this path have included enhancing personal Christian identity at work; building confidence as a Christian practitioner; providing space to reflect and to acquire the conviction that it is possible to make a difference as a result of prayer.

Next steps with Paternoster include the establishment of more pilots (one has just started at Westminster Cathedral) as well as interdenominational groups (such as with the Methodists from the Wesley Chapel at City Road, London). Some downstream issues include expanding dialogue with non Judaeo-Christian faiths and cultures. Inter-faith dialogue, through enabling group experience sharing in life matters of deep common concern, can provide a vehicle for building relations, sense making and issue-oriented collaborative learning (Charania and Walsh, 2001; Kakabadse and Kakabadse, 2003b). This would have particular applicability in the UK where the workforce has become multi-ethnic, and public services increasingly deal with citizens from other cultural and religious backgrounds.[4]

In a sense, that will be the most difficult challenge. It is one thing to assemble and make progress with a somewhat culturally homogeneous group which the Cathedral confines. It is another to reach out to other faiths, non-faiths and communities. However, this is the global challenge of the third Millennium, and it must be pursued at home before embarking on a voyage elsewhere. Focusing on the similarities present in spiritual values across the range of religious creeds, rather than on narrow (and sometimes negative) symbols and rituals, can provide an important ingredient to human dialogue, connectedness and cohesion and a counter to exclusion and possible combat.

A considerably abridged version of this chapter has been published as P. Collins and N. Kakabadse (2006), 'Perils of Religion: Need for Spirituality in the Public Sphere', *Public Administration Development*, vol. 26, no. 2, pp. 109–21.

References

Antoun, R.T. (2001) *Understanding Fundamentalism: Christian, Islamic, and Jewish Movements*. Walnut Creek, CA: Alta Mira Press.
Armstrong, K. (1999) *A History of God*, Vintage, London.

---

[4]Although there was an earlier tradition of such diversity within the British Empire.

Ayer, A.J. (1976) *The Central Questions of Philosophy*. Harmondsworth: Pelican Books.

Bayat, M. and M.A. Jamnia (2001) *Of the Sufis*. London: Shambhala.

Brandt, E. (1996) 'Corporate Pioneers Explore Spirituality', *HR Magazine*, vol. 41, no. 4, April, pp. 82–7.

Buber, M. (1937/1958) *I and Thou*, transl. by Ronald Gregor Smith, Edinburgh, T. and T. Clark, 2nd edition. New York: Scribners.

Charaniya, N.K. and J.W. Walsh (2001) 'Interpreting the Experience of Christians, Moslems and Jews Engaged in Anterreligious Dialogue: A Collaborative Research Study', *Religious Education*, vol. 96, no. 3, pp. 351–68.

Chu, Jeff, Broward Liston, Maggie Sieger and Daniel Williams (2004) 'Is God in our Genes?', *Time*, vol. 164, no. 21, pp. 54–60.

Congar, K.A., R.N. Kanungo and Associates (1998) *Charismatic Leadership: The Elusive Factors of Organisational Effectiveness*. San Francisco: Jossey Bass.

Cowley, C. (2004) 'The Cost of Being Given', The Economy Project, Heythrop College.

Csikszentmihalyi, M. (1990) *Flow: The Psychology of Optimal Experience*. New York: Harper Perennial.

Donkin, R. (2001) *Blood, Sweat and Tears: The Evolution of Work*. London: Texera.

Duffield, Mark (2000) 'The Emerging Development-Security Complex', in P. Collins (ed.), *Applying Public Administration in Development: Guideposts to the Future*. Chichester: John Wiley & Sons.

Fairholm, G.W. (1997) *Capturing the Heart of Leadership: Spiritual and Community in the New American Workplace*. Westport, CT: Praeger.

Greenleaf, R. (1973) *The Servant Leader*. Newton Center, MA: Greenleaf Center.

Jaques, E. (1965) *A General Theory of Bureaucracy*. Portsmouth, NH: Heinemann Gower.

Kakabadse, A., N. Kakabadse and A. Kouzmin (2003) 'Ethics, Values and Paradox: Comparison of Three Case Studies Examining the Paucity of Leadership in Government', *Public Administration*, vol. 81, no. 3, pp. 447–508.

Kakabadse, N. and A. Kakabadse (2003a) 'Polylogue as a Platform for Governance: Integrating People, Planet, Profit and Posterity', *Corporate Governance: International Journal of Business in Society*, vol. 3, no. 1, pp. 1–30.

Kakabadse, N. and A. Kakabadse (2003b) 'Developing Reflexive Practitioners Through Collaborative Inquiry: A Case Study of the UK Civil Service', *International Review of Administrative Science*, vol. 69, no. 3, pp. 365–83.

Kakabadse, N. and A. Kakabadse (2004) 'Religion and Research Philosophy', Research Methods Lecture, Northampton Business School, Northampton, 20 October.

Kakabadse, N., A. Kakabadse and L. Lee-Davis (2004) 'Unique Study Assesses Interactivity, Impact of Leadership Styles', *Handbook of Business Strategy*, vol. 6, no. 1.

Korac-Kakabadse, A., N. Korac-Kakabadse and A. Kouzmin (2002) 'Spirituality and Leadership Praxis', *Journal of Managerial Psychology*, Special Issue on Spirituality, Leadership, Work and Organisations, vol. 17, no. 3, pp. 165–82.

Kouzes, J.M. and B.Z. Posner (1993) *Credibility: How Leaders Gain and Lose It; Why People Demand It*. San Francisco, CA: Jossey Bass.

Lakeland, P. (2003) *The Liberation of the Laity: In Search of an Accountable Church*. New York: Continuum.

Lamo de Espinosa, E. (1990) *La sociedad reflexiva*. Madrid: CIS-Siglo XXI.

Layard, Richard (2005) *Happiness: Lessons from a New Science*. London: Penguin Press.

Miles, M.B. and A.M. Huberman (1996) *Qualitative Data Analysis: An Expanded Sourcebook*. Thousand Oaks, CA: Sage.

Mitroff, I.I. and E.A. Denton (1999) 'A Study of Spirituality in the Workplace', *Sloan Management Review*, vol. 40, no. 4, pp. 83–92.

Mommsen, T. (1958) *The History of Rome: An Account of Events and Persons from the Conquest of Carthage to the End of the Republic*. New York: Meridian Books.

Namie, G. and E. Namie (2000) *Bully at Work: What You Can Do to Stop the Hurt and Reclaim Your Dignity on the Job*. New York: Sourcebooks.

Porter, M. (2003) 'CSR – A Religion with Too Many Priests? – Dialogue with Mette Morsing', *European Business Forum*, vol. 15, Autumn, pp. 41–2.

Prasad, P. (1993) 'Symbolic Process in the Implementation of Technological Change', *Academy of Management Journal*, vol. 36, no. 10, pp. 1400–429.

Ramsden, J.J. (1991) *The New World Order*. Moscow: Progress Publishers.

Schulman, Rita, P. (2003) 'Psychotherapy and Religion: A Paradox?', *International Journal of Applied Psychoanalytical Studies*, vol. 1, no. 1, pp. 73–81.

Schumacher, E.F. (1973) *Small is Beautiful: a Study of Economics as if People Matter*, Vintage, London.

Silverman, D. (1992) *Doing Qualitative Research: A Practical Handbook*. Thousand Oaks, CA: Sage.

Tillich, Paul (1963) *Systematic Theology III: Life and the Spirit, History and the Kingdom of God*. Chicago: University of Chicago Press.

Tudway, Richard and Pascal, Anne-Marie (2005) 'Aiming for Higher Purpose in the Professional Lives of All', Ethics and Integrity of Governance: A Transatlantic Dialogue, New Development and the Ethics of Governance Stream, Programme Workshop IV, Leuven, Belgium, 2–5 June.

UNICEF (2000) *Child Poverty in Rich Nations*. Florence: United Nations Children's Fund.

Van Velsor, E. (1998) 'Assessing the Impact of Development Experiences', in C. McCauley, R.S. Moxley and E.Van Velsor (eds), *The Handbook of Leadership Development*. San Francisco: Jossey-Bass, pp. 114–27.

Whitehead, A.N. (1926) *Religion in the Making*. New York: Macmillan.

Zaehner, R.C. (2001) *The Hutchinson Encyclopaedia of Living Faiths*. Oxford: The Open University and Helicon.

15
Creating Sustained Performance Improvement

Peter A. Hunter

There are two schools of thought that drive human endeavours. The first is that we will do the right thing morally, we will treat people with respect and, in return, we too will be treated with respect. The second is more pragmatic. We need to earn money, and whatever we do to earn it is justified because our overriding concern is the maintenance of ourselves and our families.

In the past these two approaches were always seen to be mutually exclusive; our need to make money was the excuse that overrode the moral approach with the result that we were comfortable that we were not able to take the time to deal with people as individuals. In this way we have been able to build constructs that excuse our behaviour to each other on the basis that 'it is OK because we are making money'.

Here I will show that the two approaches are not mutually exclusive – in other words, it is possible to give people the support and recognition that they require without compromising our ability to make money, and I will demonstrate, through practical examples of my own work in the oil drilling industry, how individual and organizational performance increases to an astonishing degree when the managers and supervisors start to support the workforce instead of telling them what to do.

I start from the very simple assumption that 'Everybody wants to do a good job'. Few, if any, people start work and want to do a bad job. People want to be proud of what they do, they want to be able to say: 'Look at me, I did that.' They want to make a difference.

So what gets in the way? Strong structural and cultural drivers. If a good idea is ignored or disappears without trace; if others steal the credit; or if people are told, 'You are not paid to think'; if people do not feel that they are being heard, they very soon stop suggesting good ideas. This prevents individuals from making a positive contribution to the organization and can have one of two possible consequences.

The first is stress. If nobody will listen to an idea that is going to be of benefit, it is very frustrating for the originator of that idea. The harder they try to be heard, and the more committed they are to improvement, the more stressful it is.

The second possible consequence is an individual's own defence against stress – apathy. Stress is a function of caring; to avoid stress the natural defence of our minds is to cease caring; to become apathetic. Hence, an embedded reaction to a subsequent change that is imposed without consultation, even positive organization-wide improvement initiatives, is to take pleasure when things start to go badly: 'Serves them right! If they had listened to me none of these problems would have happened.' And the people who think this are often right.

In effect, the situation encountered very frequently is that we want to do a good job, but there are obstacles that frustrate us. The concept of 'Breaking the Mould'[1] recognizes this and sets out to produce an environment that actively searches for and removes the obstacles and frustrations that stop people from doing a good job. When that happens people can take pride in their work, and when they can take pride their performance becomes astonishing.

What do we need to change?

In order to create a performance improvement we have to do something different. If we don't do something different, how can we possibly expect to make a change?

That raises the first problem we have – finding out what is the thing that we need to change. Many management models have tried to find a solution with varying levels of success, from Kaizen to Six Sigma, TQM and a host of others. These models are not wrong, but they all suffer from the same failing. Somewhere in each instruction book there is a phrase that says something similar to 'The key to the successful implementation of this model is Ownership'. Then we turn the page and begin a new chapter without ever coming across the instruction that tells us how to create Ownership. It is a word that has been used and abused for years, but very few people are able to give it a meaningful definition. Without understanding what it is, how is it possible to create the conditions that allow it to happen?

I like to think of ownership as the way that we feel about something. If it is mine, I own it, I will take care of it. If it is not mine I won't take care of it, why should I? – I don't own it!

We define ownership as a feeling that gives us the ability to care about something. That definition may work in a pink and fluffy sort of way but it hardly has a place as a business strategy. Our business strategy conversation should be about percentage points, hard savings, value added and other assorted business type words. We don't want to be talking about caring. Or do we?

---

[1] P.A. Hunter, *Breaking the Mould*, 2nd edn. Milton Brodie, Scotland: Librario Publishing, 2005.

How many people have ever washed a hired car? Not many. Why should we? If the hire car doesn't belong to me, why should I wash it? It is not mine. I don't care.

And yet most of us take care of our own cars. They don't come with washing instructions but we do wash them. We take care of them and maintain them because they are ours.

After two years a hire car has a residual value of practically zero. The reason it has no value is that nobody will buy a car that has been driven for two years by people who did not care for it. After two years the hired car that we never washed is scrapped. The hire car company has no option, the two-year-old hire car has no value.

But after two years your own car does have a residual value. You can realize that value by selling the car or you can continue to use it reliably for perhaps another ten years. Suddenly the care we gave the car that we owned has a realizable financial worth. We can therefore say that the value of our care is the car's residual value, because in all other respects it is (mechanically) identical to the hire car that has no value. Now we have a solid measurable effect that is directly related to the ownership that gave us our ability to care.

At the beginning of this chapter it was asserted that we have to first understand what we have to change before we can figure out how to change it. I suggest that what we have to change is the way that people feel about their work. We have to allow them to care about what they do. We have to allow them to take ownership.

The first reaction to the suggestion that we can change the way people feel about their work is frequently that it is nonsense. How on earth can we change the way people feel and where is the profit in it? We have already seen where the profit is when people are allowed to care about what they do and changing the way that people feel about their work is something that happens every day. As often as not it is reported on the news but we don't recognize it for what it is.

In 2003 the then CEO of British Airways, Rod Eddington, was interviewed on television. He was understandably complaining about the market share that he had lost to the budget airlines, but he was also being quite bullish about it. He said that in the previous three years he had reduced his operating costs by 5 per cent. What he didn't say was that in those same three years he had made 16,000 of his staff redundant. The question that we have to ask is, 'How did the people who remained working at British Airways feel when they found out that 16,000 of their colleagues had been made redundant?' Did they feel good about it? Did it make them feel secure? Did it increase their trust in the company?

Now think back a few years to the time before the redundancies. Think about the sort of person who used to work for a national airline. The workforce was made up of people who had dreamed at school of being the cool pilot in the dark glasses relaxing in the big seat at the front of the jet flying between Tokyo and Paris, or the stewardess whose answer to the question, 'Where are you going for the weekend?' was truthfully and smugly, 'Barbados'. British Airways staff were people who had competed to get their jobs and, having won, were living their dreams and getting paid for it. They were proud, motivated, and they cared about what they did.

Three years later the redundancies had changed the way they felt about their jobs. A caring and productive workforce was changed into one that turned up for their pay cheque and had no other interest in being there.

The company had indeed changed the way their staff felt about their jobs. Unfortunately, the feelings of the workforce had been changed in the wrong direction. British Airways management had taken a caring and motivated workforce and through their deliberate actions changed them into an apathetic bunch of losers who had ceased to care about the company or the service they delivered – a change that has not remained unnoticed by those who still fly with British Airways.

British Airways are not unique in working this demotivational magic. It is happening all the time in our industries, but we fail to recognize it. To create a sustained performance improvement we need to change the way people feel about what they do, in the other direction. We have to allow them to care. We have to allow people to take pride. We have to allow them to take ownership. How exactly we can do that?

Removing the obstacles that prevent ownership

There is a recognition that lack of ownership in the workplace is a problem, yet at the same time there is confusion about how to confer this mysterious gift of ownership onto the people who need it. We often hear the phrase, 'We gave them ownership and look what happened', as if the fact of giving ownership was pure and perfect but the ungrateful workforce deliberately undermined the attempt. The real obstacle is the perception that ownership is a physical thing that can be bestowed on a grateful workforce by a generous management.

It cannot be done.

We can give someone a car but we cannot give them ownership of it. The colour may be wrong, the engine is too big or too small, there are not enough or too many doors, the level of trim is wrong, I really wanted a diesel. These are all choices that we are nowadays allowed to make about our new car and the choices are there deliberately to allow us to make them. We will perhaps then get exactly what we want, and most importantly, we have been allowed to make our own choices and, having chosen, we can take ownership. When the ability to make these choices is denied to us we cannot take ownership of the car for two reasons. The first is that bearing in mind the huge number of choices that the manufacturers make available for each model, it is extremely unlikely that the choices someone else makes will be the right ones for us. The same thing can be said at work. The man on the shopfloor knows how to do his job but it is *prima facie* unlikely that a manager making decisions about the shopfloor environment, in which he does not work, will be able to make the right decisions. The second reason is that unless we are allowed to make our own decisions we will not be able to take ownership, because it will almost certainly feel as if we are being forced to do something that someone else wants. Even if the solution that is presented to us is the right solution, we as human beings will resent being told what to do and will reject the solution.

If the car picked for us was exactly the same as the one that we would have picked for ourselves, we would still resist taking ownership because we were not a part of the decision-making process or because the decision-making process was forced upon us. For most people the view persists that we have to *do* something to others to give them ownership, but in truth we don't have to do anything to give people ownership. People want to take ownership because ownership allows us to feel pride, and pride is something that we want. What we should be doing as managers is not looking at how to *give* people ownership, we should be looking instead for the obstacles that prevent people from taking ownership for themselves. These obstacles are the things that frustrate the workforce.

Nobody wakes up and wants to have a bad day. We all want to catch the train, we all want to impress the client, we all want to be recognized for what we do. In short, we want to do a good job because when we do it makes us feel good, either from the recognition that others give us or from the simple pride that we take in knowing that we have done well. Unfortunately for each of us there are other factors that get in the way and frustrate us. The train is late, the client doesn't turn up or our efforts are simply not noticed.

Each of these frustrations can lead to stress because we are in a situation that we can't control. Our minds, however, have a mechanism to deal with stress, it is called apathy. We want to do a good job because we want the recognition that a good job deserves. We get stressed when we don't get that recognition and when the stress gets too much we either become ill or we cease to care. We know that stress is bad for us. Stress is the response that was programmed into us when we were cavemen to deal with the situation where we look up from our game of rocks and sticks to find we are just about to be pounded by an angry woolly mammoth. When stress kicks in the whole of our information processing power is concentrated on two things – fight or run away. The focus is on pure survival so our normal bodily repair and maintenance functions are switched off. In the short term this strategy is acceptable since the stressful situation is relatively short and ends in either escape (i.e. survival) or death.

In the modern world the stress from frustration at work is long term and the body has to protect itself the only way it knows how. We stop caring, because our mind subconsciously knows that we will only get more stressed if we care. Apathy is the body's defence mechanism that allows us to endure the frustrations that we encounter every day at work.

Imagine that you have an appointment with a client on the other side of the city and you decide to drive. You plan your route, allowing for traffic and the time of day. You arrive at the turnoff after a 90-minute drive and you have five minutes to spare. Your timing is impeccable, the plan worked and you are looking forward to meeting your client on time, calm and in control. You turn into the client's road and there is a barrier across the street. The only way to get to the client now is to turn around and follow a detour that is going to take at least twenty minutes.

There are two ways to overcome the frustration that is being caused by this obstacle. The first is to make a physical change. That means getting out of the car and moving the barrier. By making this physical change we remove the obstacle and, therefore, the frustration that was causing us stress. The other option is to ask the man standing by the barrier why it is there. He reveals that an unexploded bomb has been discovered further up the road and that to reach your client the only alternative is to drive around and arrive at your client late. This answer has not changed the physical circumstances at all but the understanding of why they exist has removed the frustration.

You will still arrive late, but instead of being frustrated and stressed you arrive in control and stress-free. The cause therefore of the frustrations that prevent ownership is not always a physical obstacle. Much of the time it is the lack of feedback that could provide the understanding that would remove the frustration. Note that by failing to give the feedback that would remove the frustration we create the environment that produces long term stress; by giving that feedback we can create an environment that allows people to start to take ownership.

The choice that belongs to each of us is how we treat other people. Do we give the feedback that allows them to take ownership? Or do we keep them in the dark and by so doing create frustration and apathy?

Creating the right environment for change to occur

We have established that we want to create ownership in the workforce because we understand that if the workforce own their own work they will take care of it. When people are allowed to take care of what they do they can become proud of what they do and their performance typically becomes amazing.

We have also seen that in order to allow people to take ownership we don't have to do anything to them. We simply have to understand what it is we are doing that is preventing them from taking ownership, and having understood that, we just stop doing it.

Our problem on the road to creating sustainable change is how to create the right environment for change to occur. It is all very well to understand what is stopping the change from happening, but we have also touched on the resistance that we create when we tell people what to do to implement change. This means that even though we know exactly what the problem is we cannot cure the problem by telling others what to do.

If I want to make sure that my wife never irons my shirts again all I have to do is to wait for her to do the ironing, then tell her to iron my shirt. This scenario makes us cringe because we know instinctively what her reaction will be. She certainly won't iron the shirt and there is a good chance that she will cause some physical damage to me if she happens to have the hot iron in her hand at the time. We understand that this will be her reaction in a social situation and we understand that her reaction has nothing to do with our relationship. Her reaction is because she is a human being and this is the way that human beings react when they are told what to do.

We seem to forget this very basic fact when we are at work. At work we are not allowed to make the same extreme reaction, but being told what to do still makes us feel the same way. The difference at work is that our resistance to being told what to do takes on a different, more passive form that is nonetheless equally destructive. When we are told what to do we work more slowly, we damage the machine we have been told to use, we goof off and read the *Racing Post* in the toilet, or we just tell lies and say that we have done something that we have not in order to get the boss off our back. There are many ways the workforce will get their own back on a directive boss, and most of them the boss will not know anything about.

But there is another way to get things done. At home another way is to ask for something to be done. In the shirt scenario I can ask to have a shirt ironed but then I must defend the right of my wife to say, 'No, do it yourself', because the purpose of a question is to allow a choice of outcome. When a question is asked at work, there is often no choice. If the boss asks for something to be done it is in effect an order couched in different words. Are we really allowed to tell the boss 'No, go and do it yourself'?

There is a third way to get things done that does not involve telling people what to do or 'asking'. This is to allow the workforce to care about what they do. In the ironing scenario we have to assume that being married, my wife and I care for each other. If I put on a crumpled shirt and asked 'How does this look?' she will say 'Oh, for heaven's sake give that to me!' and she will iron it. She will iron it because she cares about how I look, not because I told her to iron it or even asked her, but because she cares. In life we all have a choice about whether we care for something or not. At work we have the same choice but are often forced into apathy, because at work we are discouraged from caring by the actions of management.

Whether we care or not produces a change in our behaviour. Caring is a function of the way we feel about something. To care about what they do at work the workforce have to be allowed to change the way they feel about what they do. When trying to change the way that someone feels it is important to remember that we cannot force anyone to feel a particular way. What we can do is to create the right environment and then allow each individual to make their own decision in their own time about the way they feel. To create that environment there are a number of things that we first have to realize about how other people perceive us. When we understand other people's perceptions, then we can begin to understand how to change them.

We have discussed the natural reaction to resist when we are told what to do, but that is not the full story. When a corporate decision is taken to create a performance improvement it is normally a response to a feeling that something is going wrong. The way that change is implemented is usually by hiring an outside agency to make the change. The result of this hiring is that the manager of the workforce, who is doing his best, is confronted at some point with a consultant who has been sent by his boss to tell him what he should be doing. The effect of that confrontation on the manager is the same as a huge slap in the face. The message the manager receives is that his boss thinks that he is failing and that even though he has been doing the same job for the last ten years, someone who has no idea about what he does on a day-to-day basis is going to tell him how to do it. This seriously undermines the manager's confidence and makes him feel very vulnerable and threatened, especially when he sees the confidence that his boss has placed in the inexperienced third party consultant who has been sent to fix the problem. Consequently, with the best will in the world the manager will not be able to benefit from a transfer of expertise due to the size of the mountain of resistance that has been inadvertently built for him by his own boss.

To allow the manager to create the right environment for change to occur in his team we have first to create the environment for him that will allow him to take ownership of the change. He is a human being too and cannot perform unless he too is allowed to take ownership. Having understood how the manager is being made to feel by the best intentions of his own boss, we have gone some way to understand how to remove or avoid the resistance that the traditional approach to change creates. Here are a few suggestions that will help to create the right environment. They apply to everyone at all levels in the organization from the CEO to the cleaner. These rules are not the complete answer but their implementation will help to avoid creating some of the practical obstacles that prevent performance improvement:

Don't tell anyone what to do – people will always resist being told what to do and any perceived change will not therefore be sustained.

Don't give anyone extra work – the current expectation is that any change will involve extra work, which will generate resistance to the change.

Don't threaten anyone – the presence of a change manager or consultant is threatening to staff because their expectation is that 'change' means cutbacks and redundancies. Stand back and allow existing staff to continue to be the experts at their own jobs. Then they do not become alienated by the process of change and we allow the possibility of a 'change' that does not include 'downsizing'.

Don't try to change things – change will occur when the environment is right. Trying to force things to change will create resistance. Concentrate instead on changing the environment. When the environment is right things will change naturally and the changes will be sustained.

Support what people are doing – people want to do their best and any suggestion that what they are doing is not good enough will create stiff resistance.

Be humble – never take credit for anything. Doing so robs others of the opportunity to feel pride in their own achievement.

These are the ground rules for creating the environment that will allow change to occur. In the next section we will look at how to support this environment by finding out what it is that we are doing currently that is not working.

How to find out what is not working

We have proposed that the easiest way to improve performance is not to do something extra in order to stimulate that performance improvement but simply to find out what we are doing that is preventing the performance of others from being exceptional, then stop doing it.

It sounds so simple written on the page, but leads us to a terrible problem when we try to implement it practically, namely, how do we know what it is that we are doing wrong? How can we as managers find out what it is that we have to stop doing in order to allow our people to start performing?

The first presumption is that we do not already know what the answer is. We may think we do but if we really did, we would already be doing something about it and our organization's performance would already be improving. The answer must therefore be something that we don't know about already.

This leads us to the second question, which is really the first. Not 'What are we doing wrong?' but 'How do we find out what we are doing wrong?' The problem this question poses is at first sight very easy to resolve, we ask the workforce and they will tell us. But again in a practical situation this leads to problems in implementation.

An employee who is unhappy with the level of support or the treatment that he is receiving from management will not be particularly inclined to tell his manager the truth about how he feels until he receives so much pressure from the organization that he either explodes or quits. If he does the first, he knows that he will be branded by his manager as unreliable; if the second, he will think, 'Why should I tell the company that has treated me so badly how to improve the way they operate?' Do they deserve his help in return for the way they have treated him? I don't think so. As far as the employee is concerned management have made their own bed and they deserve everything they get. Why should he help them?

We have all had experience of the management 'Good Idea' – the flavour of the month that has been handed down from above to be implemented on the shopfloor to improve performance. When these 'Good Ideas' arrive they are greeted outwardly with the enthusiasm that the manager expects from his committed and loyal workforce while inwardly there is a huge and silent groan of despair as the workforce see yet another attempt to rip to pieces the status quo by another piece of management-driven lunacy. The originator of the 'Good Idea' is seldom challenged about its assumed efficacy or given any feedback as to how it could be implemented with better effect, even though every single person who is to be affected will have an opinion. The reason for this extreme reluctance to disagree with anything their manager says stems from the fact that the manager is the person who decides when a pay rise is due, who writes the personal development report, and who is looking for people to recommend for promotion. When a 'Good Idea' is proposed by management it is certainly easier and is largely perceived as being beneficial to go with the flow. The workforce have all seen management-led initiatives before and they know that it is only a matter of time before they fail. From the workforce's point of view, what is the point in putting one's head above the parapet to voice disquiet or make suggestions when history shows that their opinions will be ignored and the initiative is going to fail anyway? The workforce knows they don't have to do anything except wait. In many cases this passive lack of support contributes to the failure.

This situation constitutes the dilemma: if I am a good manager the workforce will tell me when I ask them that I am a good manager and there will be nothing that I need to stop doing in order to allow them to improve their performance. If I am a bad manager the workforce will tell me exactly the same thing because:

1. They do not want to say anything that might prejudice their chances when the next promotion opportunity becomes available.
2. They are sick and tired of the manager hanging around their workplace and want to be rid of him as quickly as possible, so they tell the manager what he wants to hear.
3. They do not want to get into a personal discussion about failure with someone they do not trust.
4. The manager is the person whose actions are causing them stress. The last thing they want to do is help the person who is giving them a hard time.
5. There is no point telling the truth to a manager because he never listens anyway.

If we accept the dilemma, that as managers we will get the same answer whatever we do, we are either never going to find out what we are doing wrong or we are going to have to find another way to find out.

Finding that other way

What we need to do is to get to the bottom of people's expectations. Let us start by asking, 'Why will they not communicate with management?'

Could it be that their expectation, when they tell management the truth, is so massively negative? Their expectation is, as Pavlov discovered, built on the sum of all of their previous experience. The problem has been built up over time.

As a school leaver we arrive at work full of the joys of spring, bursting with the enthusiasm and imagination of unfettered youth. We offer our ideas to management, we make suggestions for improvement and we share our experiences. Each time we do that our enthusiasm receives a blow. We never find out what happens to our ideas, nothing changes but we have no idea why not. Our ideas could have revolutionized the process. Was nobody listening? Couldn't they understand?

We go through a process of trying to find out what it was that was not working, why our ideas were not getting through, because we know that we really can make a difference, if only someone would listen.

To the detriment of our innocent enthusiasm, an expectation is slowly built up that no matter how good our ideas we will always be ignored. Being ignored is like a slap in the face, which in a social situation would not be tolerated. At work it becomes what we expect to happen every time we step up to the mark and try to give the organization the benefit of our ideas or our experience. Being ignored hurts, and we don't like being hurt, but our experience tells us that if we propose an idea, we will be ignored – so we stop doing it.

This is the response that our experience at work has conditioned us to expect. The logic goes, if we don't make any suggestions, we can't be ignored by management and therefore we can't be hurt. The environment in which we work has taught us not to make suggestions. The workforce have been conditioned by management never to make suggestions. A working environment has been created that prevents the workforce from helping the organization to improve.

To find out what is not working we have to change the expectations of the workforce. We have to create an environment in which the workforce starts to receive a positive reaction when they have an idea. It will take time to overcome expectations that have been built up in the course of their whole working lives, but when we create the right environment, the environment that produces the positive consequences of a suggestion, we will start to find out what is not working, and, more importantly, what we need to do about it. Hence, the key to finding out what is not working lies in creating that environment.

We can then start to realize the value inherent in our workforce and allow them to start taking the first steps along the road to ownership.

How to create performance improvement

So far in this chapter we have seen how the environment at work has created a situation in which employees are actively discouraged from making suggestions. On the surface there are reward schemes and suggestion boxes galore, but they do not address the issue of the environment that has been created that discourages people from offering to share their experiences or ideas for the benefit of the organization. Putting up a suggestion box does not change the way that people feel about what they do. The suggestions made will still be ignored and the workforce know this so they will not make suggestions, in order to avoid being ignored. To reiterate, we have to create the environment where staff will come to expect that they will get a positive consequence when they offer a suggestion.

We have to do something different and the positive consequence that we offer does not have to be money. We are used to the reward scheme that provides a financial incentive but as human beings we are fiendishly adept at achieving the reward without changing what we do. The purpose of the reward as a driver for behavioural change is therefore defeated. The financial reward is notoriously difficult to administer fairly, and because we like to achieve the prize all the time it soon becomes an expectation. This then becomes a negative consequence when it is not achieved, instead of being a positive consequence when it is.

Therefore the first thing to consider is that if the reward is not money, what can that reward be?

The reward that cannot be bought costs nothing. Imagine your department is due for a business review and you are well ahead of the curve with your preparation. On Friday afternoon it is announced that the directors of the parent company will be in the country for a board meeting. To allow them to be present at the business review it will now take place on Tuesday instead of the following Friday, Your boss asks you to bring your schedule forward. This requires you to work all weekend to be ready. Your efforts allow you to make the presentation on time and you are relieved that the directors do not appear to be displeased. It is a familiar story of response to pressure that is both difficult to resist and increasingly expected. Now one of the directors walks across as you are packing away and says, 'I'm sorry I couldn't rearrange my schedule to fit in with your original programme, thanks for your presentation, you were impressive.'

Now, how do you feel? Is there any amount of money in the world that would give you the same feeling of pride and self-respect? The effort to give that feedback cost the director a few seconds of his time but the result is that now you can leap tall buildings. In other words, feedback which is Appropriate, Positive and Timely costs nothing.

This is a single instance of one particularly talented manager delivering praise exactly where it is needed at exactly the right time. With our typically large and fragmented departments could we possibly be sure of having that sort of effect with our own workforces? The answer, as always, is that if we are not having that sort of effect on all of our staff right now then we never will, unless we change something that we are doing. We know what the effect of Appropriate, Positive and Timely feedback is, we just need to decide what we have to do to give it.

The simplest way of giving it is called Planned Spontaneous Praise. This is a model in which the supervisor/manager decides to do one extra thing every day. That one change in his behaviour is something that he decides on the way in to work in the morning and is 'the thing that he is going to catch someone doing right', for that day. It does not matter what that thing is, whether cleaning the coffee station, filing the invoices, or sweeping up around a machine. Having decided what that one thing is the manager spends time walking around trying to catch someone doing it right. If he catches someone he gives Appropriate, Positive and Timely feedback: 'Thanks Jack, I appreciate the extra effort you've put in here'. Then he walks away.

If the manager doesn't find anyone then he says nothing and thinks of something else for the next day. This stops the workforce from seeing praise as an expectation. When they get praise it gives them a win for their effort, praise which they may never have had before. In time people's behaviour will change to allow them to achieve the feeling that praise gives them. Even if they can't leap tall buildings they will start to feel better about what they do, and the journey towards pride and responsibility has been started.

The above is a simple model that relies on the Supervisor/Manager doing something consistently differently to achieve a result different from what happened before, and that result is to give people a sense of pride and self respect. One of the things that we know we are not very good at is changing what we do unless we can see a win for ourselves. From the viewpoint of the manager this simplistic approach may feel like the right thing to do, but it is difficult to continue unless we can see a return on the investment of our time, and no matter how good it feels it is always going to be difficult to put a value on the result. But using the same process we can include the creation of the correct environment as part of our Planned Spontaneous Praise strategy.

We know we need to give staff a positive response for submitting ideas and we know that response should always be positive because it is this response that creates the feelings that turn into pride and ownership. This is great if the idea is a good one, but how can we be positive if the ideas we are given suck?

Consider, nobody is going to suggest an idea that they know is not going to work. The reason for submitting an idea is to get the recognition and feedback that is going to make them feel good, because they believe their idea is good. If the idea is not going to work it is most likely that it is for a reason of which the originator was unaware. In this case the correct and positive feedback is, 'No, we are not going to use your idea, and here is the reason why not'. This is a positive response that gives respect to the individual who knows that his idea has been given weight and consideration. It is moreover the response that will make him go away with more information than he had before. He is feeling respected and therefore will be looking for another solution to the same problem that will work, or the solution to an entirely different problem, because his input has been recognized, he has been supported and it makes him feel good.

It is important to remember that one positive response will not reset an existing expectation. We are trying to set a new expectation to overcome the one that has been built up through a whole working life of negative feedback. To do this we have to keep repeating this positive response until the individual's negative expectation is overcome and they start to believe that this is the way they are going to be treated in future.

This is when their expectation changes – when each individual decides that we have created the environment that encourages him or her to offer the organization the benefit of their experience. As long as this expectation continues to be reinforced the individual's sense of pride in his own accomplishments will continue to grow, and so will his feeling of ownership.

When people take ownership their performance becomes amazing. To create the performance improvement, first we have to create the conditions to allow ownership. Without ownership any performance improvement will be ordinary and temporary. With ownership it will be astonishing and sustained.

How to stop people from performing as well as they can

We have been concentrating on how to create a sustained improvement in performance. One of the things that we identified was that in many cases we don't have to do anything extra to people for them to be as good as they can be, we just have to stop doing the things that prevent them from being as good as they can be. These things are called blockers and represent obstacles placed by management in the path of the workforce that prevent them from performing.

The biggest obstacle to anybody's ability to perform we have called the 'Directive Blocker.' This is the ability that we all have to affect somebody's performance by telling them what to do. At the base level this is the effect of the pointed finger that says, 'Don't argue, just do it'. By telling someone what to do in this way, i.e. by being directive, we make people feel threatened and therefore defensive.

The effect of being on the wrong end of the directive finger is that the hairs immediately stand up on the back of your neck and the blood rushes to your face. Our internal system has in effect not had a software upgrade since the Stone Age and the signals that are now being generated are that your body is ready for a fight.

In a social situation we seldom use the directive behaviour of the pointed finger because we instinctively know that the response will be confrontational. We do not want to put ourselves into the situation where someone else will try to defy us or want to fight, although we might sometimes still try to use this behaviour irrespective of the damage it causes, because in common with the manager we do not know of any other way to get the job done.

We may recall the effect of this directive behaviour when it was shown to us, or we may have inflicted it on our own children – 'I said tidy your room, and when I say tidy your room I mean now!'. Has this directive behaviour ever resulted in anyone tidying their room, or has it simply led to confrontation and even destructive behaviour?

At work the artificial hierarchy that we create protects the manager from the consequences of his confrontational behaviour. Being insulated from the workforce's natural desire to fight, the manager may feel quite happy about causing people distress with his behaviour in the comfortable knowledge that they can do nothing about it, or their distress may be so well hidden because of the fear that the manager has generated that he may not even realize that he is the one causing it. At school this behaviour is called bullying and is treated very seriously as a result of the stress and physical consequences that it can engender in the bullied individual. At work this behaviour is still bullying, but it is regarded as simply what we have to put up with every day if we want to continue being paid.

It is true that nothing can be done to the manager who causes the stress by the person who has been stressed, but that still leaves us with a human being whose blood is up and, due to the age of the software that is running the program in our heads, is in serious need of some action to satisfy the heightened state of alert in which his body has been placed. It is this unresolved need for action that causes the problem. The body is stressed and requires action to relieve the stress.

In the Stone Age this meant either run away, or stand and fight. The body has switched into an emergency mode designed to cope with either. The normal maintenance functions and the ability to think logically are put to one side while the body prepares to battle for its life. In the modern world we are no longer allowed to resolve stress through violent action, so the body has to find another way to get rid of the stress. If we do not resolve the stress the body will start to suffer damage from a prolonged period in this emergency state when the body has shut down its normal maintenance functions. It is this physical need to seek resolution for stress that prevents us from performing as well as we can. The form that resolution takes varies but it is never positive. The individual, in order to remove the unresolved stress that is poisoning his body, may go away and break the machine he has been told to operate, or he could work slowly, work badly or not work at all. Our prehistoric operating program has to receive the destructive satisfaction that will allow it to turn off the stress that will, if allowed to continue, cause long-term physical damage

In order to preserve itself in the face of unresolved stress the body must perform destructively. It is this behaviour caused by the directive blocker that stops people from performing as well as they can. By telling people what to do we create the environment that prevents them from being able to do it.

Our primary problem is not how to stop this destructive behaviour; it is how to stop the directive behaviour that is causing the stress in the first place. The traditional way to stop someone doing something is to tell them to stop doing it. Unfortunately, this is the exact behaviour that caused the stress in the first place. This makes behaviour almost impossible to change through training, since training usually involves a large proportion of directive behaviour (i.e. telling people what they ought to be doing). The problem remains, how to allow someone exhibiting this sort of behaviour to understand how destructive it is and what the alternative behaviour is that would achieve a better result.

If we have deduced that telling people what to do is wrong, how are we going to tell someone that, if telling people what to do is wrong? The answer is to allow them to find out for themselves. Experiential learning is the most powerful mechanism we know for transferring knowledge. Compare it with traditional learning. Learning is a process of transferring knowledge from one individual to another. In the classroom we are placed in a situation where we are assailed by facts whose sole use is to be regurgitated on a single occasion called an exam when our ability to do so will be assessed by a pass or fail. There is evidence that less than 10 per cent of the information transferred in this traditional way is retained for more than one month. On the other hand, there is general acknowledgement that information is much more likely to be retained if the learning experience is made interesting, by creating experiences for the student that are positive and allow a much greater retention by either making the student want to learn, or at the very least reducing the students' resistance to learning. The third and most powerful way to transfer knowledge is for the student to find out himself, to involve the student in the situation from which he learns. This is called experiential learning. If a child is told not to touch something because it is 'hot', the child has no reason to associate the word 'hot' with harm. If a child is shown a fire and told not to go near it he may be persuaded, but will he actually understand the reason he is being given this lesson? If a child feels the heat of a fire he may not even know that he is learning but his experience will, for the rest of his life, tell him not to go too close. In summary, involve him and he will understand; tell him what to do and you will alienate him.

What happens when people are allowed to care about what they do?

Instinctively, we know that giving people respect and valuing them is the right thing to do. We have been able to see why, when you treat someone as if they are valuable, that is what they become. We have somewhat clarified our understanding of people and what motivates or demotivates them. In this section, we describe some real practical results obtained when the workforce on an oil rig in South America were allowed to care about what they did.

In one operation, called 'skidding the rig', the workforce, who had been described initially as 'intimidated and silent', were allowed to take control of their own performance. Three months later they were described by the same commentator as 'knowledgeable and proud'.

A drilling rig can only drill one well from any given location. When a well is completed the rig has to be moved in order to start the next well (for the rig in question the distance was about 15 metres). The rig has no wheels and is manoeuvred with large hydraulic rams from one location to the next. The operation to move the rig from one position to the next is known as 'skidding the rig'.

The chart below (Figure 15.1) shows how in the first three weeks of a 'Breaking the Mould' implementation, the crew's performance in this operation went from 8.5 hours to less than one hour – an 800 per cent performance improvement in three weeks. That performance improvement was then sustained for the next seven months.

The improvement was created by the workforce themselves, who, instead of being told what they should be doing, were asked what it was that they needed in order to do their jobs better. This approach involved the workforce in the control of the process. By listening to and using the workforce's own suggestions the value and respect that they began to feel started to turn into ownership.

In the first two days the workforce gave 74 different suggestions for improving the operation. By incorporating their suggestions into the operation and

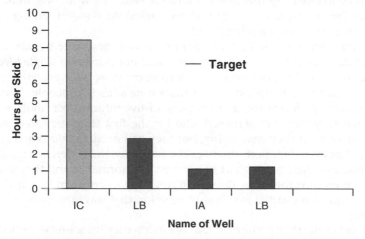

Figure 15.1 Average time per skid for successive wells

giving the workforce positive feedback about the value of these ideas, performance began to improve, as recorded in Figure 15.1. Not all of the ideas were used, some were impractical and some were duplicated, but each had two potential benefits:

1. Those that were used had a measurable practical effect on the way that the operation was carried out;
2. All of the ideas, including those that were not used, were an opportunity to give feedback to the originator. It was that feedback that changed the way the originators of the ideas felt about what they did.

It might be argued that this performance improvement was not a function of ownership at all but the application of 74 new ideas to improve the process of 'skidding the rig'. It would be easy on the surface to support this argument were it not for a very curious thing that happened shortly after that initial performance improvement was made. The same workforce, having become proud of the massive changes they had made in the rig-skidding operation, turned their attention to another operation called 'running the liner'.

When a well is drilled the bit is withdrawn and the rock formation that has been drilled is now exposed. Unsupported, over time this formation will collapse into the well bore, blocking it and preventing oil production. To keep the bore open a steel liner is run into the well, which supports the formation. In this case the liner had a diameter of 7¼ inches. The liner is run into the well in thirty foot lengths which are screwed together on the drill floor. The operation to screw the joints of liner together and run them into the well is known as 'running the liner'.

These wells were 6,000 feet deep. Hence 200 30-foot-long joints of liner had to be screwed together and fed into the well. The workforce were asked exactly the same question they had been asked for skidding the rig – what did they need for running the liner?

The crew, who on the back of their previous success were by now highly motivated, thought long and hard, but could not think of a single idea that would improve this operation. All the equipment worked, everything they needed was where it should be and there were sufficient people. Moreover their current performance, at an average of five minutes per joint, was the best that they had ever achieved, and for the first time they were feeling good about what they were doing, but they had no suggestions at all about how to improve their performance. The only physical difference on the rig was that now there was a chart of the crew's performance and they could at any time see how they were doing. No comment or criticism was made. The chart simply represented existing information that was now made available to them.

The next time they performed that operation they increased their performance by 25 per cent – to an average of three minutes 45 seconds per joint, and the next time it improved to three minutes 20 seconds, then to two minutes 30 seconds per joint. In terms of performance improvement the crews had been running at 12 joints per hour (five minutes per joint) and now they were working at 24 joints per hour (2½ minutes per joint), a total performance improvement of 100 per cent in the space of three runs (see Figure 15.2).

The workforce were now working at almost world record speed (25 joints per hour) having made no changes at all to the way that the physical process was carried out.

The only difference between running at five minutes per joint and running at two and a half minutes per joint was the attitude and behaviour of the workforce. Running at five minutes per joint they would lean on the rail and, looking out at the jungle, would swap gossip and tell tall tales. When they were running at two and a half minutes per joint they did exactly the same thing, they leaned on the rail and gossiped. The difference was that now while they were waiting for the next joint they did not look out at the jungle. They looked inwards to the rig floor where the pipe was being prepared. They knew exactly when they were needed and nobody had to call their attention back to the job from the jungle. As soon as the crew were required they were ready, the evidence of the effect of their attention being the sustained change from five minutes per joint to two and a half minutes per joint, a 100 per cent performance improvement.

There was no change at all in the physical process – the workforce had simply been allowed to feel proud of what they did. That was the only difference. No workshops, no questionnaires, no analysis, no training. The workforce had always wanted to do a good job but previously they were not allowed to because of the lack of recognition and support that they received. When

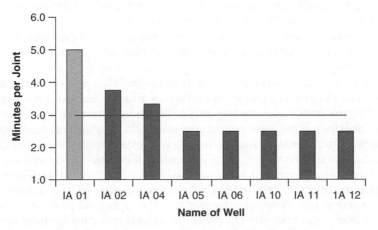

Figure 15.2 Running times per liner joint for successive wells

they were given the recognition and support that they needed to do a good job their performance became amazing.

The lesson? To improve performance it is not the process that is important. What is important is the people who apply the process and how they are allowed to feel about what they do. We all have the ability to affect the way that people feel about what they do. When we make them feel bad their performance is ordinary. When we recognize and support them then they start to feel good about what they do and their performance becomes extraordinary.

We all have a choice: do we continue to achieve ordinary results? Or do we choose to produce the extraordinary?

How to measure change

To know that we have created a performance improvement we first have to measure our performance. Without this benchmark we cannot say what the effect has been of the changes that have been made. The problem with measuring something like this is that the process of measuring always changes the thing being measured. If we are measuring the performance of an individual on the production line and they know it, the change in their performance is normally positive and this change is known as the 'Hawthorne effect', so-called as a result of work undertaken in the late 1920s at the Hawthorne plant of the Western Electric Company in Illinois. This series of researches, first led by Harvard Business School professor Elton Mayo along with associates F.J. Roethlisberger and William J. Dickson, started out by examining the physical and environmental influences of the workplace (such as the brightness of lights and levels of humidity). The study was only expected to last one year, but it was extended to five years since the researchers received a setback each time they tried to relate the manipulated physical conditions to the workers' efficiency. Namely, the researchers increased the lighting level and recorded an increase in the workers' productivity; the researchers decreased the level of lighting and again recorded an increase in productivity; and then they returned the lighting to the original level and still recorded an increase in the level of productivity.

It took the researchers some time to figure out that productivity did not depend on the level of lighting. What they eventually concluded was that the act of measurement itself was responsible for the variation in the levels of performance, their reasonable conclusion being that the workers were pleased to receive attention from the researchers who expressed an interest in them. The individual always wants to be recognized for doing a good job, and as a result, when he knows he is being watched he will make an extra effort so that his performance is judged to be good. The Hawthorne effect is a short-term phenomenon that disappears the moment the individual perceives he is no longer being watched. The effect can be likened to a car travelling along a road infested with speed cameras. The individual measurements appear to show good performance, but the average speed is still in excess of the limit since most drivers speed up between the cameras.

Another result of the act of measuring is that it can have a negative effect on the ability of the individual to perform. This happens when a target is imposed on the workforce by a third party, normally management. The target is seen by the workforce as giving management ammunition for them to criticize the workforce's failure to reach an unrealistic and arbitrary level of performance that was set by a manager with no practical experience of the job. Unfortunately this is quite a widespread practice.

The fact remains that we cannot realize the efficacy of any initiative without measuring performance, yet what we are suggesting is that the fact of measurement will create a set of data points that are unreliable as a measure of that performance. The above is true if we impose a set of standards and create targets for others to be measured against. However, if instead of imposing the target we allow the workforce to select their own target then the result is completely different.

The group of oilfield workers in South America was carrying out the rig skid mentioned above in an average of eight and a half hours. Their manager thought that he knew what their performance should be so he set a target for them. He said that once in his life he had seen the same operation carried out in only two hours. Based on this experience, he set two hours as the target for his workforce i.e. the horizontal line on the rig skidding chart (Figure 15.1). This anecdote would normally be used as an example of a manager setting an unrealistic target that his workforce could not possibly achieve. Their non-achievement would then act as a demotivator causing even worse performance, and we could quite smugly blame the manager for causing his workforce to fail by having set them an unrealistic target. Yet if we know that setting a high target will act as a demotivator, why do we set it?

Managers have a pervading need to set targets for the workforce. This need is driven from the top and percolates down to the workforce, who are invariably told what their performance should be by people who have never done their job. As we have already seen, the fact of telling the workforce what to do will affect their ability to do it. This is partly due to our natural resistance to doing what we have been told to do, but it also stems from the way in which managers use measurement. Managers in general are not very good at looking for the positives in statistics. If we are presented with a set of figures we will automatically look for the instances where the target has not been achieved, rather than when it has. This negative use of the data means that the expectation of the workforce when presented with a measurement is to assume that the data is going to be used to criticize them. The result is that record keeping will be imperfect and the data skewed wherever possible by the data gatherer in order to accentuate good performance and hide or minimize the effect of poor performance.

In the case of the rig-skidding operation the target that the manager set was never communicated to the crews. Instead, specifically to avoid the resistance that setting the target would have created for the crews, their performance was simply recorded without comment or criticism. When the workforce could see how they were doing and the negative association with the measurement function was removed (they were no longer criticized) they began to take notice of the data. They started to realize that what they did was measured and that they could have an effect on their own performance. Someone was paying attention – and a change was starting to take place. The workforce performance started to improve and as it improved they started to take pride in that performance. In three weeks the performance of this routine task went from 8½ hours to 55 minutes, without anyone telling anyone else what they should be doing. They did it for themselves and they were proud of what they had done. The two-hour target that was thought to be unachievable was simply ignored. That target was not communicated and the workforce simply improved until they were doing as well as they could, accomplishing the task in under one hour. In time, the workforce accepted their own informal target of one hour and would judge the success or otherwise of an operation against that measure. When they failed to achieve their self-imposed target (100 per cent better than the best their manager had ever seen), there were no recriminations or blame. Instead there was a simple endeavour to find out what had happened and a search for a solution that would stop it from happening again.

The crews had come to understand that failure was not a cost. Instead, failure became seen by them as an investment that was repaid with the lessons that they could learn to improve their future performance. Suddenly, there was no more blame culture.

Performance must be measured, but it is what we do with the data that makes the difference. We can use the data to browbeat the workforce, ensuring that targets are not met and continuing to suppress their natural desire to do a good job. Or we can use exactly the same data to generate pride and the sense of value that will sustain the inevitable performance improvement in the long term.

In other words, we can choose what we do with what we have got. The performance that we achieve is the product of the environment that we create. If we assume that people want to be able to do a good job, we simply have to create the environment that allows them to do it. The right environment can be created by listening to the workforce and finding out what they need to be as good as they can be. There will be physical requirements too, but most of the time what the workforce really need is support and recognition. As W. Edwards Deming remarked, 'Remove the barriers that stop people from being as good as they can be, and count the smiles on Monday morning.' We can put it even more succinctly: 'Give the workforce what they need to do a good job, then let them get on with it.'

Epilogue: Spiritual Motivation for Leadership

Shuhei Aida, Jeremy Ramsden and Andrew Kakabadse

> How will new capitalism evolve and how will evolution change current notions of corporate management? This question, so unanswerably – at the time – posed by one of us fifteen years ago,[1] can now be answered: we advocate 'Spiritual Motivation Management' based on the conjunction of Spirit/Mind/Body.

The structural changes engendered by the development and penetration of global cyber (or digital) economies have caused industry, academia and political establishments to question seriously how capitalism will evolve and how this will affect notions of corporate management. Fundamentally, both dialogue and an examination of this development are required, whose terms of reference should be economic ethics and the spirit of capitalism, taking note of the perspectives of legal and economic science.

Common features of the Japanese virtues embodied in bushido, which is somehow embedded in our genes, and British 'gentlemanly behaviour' have been noted; these features are rooted in the conjunction of Spirit/Mind/Body. It is our intention to advocate this essentially old but at the same time novel philosophy to develop leadership and management ethics that could be accepted not only by eastern but also by western countries.

Spiritual Motivation, we maintain, has the Seven Principles of Bushido as basic elements: Rectitude, Courage, Benevolence, Honour, Respect, Honesty and Loyalty. Each of them is individually independent; for example, loyalty that was not independent of the other virtues was considered as false loyalty.

These seven principles turn out to have a remarkable commonality with the so-called 'Nolan Principles', which emerged from the deliberations of the Committee on Standards in Public Life, set up by the then UK Prime Minister, John Major, in 1994 (Lord Nolan was the first chairman). The principal achievement of that committee has been the enunciation of the *Seven Principles*

---

[1] J.J. Ramsden, *The New World Order*. Moscow: Progress Publishers, 1991.

of Public Life, namely Selflessness, Integrity, Objectivity, Accountability, Openness, Honesty and Leadership.

In cooperation with the Cranfield University School of Management, it has been decided to set up a Japan–UK joint research project aimed at the enhancement of individual spiritual motivation by bringing to light the similarity of *Bushido* and the *Principles of Public Life*, rooting the latter in traditional gentlemanly behaviour, to benefit the cultivation of leadership of corporations and other organizations.

Bushido in Japan was a philosophy and set of principles by which people in the leaders' class conducted themselves in the era from the Edo (1590–1868) to the Meiji (1868–1912) periods, when modernization occurred.[2] In contemporary Japanese society, the true significance of bushido is not actually well appreciated. Nevertheless, modern Japan has produced many remarkable philosophical pioneers of bushido such as Saigo Takamori (1827–1877) known for the philosophy of *'Keiten Aijin'* or 'Revere Heaven; Love Man', Tohyama Mitsuru (1855–1944) known for *'Gen'yosha'*, Yamamoto Tsunetomo known for *'Hagakure'* (1716) and Nakamura Tempu (1876–1968) known for 'Unification of Mind and Body'.

A comment on a recent series of corporate scandals in Japan by Hiroshi Okuda, chairman of the Japan Federation of Economic Organizations, is still fresh in our minds. He said 'Let top leaders seek how to conduct themselves by deferring to bushido.' The Hollywood movie *The Last Samurai* has generated some publicity of bushido principles in western countries. *Bushido, the Soul of Japan* by Nitobe Inazo (1862–1933), published in 1900, and English translations of *Go Rin No Sho* or *The Book of Five Rings* by Miyamoto Musashi (1584–1645) are again being read and bushido is beginning to be understood. It is opportune now to again explore the philosophy of bushido, which constituted the spiritual foundation for the modernization of Japan.

The principles that make bushido are fundamentally indispensable for top management in leading companies in modern society. However, a global survey must conclude that such principles are seriously lacking in current business schools. We advocate the creation of a philosophy in an integrated manner, based on the thoughts and actions of the distinguished predecessors who have expounded bushido. The objective of spiritual motivation management research is to establish a training course (see Figure E.1) that will allow leaders, managers and experts to acquire competence in the application of these principles. In this course we hope not only to develop efficient and effective management skills, but also that the whole concept of a human being, based on universal and enduring principles of bushido, will be instilled as 'implicit wisdom', bolstered by the ethos of bushido as a practical philosophy.

---

[2] Although bushido originally embodied rules for warriors, after the establishment of generally peaceful conditions in the Edo period, it became an ethical code for rulers, influenced by Confucianism, Buddhism and Shinto.

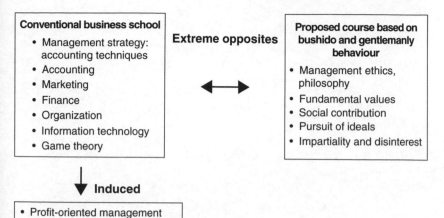

Figure E.1 Diagram comparing conventional and proposed management courses

Index